LIONEL

America's Favorite Toy Trains

Gerry and Janet Souter

MBI Publishing Company

"To our kids: Damienne, Allison and Collin,
Who help keep us young in spirit"

First published in 2000 by MBI Publishing Company, 729 Prospect Avenue, PO Box 1, Osceola, WI 54020 USA.

© Andover Junction Publications, 2000

Photography by Gerry Souter except as noted.

Book editing, design, and layout by Mike Schafer and Maureene D. Gulbrandsen Andover Junction Publications, Blairstown, New Jersey, and Lee, Illinois.

MBI Publishing Company books are also available at discounts in bulk quantity for industrial or sales-promotional use. For details, write to Special Sales Manager at Motorbooks International Wholesalers & Distributors, PO Box 1, Osceola, WI 54020-0001 USA.

Library of Congress Cataloging-in-Publication Data available ISBN 0-7603-0505-6

Front cover: Lionel's *Hiawatha* locomotive and passenger train rounds a curve on the layout of noted Lionel historian Chris Rohlfing. Manufactured in 1935, this so-called "scale model" was designed to run on O-72 wide-radius track and was pricey for its time. Nonetheless, the train was very popular and graced the cover of Lionel's 1935 catalog. *Chris Rohlfing collection*

Frontispiece: If ever there was a signature locomotive for Lionel, it was the Santa Fe rendition of Electro-Motive's F3-type diesel-electric. Its popularity astounded even Lionel's founder, Joshua Lionel Cowen. *Steve Esposito collection*

Title page: Trains stand at the ready on Stan Roy's fabulous Lionel Layout. The pike features Lionel products from all eras after World War II. *Stan Roy collection*

Verso page: Lionel's No. 636 *City of Denver* articulated steamliner. This O-gauge model based on a Union Pacific prototype came out in a four-car set and complemented the Union Pacific M-10000 and *Flying Yankee* streamliner models that helped pull Lionel out of the red. *Don Roth collection*

Back cover, lower left: Model ZW transformers hum over the layout of Mike Moore as a Southern Pacific Daylight-type steam locomotive pauses while a Budd Rail Diesel Car set scoots overhead. Mike's giant Lionel layout reflects the different eras of the mighty toy train manufacturer.

Back cover, upper right: Lionel's signature locomotive was its Santa Fe Electro-Motive F3 model issued after World War II. Joshua Lionel Cowen figured it would be a flop, because it didn't have the action of a steam locomotive. Instead, it became Lionel's best-selling locomotive ever. *Andover Junction Publications*

Back cover, lower right: The 1948 Lionel catalog featured the company's ubiquitous Pennsylvania Railroad steam turbine locomotive passing a streamliner heading in the opposite direction. This locomotive, in O gauge and O-27 gauge, sold in the thousands and was a consistent performer. *Jim Flynn collection*

Printed in China

Contents

Acknowledgments
Page 6

Preface
Page 7

Chapter 1 **An Electric Cheese Box**
Lionel's Primordial Years:1900-1919
Page 11

Chapter 2 **Struggle to Triumph**
Lionel Climbs to the Top: 1920–1940
Page 35

Chapter 3 **War and Postwar**
The Enemy is Joined: 1941–1957
Page 67

Chapter 4 **The Fox in the Poultry Car**
An Empire Derails: 1957–1969
Page 103

Chapter 5 **The Fundimensions Era**
The "Grain Grinders" Give it Their Best: 1969–1986
Page 113

Chapter 6 **"Train Guy" at the Throttle**
The Kughn Years: 1987–1996
Page 127

Chapter 7 **And Now, Lionel L.L.C.**
Thriving Market, Tough Competition: 1996–1999
Page 141

Index
Page 156

Acknowledgments

Without the help and encouragement of the following friends, experts, and colleagues, this book would not have been possible.

Arlington Heights Society of
    Model Engineers
Arlington Heights, Illinois

Dan Basore
Antique Fishing Gear
Warrenville, Illinois

Neil Besougloff, editor
Classic Toy Trains Magazine
Kalmbach Publications, Inc.
Waukesha, Wisconsin

Roger Carp, author
The World's Greatest Toy Train Maker
Kalmbach Publications, Inc.
Waukesha, Wisconsin

Jeffrey L. Cohen
MDK–K-Line®
Chapel Hill, North Carolina

Andy Edleman, vice-president–marketing
MTH Electric Trains/Rail King™
Columbia, Maryland

Jim & Debby Flynn
Marx Trains™
Addison, Illinois

Tom Groff
The Choo-Choo Barn
Strasburg, Pennsylvania

Bob Hanselman
Downers Grove Hobbies, Inc.
Downers Grove, Illinois

John Hetreed
Arlington Heights, Illinois

Ron Hollander, author
All Aboard!
Workman Publishing, New York

Bruce Malmin
(3-D camera collector)
Arlington Heights, Illinois

Patrick Martin
Palatine, Illinois

J. P. Miller
Williams Electric Trains
Columbia, Maryland

Tom McComas
TM Books and Video
New Buffalo, Michigan

Mike Moore
Toys and Trains Hobby Shop
Morton Grove, Illinois

Jerry Price, president
Toy Train Operating Society
Pasadena, California

Kelly Rice
Weaver Models
Northumberland, Pennsylvania

Chris Rohlfing
Addison, Illinois

Don Roth
Arlington Heights, Illinois

Stan Roy
Glenview, Illinois

Mike Schafer and Steve Esposito
Andover Junction Publications
Lee, Illinois, and Blairstown, New Jersey

Barry Stevenson
Arlington Heights, Illinois

Train Collectors' Association
    John V. Luppino, operations manager
    Gary Lavinus, chairman, Education &
        Museum Committee
    Jan Athey, TCA librarian
    and the patient TCA museum
        volunteers
Strasburg, Pennsylvania

Mike Wilson
Arlington Heights, Illinois

The long list of acknowledgments we have provided cannot adequately thank the number of contributors to this book. For an in-depth look beyond the scope of this work at the period of Lionel's growth between 1900 and 1981, there is no better book than Ron Hollander's *All Aboard* (Workman Publishing Company). The Greenberg Series of toy train collectors' guides, with their history clips and descriptions of hardware, is also a gift to any serious researcher as were the conversations with their many authors. Roger Carp's book, *The World's Greatest Toy Train Maker* (Kalmbach Publishing Co.) provides a rich background look at the company by former Lionel employees. We were also blessed with help from an impressive group of experts who offered us many new perspectives. The Train Collectors Association Museum in Strasburg, Pennsylvania, opened its doors and archives to us as it did when we wrote and photographed *The American Toy Train.* A special thanks goes to Gary Lavinus, the museum's patient and knowledgeable curator, for long hours with late night photography; Jan Athey, who opened the TCA library to us, and John Luppino, the manager of the museum and good friend. Down the road from the TCA Museum, we discovered just how much fun a really huge three-rail layout can be at Tom Groff's Choo Choo Barn. Jerry Price, president of the Toy Train Operating Society was also a constant supporter and contributor to our efforts. His critiques and insights into the hobby made quite a chunk of this book possible. We needed the support of our editor and art director, Mike Schafer (who is also our American Flyer and prototype expert) and his assistant (and sister) Maureene D. Gulbrandsen. And special thanks to Steve Esposito, the boss of Andover Junction Publications, who has always been in our corner. Lionel dealers gave us their experiences and Lionel fans gave us their enthusiasm.

Finally, we would like to thank the folks at Lionel L.L.C., the current stewards of the Lionel name and reputation. They supported our work on *The American Toy Train,* but were unable to lend a hand with this volume, as they were committed to a book of their own. But they have managed to keep the Lionel name alive so that this work is not a eulogy, but a continuation of the celebration of that trademark from a journalist's point of view.

Author's note: A significant portion of the research documenting the Kughn Years came from the generously granted use of material from an unpublished article written and copyrighted by Jerry Price, a copyright and trademark lawyer and president of the Toy Train Operating Society. Mr. Price's insight into these years comes from relationships, both business and personal, with many of the key decision-makers that shaped this period in Lionel's history including Richard Kughn, Jerry Williams, and Mike Wolf as well as many of the dealers, hobbyists, and supporters of Lionel. We gratefully acknowledge his expertise and contribution.

Preface

We came to this project directly from our work on *The American Toy Train* (MBI Publishing Company, 1999). As with that book, we were outsiders looking in, but this time we had a year of toy train research behind us. In this previous work, once electricity replaced a piece of string, steam or a wind-up key as motive power, Lionel dominated America's toy train evolution. The name has had a life of its own through 100 years of manufacturing history. In the volatile toy business, this brand name longevity is very rare. For us, the history of Lionel was an extension of our previous book, but now in the space allotted for this volume, we could look closely at the one company that drove the entire market for electric trains. To virtually every reader, Lionel means "electric train."

This marketplace stature has existed for about 90 of those 100 years. Only today does the Lionel name, as part of Lionel L.L.C., struggle amidst a group of competitors who claim equal and greater market share. But all of Lionel's competitors are johnny-come-latelies, born into the adult world of demanding collectors and train layout operators where nostalgia and high-priced technology mix to form part of model railroading, the fastest growing hobby in the U.S. Lionel trains had always been toys for kids.

A hundred years ago, Joshua Lionel Cohen built a battery-powered cheese box on rails used to attract kids and parents to a toy shop window—not to buy the train, but to buy the toys. Joshua was ready to stumble again. Earlier in his brief career, he had invented a battery powered, hand-held light. What did he do with it? He stuffed it into a flower pot to shine on the posies—a flower pot illuminator. After rotten sales, he gave the idea to an associate who called it the Eveready Flashlight and later died a rich man. When Cohen was at school, he invented an electric doorbell, but was talked out of it by his short-sighted instructors. This was 1900; electricity was the hot ticket. You could buy an electric car, an electric lamp; you could even buy an electric belt that promised to relieve a hernia. Joshua was in on the ground floor looking for that one big product that would make his fortune. He created an electric fan that couldn't stir a breeze nor open a pocketbook and now he had this idea for a window-dressing gimmick. Then a toy shop customer bought the cheese box right out of the toy store window and took it home to his kid for Christmas. Joshua was amazed. He had been counting the number of shop windows he could decorate. Now, he could count the number of people in New York who had $4 to spend on their kids for a holiday present.

He called his cheese box the *Electric Express* and once he became convinced of its potential, he never looked back. Joshua put on his helmet and pads, Americanized his last name to "Cowen" and launched the Lionel Manufacturing Company into the sedate, gentlemanly world of his competition. Who he didn't confront with innovative and imaginative products he annoyed with vitriolic bombast. When the competition came up with a better idea, he out-advertised them. Never the cheapest, Lionel was always the best . . . according to Lionel. When the other manufacturers formed a toy-makers association in 1916 to sponsor a tariff against the importation of German goods, guess who was not invited to join—the upstart window dresser. The company to which he had affixed his middle name grew at exponential speed while his rivals

In 1954, father and son bond across the tracks of a busy Lionel railroad. Inside the colorful catalog, new 6464-series boxcars were introduced and the Fairbanks-Morse Train Master diesel locomotive was a featured player. *Jim Flynn collection*

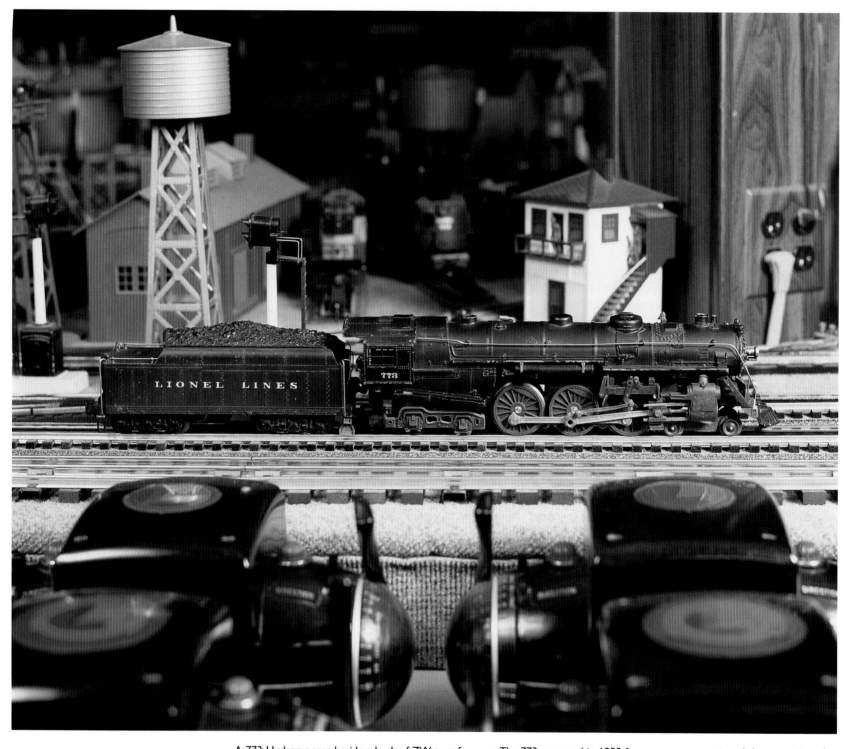

A 773 Hudson poses beside a bank of ZW transformers. The 773 appeared in 1950 for one year as a stripped-down version of the original 700 series (700E and 763) prewar scale models. The 773 was revived in 1954 and 1956 and is popular with collectors today. *Chris Rohlfing collection*

groped along in his wake, occasionally challenging, then disappearing again.

And so the story went through decades of a boom and bust economy, two world wars, and a death spiral decline in the toy train market as the 1950s rolled over into the 1960s. At even the lowest, bottom-feeding point in Lionel's fortunes, the name alone, to whatever it was applied, was worth an uptick and a few cents more on the stock offering, a lift in investor enthusiasm, a recognition that was immediate.

To adult toy train collectors and operators, Lionel will always be the orange-and-blue boxes beneath the ribbons and wrapping paper, the smell of warm oil and glowing electric lamps, the rush and clatter of metal wheels on tinplate three-rail track, the hum and buzz of operating log loaders, coal dumpers, and tiny gate-keepers, the rise and fall of bridges, puffs of smoke, and the sound of a steam whistle or diesel horn at the push of a button.

But the term "toy" train has become ludicrous in a market where locomotives can cost over a $1,000 and rolling stock as high as $100 apiece. Kids are only part of the market today, and generally only because they inherit their enthusiasm from their parents or from exposure to train clubs who are willing to grant them operating status. Lionel's advertising slogan from the 1950s, "Which Lionel do you want, son?" seems quaint and out of step in today's world of computer games, action figures, and models of hot cars and even hotter aircraft. Lionel continues to survive as a player amidst a group of competitors who have forged their own identities and reputations for quality products. But it must be galling to those competitors to know that when a father brings his son into a hobby store—trains have always been a "guy thing"—and that Dad's brain's synapses register the word image "electric train," a nanosecond later, they also flash "Lionel."

However brief our examination of Lionel's history to date, it is made with respect for the founder, Joshua Lionel Cowen, who established the reputation; for General Mills, which kept the company afloat during the dog days; for Richard Kughn, who later rescued the company; and for today's management who keeps those orange-and-blue boxes on the shelves. Behind the front men, thousands of assembly-line workers, designers, and dreamers have labored to create an everlasting world of miniature railroading where we are all kids again every time the power is switched on. Here's to the bright future of Lionel.

—Gerry and Janet Souter

There's no better way to watch a big tinplate locomotive than eyeballing it coming down the three-rail track. This young man has the perfect view that kids of the 1920s and 1930s had as the big-shouldered steamer clatters down the straight ready to swing into an impossibly tight curve, valve gear flashing, in a blur of color and action.

From lowly cheese boxes, mighty trains grow: Lionel had come a long way from its *Electric Express*-powered wooden gondola when it introduced its first O-gauge locomotive in 1915. The Model 700 locomotive, based on the prototype New York Central System's then-new S-motor electrics used to shuttle trains in and out of the new Grand Central Terminal, is shown here pulling a short string of 600 series passenger cars dating from the 1920s. This diminutive precursor to what became Lionel's main product line was built like a tank and many of the motors are still running today. *Train Collectors Association Toy Train Museum, Strasburg, Pennsylvania*

chapter 1

An Electric Cheese Box

Lionel's Primordial Years: 1900–1919

The twentieth century and the history of Lionel electric trains began *con brio*—with a rush of enthusiasm. Cuba had been liberated in the Spanish-American War of 1898, the United States was now an international power, and President McKinley governed as a man of the people. Meanwhile, Theodore Roosevelt was a force of nature awaiting his turn on the world stage as president. Women wore picture hats and long skirts as they stepped gingerly around horse droppings and up into electrified trolley cars. The gas buggy was considered an eccentric oddity, although William K. Vanderbilt—of the New York Central Vanderbilts—managed to drive his auto into a fish delivery cart at 51st Street and Fifth Avenue during the week of New York City's first automobile show.

Most homes were still lit by gas—or kerosene in rural areas—but the magic of electricity had worked its way into public spaces and the more affluent residential neighborhoods. Pitchmen sold "electric belts" to cure impotence, and the Cincinnati firm of Carlisle & Finch had been selling toy trains that ran on electrified track for two years.

Toys were big business in the U.S., but Germany and England still made the high-ticket items. Kids played with tin, wood, cast-iron, and rubber toy trains powered by hand, live steam, and spring-wound clockworks, but toys that responded to the touch of those invisible volts and watts were still considered expensive "electric novelties."

Of all the cities in the nation, New York was the center of electrical innovation. Into its docks poured not only immigrants from Europe, but also imported goods in high demand by the wealthy and upwardly mobile middle classes. Marketplace energy was high as new fortunes were being made. Hundreds of fledgling businesses flourished, went bust, and rose again with another product or service. In this atmosphere of well-heeled enthusiasm, anything "electric" had an immediate cache with both investors and consumers.

Into this rough-and-tumble New York marketplace, where new patents were dealt daily like playing cards, stepped a young man with a gift for both invention and marketing savvy. By 1899, Joshua Lionel Cohen had already filed his first patent, No. 636,492, for a battery-powered igniter used to fire photographers' magnesium-based flash powder. A year later, this success led to a Navy contract for 24,000 mine detonators triggered by electrically fired fulminate of mercury blasting caps. He managed to fill that order without decimating a few square blocks of Manhattan. His constant search for saleable products—or that one saleable product that would make his fortune—came

The "electric cheese box" that started it all. The *Electric Express* gondola of 1902 was of wood construction, almost literally a cigar box on wheels. The box rode on a four-wheel frame powered by a fan motor that Joshua Lionel Cohen had used in his line of (rather unsuccessful) cooling fans. Wire steps and grabirons were hammered into the wood. It rode on steel track comprised of strip metal and slotted wooden ties which had to be assembled by the buyer. *Train Collectors Association Toy Train Museum, Strasburg, Pennsylvania*

Toy train offerings of the late nineteenth century, back to front: The Stevens dockyard steamer of 1845 is a typical "dribbler" that leaked at the seams—which kept it from blowing up as water levels got too low. It also was very slow to cool down between runs. The 1860s wooden Bliss engine is a "dragger" (i.e., "powered" by pulling it with a string) assigned to a set of wood coaches called the *Chicago Limited*. Its detailing is largely lithographed paper glued to the wood. A typical cast-iron locomotive is represented by a Kenton model of the ubiquitous No. 999 *Empire Express* locomotive that set a world speed record. Cast-iron models were first patented in 1880 and were still popular in the 1920s and 1930s. Last, an Ives 1884 wind-up represented a stride forward in that company's conservative thinking. The weight of the cast iron required a powerful spring mechanism to haul any kind of train. *Train Collectors Association Toy Train Museum, Strasburg, Pennsylvania*

from an indulged childhood and the persistent work ethic of his family.

Hyman Nathan Cohen and his wife, Rebecca, arrived in New York shortly after the Civil War. No penniless refugee, Hyman had already emigrated to England from his native Suvalk, an embattled village in a Jewish settlement zone between the border of Poland and Russian Lithuania. He had successfully operated a hat manufacturing business in London before embarking for the U.S. Rebecca had also worked hard in the Old Country and possessed the same spirit as her husband. They were a formidable couple, set a kosher table, and were comfortably well off when little Joshua arrived on August 25, 1877.

The world around young Joshua Cohen moved at the speed a horse could trot, and when the sun went down, raw flame from oil or kerosene lamps lit the over-decorated rooms of the Victorian period. Gas jets were being installed in new homes and office buildings, fed by huge reservoir tanks spotted throughout the city or from coal gas tanks that were refilled at the back door. Tall sloop-rigged and square-rigged sailing ships crowded the New York docks alongside the sleek sidewheel steamers, creating a forest of wood spars above a dense haze of coal smoke and pungent odors from salted fish, raw hides, pine resin from Minnesota lumber, wheels of Dutch cheese, and the well-stirred effluvia of densely packed mankind and horseflesh.

Hyman enjoyed the status of a successful businessman—having added real-estate interests to his hat business—and enjoyed his leisure time discussing the Talmud with other Jewish patriarchs in the community. Rebecca established a piecework shop on Hester Street and saw to the spiritual and secular education of Joshua and his eight siblings. Being next to the end of the line in this mob, Joshua chose to quietly pursue solitary pleasures rather than fight for attention. At around age seven, he discovered wood carving, specifically carving models of steam locomotives.

To kids of the 1880s, these smoke-belching, ground-shaking behemoths represented speed, power, and dreams of travel to far-away places. There was nothing faster than a steam locomotive. Just watching something that big go that fast, hammering across a road crossing, whistle screaming, drive rods blurring, steam streaming from valves and pistons, and smoke ripping from the stack in explosive blasts like drumfire from artillery seemed to suck the breath from small boys and dazzle the eyes of their fathers. Joshua studied the steam locomotive's brute bulk and its necessary mechanical parts and attempted to replicate them in wood with his pocket knife.

Trains available to kids Cohen's age in the 1880s were made from cut and soldered tin and powered with a wind-up motor, or they were carved from wood with details lithographed onto paper and glued to the sides. Some were working miniatures of their prototypes, powered by live steam. These leaky little steamers—or "dribblers"—reflected the educational trend in toys of the period demonstrating the theory of steam propulsion. An alcohol lamp wick heated a boiler of water to produce the steam. This steam gathered in a "steam chest" until sufficient pressure had built up to open a valve and force the piston to move, which turned a wheel by means of a drive rod. Repetition of this action moved the little steamer across the dining room floor—often with its wheels locked into a turning circle to avoid scarring the parlor furniture.

At one point in his adolescence, Cohen decided to set aside his whittling tools and build his own steam engine. This tale became a favorite of the founder of Lionel Trains. While some journalists claim Cohen tried to whittle a wooden steam-powered engine, the story that seems to hew closest to the truth comes from a 1947 *New Yorker* article by John Lewis Taylor.

> "As far as possible, he stuck to his whittling and then branched out to more elaborate miniature construction. His first real success was a steam engine that had, as the boy suspected all along, a trivial flaw or two and finally blew up in the kitchen, removing most of the wallpaper."

You can almost hear the older Joshua embroidering this story with shining eyes and gestures. Those little steamers rarely "blew up." Their seams weren't that sturdy. Mostly, they melted when the water boiler went dry. More likely, he scorched the wallpaper when the alcohol lamp tipped over, but which story makes the best tale? Sorting truth from fiction becomes a toss of the dice when looking at his early life because he never lost that childhood exaggeration side of his character when he became an adult. He loved telling tales to an audience.

One thing is true: he was no scholar. After years of fending off truant officers, Hyman bundled young Joshua off to the Peter Cooper Institute where the boy studied mechanical and technical subjects. There, he discovered electricity and, according to yet another tale told to John Lewis Taylor, put the mystical power source to work as "the world's first electric doorbell" driven by a semi-dry cell battery. But his genius was thwarted by his instructors who offered, ". . . nothing will replace old-fashioned knuckles."

Cohen later puttered ineffectively around City College and then enrolled in Columbia University at age 16 to study engineering. While his classmates dreamed of suspension bridges, tall buildings, and huge reservoirs, Joshua was a merchandiser at heart and hunted for an invention that would make his fortune. After one semester, he bolted from Columbia to apprentice at the Acme Electric Lamp Company at 1659 Broadway. During the day, he dutifully assembled battery lamps, but he used his free time to come up with ideas for using batteries in new and different ways. Watching photographers take indoor pictures with their clumsy equipment led to his first success.

At the end of the nineteenth century, photographic film required considerable light to make an exposure. Indoors, or under poor light, photographers used magnesium flash powder to create a bright burst to illuminate subjects while the shutter was held open. One method was to blow the powder through a tube across an open flame. This worked as long as the cameraman didn't inhale during the process. On June 6, 1899, patent No. 636,492 was filed for a device that used the spark from dry cell batteries to ignite a trough of magnesium powder. It was Joshua Lionel Cohen's first patent.

The U.S. Navy was looking for a reliable fuse to detonate marine mines, and they called in Cohen to demonstrate his electrical flash powder igniter. After sleeping all night on the train to Washington he arrived wearing a rumpled suit and carrying a ratty shoe box under his arm containing his flash powder ignition equipment, ready to dazzle a board of admirals. After first convincing the officers he was not a messenger boy, he next proved the reliability of his electric igniter and walked out the door with a $12,000 contract to produce 24,000 mine detonator fuses. He and a lad

Before turning to electric trains, Joshua Cowen invented this electric fan. It was not a very good fan and came out just in time for New York's winter when no one wanted a fan, electric or otherwise. Next, he had an idea for an electric "train" (operating gondola, actually) and called it a Lionel—his middle name. It was powered by one of the fan motors (page 11). *Train Collectors Association Toy Train Museum, Strasburg, Pennsylvania*

As a boy growing up in metropolitan New York, Joshua Cohen lived near the New York Central & Hudson River Railroad main line into Manhattan, which was also used by New Haven Railroad predecessor New York & New Haven. Like many boys of the era, he was no doubt enamored and inspired by the high-stepping passenger steam locomotives of both roads, marching in and out of Grand Central with an incessant parade of through limiteds and commuter trains. This NYC&HR Atlantic-type (4-4-2) locomotive, shown at Pleasantville, New York, on the old New York & Harlem line typified small but fast steam passenger locomotives around the turn of the century—the perfect prototype for toy trains. *Railfan & Railroad collection*

hired from Acme assembled the fuses, packing each one with volatile fulminate of mercury used to fire the gunpowder in rifle cartridges and artillery shells. The sweaty task accomplished, he hired a horse and wagon and gingerly delivered the lethal cargo on time—and without leveling three blocks of Lower Manhattan.

With this money in hand and a second patent filed for "... improvements in Explosive Fuses," Joshua and former Acme employee Harry C. Grant set up shop on September 5, 1900, in a loft at 24 Murray Street to manufacture "electrical novelties."

The venture did not jump off to a rousing success. Cohen invented a battery-powered fan that wouldn't stir a breeze. Next came a tube containing a dry cell battery with an Edison light bulb screwed into the other end. Push a switch and the bulb lit. *Voila!* He stuffed the tube into a flower pot to illuminate the posies. New York restauranteur Conrad Hubert sold his restaurants and took to the road to sell the electrified flower-pot illuminator. Possibly watering the flowers caused problems with the batteries, as Cohen gave up on the idea and sold it to Hubert who turned the illuminator into the Eveready Flashlight ... and left six million dollars to charity when he died in the 1920s. Cohen returned to the small motor that operated his sad little fan. The motor might have other possibilities. Not being a sedentary thinker, Cohen took a walk.

Near the end of the last year of the nineteenth century, a casual walk through the narrow streets of Lower Manhattan was an adventure. Horse-drawn trolleys clattered past on rails screwed down onto the cobbles. Little Forney steam locomotives puffed black smoke and cinders as their drive wheels and the steel wheels of their wooden passenger cars squealed overhead along miles of elevated tracks. Below them, electric trolley cars waited impatiently for delivery wagons drawn by teams of massive draft horses. From the distant Grand Central Station, departing whistle whoops were heard escaping from the vast train sheds as transcontinental and local steamers chugged toward the main lines out of town beneath a smoke-shrouded copper penny sun.

High-collared and derbied workers bundled in velvet-trimmed overcoats came down the steps from City Hall and crowded the sidewalks looking for lunch and a nickel beer among the restaurants and saloons that reached out with seductive aromas. Push-cart vendors guarded the curbs peddling steaming sausages and roasted chestnuts in small paper sacks from carts already decorated with Christmas bells and sprays of holly. Winter had come early and New York City was chilled to the bone.

It's not hard to imagine the short, serious-looking Joshua Cohen—with a derby protecting his head, a muffler around his neck, and hands thrust into his pockets— dodging the lunch crowd on the sidewalks. He turns down Cortlandt Street about six blocks from his loft office and heads toward the Hudson River, trying to think above the Dickensian chaos. For a moment, he pauses beneath the awning of a shop window and looks at the serene scene beyond the glass. "FINE TOYS" sold by "ROBERT INGERSOL–PROP." peer back at him. An acrobat on a trapeze is arrested in mid-swing. Toy tin soldiers present arms as a silent salute. A wind-up doll stands, arms outstretched, her tottering stride halted by her fickle clockworks, cogs, and gears. Behind Cohen, the crowd bustles past. Christmas and Hanukkah are approaching. The year 1900 has signaled an unprecedented gift buying binge that began right after Thanksgiving. The newspapers predict Americans will spend over $50 million dollars on Christmas gifts alone. Window trimmers at the large department stores have created animated delights with clockwork motors, smoke, and mirrors that are so seductive that crowds stand in bunches ten to fifteen deep to glimpse the marvels. The toy shop window in front of Cohen needs something happening in it to cause people to stop and look—maybe something electrical that can be driven by his little motor.

This story has been told and retold many times from the imagination of different writers. No one knows what really happened and the least reliable source is Lionel's founder. But what is known is on that chilly day in late 1900 Joshua Cohen sold Robert Ingersol on the idea of a battery-powered electrical window display and then went off to build it. Remember,

Cohen had already convinced the Navy he knew all about mine detonators and talked Conrad Hubert into selling off his restaurants to go on the road peddling illuminated flower pots. Cohen was a born pitchman.

He came away from that window with the idea of an electric car—or at least a carlike device that would add movement to the static window display by circling on rails. Anything that ran on rails was considered state-of-the-art for efficiency and speed. Number 999, the famous New York Central & Hudson River Railroad locomotive assigned to the *Empire State Express*, had achieved a 112 MPH speed record. New York City was criss-crossed by rails. Cohen had played with his carved wooden locomotives as a child. He had grown up in his parents' house near 104th Street and Madison Avenue where, a block away, high-stepping "Ten-Wheeler" and Atlantic-type passenger locomotives of the New York Central & Hudson River shared tracks with trains of the New York & New Haven. Beneath his feet a new subway scheme was pushing electrified rails through a tube deep underground. Steam trains and trolleys were part of the American landscape as were the homely gondolas that were part of electrified maintenance trains, but, he might have thought, it would be quite another thing to see one clipping around in a store window.

As first conceived, the *Electric Express* was never meant to be a toy. He and his young partner, Harold Grant, assembled a shallow wooden cigar box made of birch, 15$\frac{1}{8}$ inches long, 4 inches wide, and 4$\frac{1}{8}$ inches high, painted red and supported on a cast-

Continued on page 18

Carlisle & Finch was a respected toy train manufacturer predating Lionel. Shown is C&F's No. 57 suspension bridge accommodating a No. 4 locomotive and caboose. Normally, there would be center support piers, but the cast-iron structure was very sturdy. Like Lionel, the company name survived into the new millennium, but unlike Lionel it was no longer associated with toy trains. *Carlisle & Finch*

Carlisle & Finch—
Electric Toy Train Pioneers

Electricity was still in its infancy in 1893 when Morton Carlisle and Robert S. Finch launched their electric equipment repair company. It wasn't long before the 21-year-olds decided that there was money to be made in manufacturing electrical products as well. Inspired by the German clockwork trains so popular in America at that time, they decided to take the technology one step further and developed electric trains that got their power from batteries connected to the track rails.

In 1896 the company offered its first toy, a four-wheel electric trolley car. Carlisle & Finch produced 500 of these, never anticipating that they would receive orders for 1000! This first car clicked around a three-rail track, but later that year the company, with an eye toward more realism, converted to a two-rail configuration with the rails set two inches apart. They established two-rail trains and trolleys as their major product from then on. Although Carlisle & Finch was not the first to conceive of toy trains that ran on electrically powered track—Jehru Garlick of Patterson, New Jersey, was the first—they were the first to successfully market and mass produce their product. And for that, they are considered to be the pioneers of the electric train in America.

The reasons for the company's success was simple. First, they advertised in *Scientific American* magazine, a prestigious journal committed to publishing innovations in science supported by a well-heeled subscription list. C&F also employed sales agents in several cities across the U.S. as well as England, Venezuela, and Australia. In addition, C&F trains were relatively uncomplicated and priced to sell to an emerging middle-class market with fairly deep pockets.

Carlisle & Finch's most popular product was the No. 4 steam-type locomotive introduced in 1899. A gondola and boxcar completed the set. The company evidently took pride in high-quality detailing. Its No. 45 4-4-2 Atlantic-type locomotive and tender—a copy of that assigned to New York Central & Hudson River's *20th Century Limited*—has been touted as one of the most beautiful and proportionately accurate toy locos ever made. In fact, C&F used a photograph of the actual engine's prototype in its catalog for two years.

From 1903 to 1908 the Carlisle & Finch line was expanded to include passenger and freight cars for their steam locomotives, four-wheel trolleys, a motorized derrick car, a freight-loading platform, a large truss bridge, a terminal station with solenoid-operated semaphore signals, and a cast-iron suspension bridge.

Although C&F offered top-of-the-line quality in rolling stock and accessories, its track designs tended to be cumbersome when compared to Lionel or the other contemporary manufacturer, Voltamp. Until 1908, Carlisle & Finch tracks consisted of metal strips that the customer would bend and then attach to a wooden frame using small nails. The company offered pre-assembled sectional track in 1908, but the 15-inch radius curves didn't accommodate its own No. 45 steam engine. In addition, there were electric anomalies. C&F never made a working headlight and the power to

The Carlisle & Finch 1897 catalog cover featured the company's hand-cranked dynamo that was used to run a train when no electricity was available. Little Tommy could crank until the *Coast to Coast Limited* reached its station or he blacked out. *Train Collectors Association Toy Train Museum, Strasburg, Pennsylvania*

Carlisle & Finch created trains in this Cincinnati, Ohio, factory. The locomotives and rolling stock were made of sheet brass, stampings, and wood, requiring considerable handwork. For 23 years, C&F trolleys and trains were sold around the world. *Train Collectors Association Toy Train Museum, Strasburg, Pennsylvania*

the tracks still came from batteries, either chromite dry cells, or the wet-cell glass-jar batteries with zinc and carbon electrodes and chromite solution that had been originally offered in the early 1900s. By 1908, Lionel had come out with a cleaner and more efficient transformer that used house current, yet C&F still recommended dry cells. However, C&F did produce dynamos.

In an interesting marketing move to reach homes that had not yet been blessed with electricity, C&F introduced a hand-cranked dynamo that produced sufficient juice to power a train until it reached its destination or the "power manager"—read, little brother or sister—gave up cranking from sheer exhaustion. Another dynamo scheme used a connection to the tap at the kitchen sink and water power to propel the young engineer's *Express* to Chicago, its speed dependent on gallons-to-the-watt.

The years following 1908 saw increased competition in the electric toy train market now that Lionel was firmly established along with Voltamp, Knapp, and Howard. Carlisle & Finch attempted to keep its prices steady and competitive, but that became increasingly difficult. The company cut back on hand-assembly production costs by simplifying some of its models, including the No. 45 locomotive, the 19-inch No. 2 1903 interurban, and its No. 34 steamer.

In June, 1914, World War I broke out in Europe, and American industry quickly began focusing on wartime production. C&F soon found that government contracts for marine searchlights and related materiel were far more lucrative and less competitive than toy train manufacture. From 1916 on, the company dropped its train line to manufacture searchlights. The irony was that the company which never built a working headlight for its locomotives ended up building searchlights for navigation aids.

In 1934 the company, now under the leadership of Robert S. Finch's son, Brent S. Finch (Carlisle had sold his interest in the company to Robert Finch in 1926), made several prototype toy train models, but decided against devoting time and materials for full-scale manufacturing. It is uncertain why the line was abandoned; perhaps C&F felt the retooling costs wouldn't generate enough profits, especially since the country was in the throes of the Depression.

A footnote to the Carlisle & Finch story is the Centennial Plaque dedication which took place at the company's headquarters in Cincinnati on September 14, 1996. Seventy members of the Train Collectors Association met to present a plaque to the descendants of Robert S. Finch honoring C&F's initial run of America's first successful mass-produced electric toy trolleys. As stated in the dedication speech, ". . . Carlisle & Finch is testimony to the idea that ingenuity, good product development, and marketing can lead to bigger things and . . . the spirit of its ingenuity lives on in the company of today."

No. 9. Railway Station, with Automatic Signals.
PRICE, $1.50.

Length, 12 inches; height, 6 inches.

Signals are operated by electro magnets, are positive in action and show what block the car is on. Indispensable for show window displays. Intensely interesting when used in connection with any of our railway systems.

Weight in box, 4 pounds.

No. 14. Rail Connector.
Price, 5c. each. By mail, 6c.

In order to make electrical connection between the ends of the rails when two or more sections of track are used, it is necessary to either solder wires to the rails and twist these wires together, or to solder the rails themselves together, or what is probably the best way is to use these Rail Connectors. They may be applied instantly, or removed with equal ease. The two rails are placed with their ends abutting and two set screws allow screws allow be on the ou the wheels.

The Carlisle & Finch railroad depot in this ad featured semaphore signals operated by solenoids wired to the track. The lithographed tin building was lettered "Buffalo" (New York) and, as with all C&F products, was well-proportioned and realistic. *Train Collectors Association Toy Train Museum, Strasburg, Pennsylvania*

By 1916, Carlisle & Finch had seen the light—literally. When its toy train line began to lose money due to competition and manufacturing costs, the company devoted its efforts to navigational aids and searchlights for the government—which is its business today.

Continued from page 15

iron framework that rested on four sprung wheels.

In design, it resembled the maintenance cars that were loaded with tools and supplies towed around the city by work trolleys. The electric motor undercarriage closely followed the pioneer design of Frank J. Sprague, creator of the first wholly successful trolley line in 1888 and adopted by most traction companies. Cohen's little motor was placed between one set of metal wheels and was powered by battery electricity sent through wires to two strips of thin steel track 2 7/8 inches apart, bedded in slotted wood ties. Curiously, Cohen had not adopted the three-rail distribution system used in New York City and Washington, D.C, trolley systems whereby power was fed from a concealed conduit that ran down the center of the track. The *Express* had one speed with a reverse mechanism and

The Carlisle & Finch coal-mining train of 1899 was still a step above Lionel's offerings of the period. It ran on two-inch-wide steel strip track connected to a cordwood stack of dry batteries. It had two speeds in this pre-transformer era: full speed and stop. *Train Collectors Association Toy Train Museum, Strasburg, Pennsylvania*

No. 3. Coal Mining Locomotive and Train.

PRICE, $5.75.

5 to 6 VOLTS.
¾ AMPERE.

This represents a modern hauling plant as used in our large coal mines. The motor is self-starting, and on top of locomotive is a lever connecting with a reversing switch, by means of which the train may be run backward or forward.

Connection is made from the motor to the wheels by means of double reduction spur gearing with accurately cut teeth. The wheels are spoked, two inches in diameter, and made of iron.

The locomotive is very powerful. It will climb grades and haul the three cars heavily loaded. It will haul 10 to 12 empty cars on a straight, le el track. The speed is somewhat less than that of the railways Nos. 1 and 2.

The equipment consists of locomotive, three coal cars, 18 feet of 2 inch gauge track, and four dry batteries,.
Coal cars are iron, with iron wheels. They will stand hard usage. The track may be arranged in any shape. It is better to see that it is level, as the locomotive will run easier and be easier on the battery when track is in this condition. Oil all moving parts of locomotive and train frequently.

Length of train, 18 inches.
Weight, complete, boxed, 13½ pounds.
Coal cars, 25 cents each. By mail, 35 cents.
Track and Ties in 9 ft. lengths, 35 cents. By mail, 50 cents.
Extra dry batteries, per cell, 25 cents.

the little car was designed to carry goods around a circle of track and draw the attention of passersby to the shop window.

It is not known if Cohen simply pinched his idea from the manufacturers of toy electric trains currently doing business. The first electric train in America was built by a Vermont blacksmith named Thomas Davenport in 1835. Power came from three wet-plate batteries at the center of a circle of elevated track. The battery cables went directly to the connectors on the motor in an open gondola car rather than to the track. The car circled the batteries at the end of this wire tether with four wheels on two rails. Everybody laughed at him, and he went back to shoeing horses.

The German toymakers in Nuremberg had experimented with electricity for some years, and the firm of George Carette and company had shown an electric trolley at Chicago's 1893 World's Fair. Electric motor-makers Carlisle & Finch of Cincinnati had marketed its own "electric novelty"—a brass trolley running on two-inch-wide, three-rail track—in 1896. By 1899, C&F was selling its No. 4 steam locomotive, freight cars, and their No. 3 Coal Mine Engine towing three dump cars. All their motive power had three-pole motors with reversing levers and ran off clusters of dry-cell batteries. Before the century's turn, Carlisle & Finch had abandoned three-rail track for two-rail strip track not unlike Cohen's. The mine train cost $6.25 with one set of four batteries and 18 feet of track and ties. That was a heavy hit to the pocketbook in the 1900s for a childish indulgence, so Carlisle & Finch limited its market to the pampered offspring of America's monied class.

Cohen sold his one-of-a-kind *Electric Express* to Ingersol for four dollars. To his surprise, Ingersol promptly sold it to a customer and went to Cohen with an order for six more. Cohen and Grant then set up a cottage industry in their loft office, farming out the wheels, the carbodies, and the cast-iron undercarriage frames to piecework fabricators scattered through Lower Manhattan. They probably established an assembly line, finishing the boxes that were supplied (it is surmised) by a company that made cheese containers, dipping them in red or brown paint and letting them hang dry while the four-wheel power truck was assembled. Track was cut from strips of thin steel to be assembled with wood ties four inches wide, one inch thick, and a half inch high with two sawed slots 2 7/8 inches apart.

This was a simple solution, but it suffered from a number of problems. First, the surface from which the wheels received their electric power was a razor thin 1/16 inch, resulting in start/stop jerky running over any uneven or rusted surface. Next, connection between the beginning and end of the strip track sections was provided by a crude offset connector that could flex out of position and stop the train. The only "layout" available to the purchaser was a simple loop or an oval, and the steel strips, once curved, proved difficult to straighten without kinking. In their second catalog, issued in 1902, they cautioned against creating a circle, since friction applied to the constantly turning wheels would run down the batteries prematurely. At some point, they must have realized they were also in the battery-selling business and left that caution out of subsequent catalogs.

Batteries were provided at $1.20 for four that ran the little car in circles for 10–15 hours. Though Thomas Edison had wired one square mile of New York City for electric power in 1881, by the early 1900s electrification was far from common across the country. Even in homes where the income was high enough to afford a $6 Lionel train—$10–15 a week was considered to be a good take-home pay—electric light sockets provided the only outlets. Out of necessity, both Lionel and Carlisle & Finch offered the purchaser an opportunity to use direct house current to run their electric trains.

Here's the picture: Billy sits on the dining room floor with two square glass jars, lead plates that will fit in the necks of the jars, a coil of wire, a pitcher of water, and a 32-watt light bulb in a socket at the end of wires that will screw into the lamp fixture above the table. He also has his pocket knife and a brown glass bottle of sulfuric acid bought at the corner drug store. With his knife, he skins the insulation from one of the light-bulb wires and attaches two lengths from his coil between the bulb wire and two of the lead plates which he places in the jars. He bends a third plate into an upside-down U-shape and dips each end of the U into one of the jars. Two other lengths of wire are run from the plates to each of the track's rails. Carefully, Billy pours water into each jar from the pitcher. And, finally, he removes the glass stopper from the sulfuric acid bottle and adds the required measure to the water. He remembers Joshua Cohen's specific written instructions, "Never add water to the acid in any event, but pour the acid on top of the water." Oops, he spills a drop on the floor. Hissing and sputtering, the acid quickly eats through the carpet, the varnish on the wood flooring and down into the rock maple, leaving a wisp of smelly smoke behind. Hope Mom doesn't see that hole. Oh, well. He screws the bulb's plug into the lamp socket and his Lionel *Electric Express* begins to circle the track.

Any toy manufacturer who brought out such a "power kit" today would find themselves behind bars in the basement of some maximum security prison, but in the early 1900s playing with toys operated by live steam or electrical current from acid wet cells was considered educational. And it probably was, for better or worse.

Regardless of the drawbacks, orders began pouring in, and Cohen was authorizing distributorships for the little box on rails. Though he still thought of it as a shop-window display, he realized people were buying it as a toy and hedged his bets in his first catalog, published in 1901. An electric trolley was added to the catalog's lineup by attaching the power undercarriage to a 16½-inch-long open-air trolley body originally manufactured as a key-wind floor toy by Morton E. Converse Company in Massachusetts. Cohen referred to his electric novelties both as "toys" and as "window displays." As if reluctant to become known as a "toy manufacturer," he also referred to his "goods" as "miniature electric cars" to be used for the study of the properties of electricity.

The first Lionel accessory was offered in the 1902 catalog—a suspension bridge two feet long and 10 inches high, assembled from a kit costing $1.50. Cohen began what would be a lifelong pursuit of hyperbole and exaggeration in his advertising by calling the bridge, ". . . an exact reproduction of suspension bridges found all over the country." In the 1902 catalog, he also instituted an advertising policy that would eventually mature into virulent attacks on his "impertinent" competition by stating, ". . . our goods should not be conflicted with any other on the market— they are in a class by themselves." On the cover of this slim and skinny publication, beneath a picture of the trolley car, the new company name appeared for the first time—Lionel Manufacturing Company, Incorporated.

Why call the company "Lionel?" In later years the founder said, "I had to name it something," and chose

With a nod to homes not wired for electricity, this Carlisle & Finch water-powered dynamo turned the kitchen spigot into an electricity source. Water turned the wheel—just like an old mill—and produced enough juice to run an electric train. *Train Collectors Association Toy Train Museum, Strasburg, Pennsylvania*

ELECTRIC TROLLEY CAR.

(Catalogue No. 300.)

(Actual size, 16½ inches long; weight, packed, 12 pounds.)

By reference to the above cut it will be noticed that these cars are built on the lines of the regular electric trolley cars. Every feature is carried out to the minutest detail. A full description of the parts follow:

The CAR BODY is constructed of cold-rolled steel, and is 16½ inches long. It has 6 seats, all of which are reversible, as are the signs at the top. It is finely enameled and lettered.

The CONTROLLER in front, which starts, stops and reverses the car, is an exact reproduction of those ordinarily used on large cars. It is cast of brass and nicely finished.

The MOTOR is designed to attain high speed and hauling power, and at the same

3

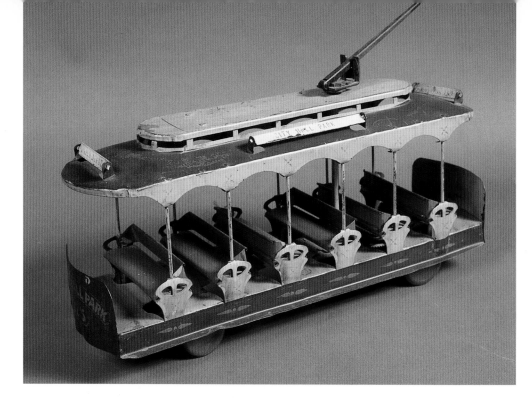

This is the Converse trolley that was put on a Cohen motor chasis to create Lionel's first electric trolley. The Lionel trolley sported a different paint job, but subcontracting the coachwork allowed Cohen to quickly put a new product on the market using the same motor as that which powered the famous *Electric Express. Train Collectors Association Toy Train Museum, Strasburg, Pennsylvania*

The No. 300 Electric Trolley Car in the 1902 Lionel catalog was a faithful reproduction of the cars that ran up and down New York City tracks, drawing power from a center rail or by means of a cable. The trolley body was borrowed from the Morton E. Converse Company in Massachusetts, then repainted to suit Cohen. *Train Collectors Association Toy Train Museum, Strasburg, Pennsylvania*

Lionel's No 340 suspension bridge was a kit-built affair priced at $1.50 and was a quick way to offer an accessory without factory assembly cost. Of course, Cohen trumpeted that it was "... an exact reproduction of suspension bridges found all over the country"—classic hyperbole of the era that would drive all Lionel advertising. *Train Collectors Association Toy Train Museum, Strasburg, Pennsylvania*

his middle name. "Lionel" was a family name and it was also a "neutral" name with no ethnic connotations. Anti-Semitism was firmly rooted in manufacturing business circles of the time. Cohen didn't want anything to stand in the way of his company's success.

From a loft in Lower Manhattan, this young man in his early 20s began manufacturing and selling electric toys into a market that swelled with powerful competition. But a closer look at his competitors in the toy train field is revealing. Ives was a powerhouse toymaker with a line of wind-up toy trains, sectional two-rail track, and accessories. The Germans—Bing, Carette, and Maerklin—offered complete railroads of track, illuminated buildings, stations, semaphores, and trains running off both key-wind and electric power. Other American electric train manufacturers emerged alongside Lionel and Carlisle & Finch in those prewar days. Knapp, Howard, and Voltamp sent beautiful locomotives and accessories into the growing marketplace. American Flyer in Chicago had a ready market for its key-wind train sets and would persist as a Lionel competitor for the next 50 years.

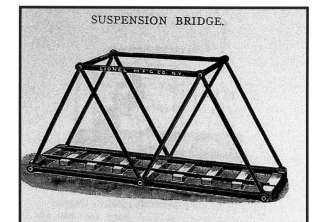

SUSPENSION BRIDGE.

(Catalogue No. 340.)

(Actual size, 2 feet long, 10 inches high.)

This bridge is an exact reproduction of the suspension railroad bridges to be found all over the country. It is 2 feet in length and 11 inches high. The braces which form this bridge are all apart, so that the user may have the advantage of setting it up. Each brace is numbered, so that no error can be made.

This accessory adds to the attractiveness of the road. It may be elevated to any height by placing some of the ties underneath it.

Price complete, boxed.................$1.50

13

This line-up shows Lionel's rivals as they existed in 1910. From rear is the Voltamp model 2100 Baltimore & Ohio engine built from 1908 to 1910, a beautifully proportioned locomotive. The Carlisle & Finch No. 34 engine introduced in 1910 became the mainstay of the C&F line until 1913. The shiny brass boiler Electoy built from 1910 to 1912 compared very favorably with the Lionel No. 5 tank engine shown with its added-on tender. Lionel prevailed in a tough, upscale market, but first-rate competition drove the company to be the best. *Train Collectors Association Toy Train Museum, Strasburg, Pennsylvania*

But Ives, which offered many toys, was content with its miniature train market share and was slow to adapt the new electrical technology. The Germans had snob appeal—it was then fashionable to "buy German" when it came to toys—but they relied on friendly trade relations with America. American Flyer was more of an Ives competitor with its similar-looking key-wind sets. Howard Miniature Lamp Company and Knapp had limited offerings. Only Voltamp, with its beautifully proportioned steam locomotives and extensive accessories, came close to offering Lionel and Carlisle & Finch a run for their money.

Of the group, however, none of them matched the dogged competitive muscle of Joshua Cohen. All around him, he saw fortunes being made by the industrial and banking aristocracy of the time riding a wave of new century prosperity. He finally recognized that these toy trains were his shot at success. He could be the greatest railroad builder of them all—laying thousands of miles of track. So what if the rails were only $2^7/8$ inches apart?

His second year of production in 1902 saw the addition of a switch, a 6-inch wood crossing that permitted a figure-8 track configuration, and an end-of-spur bumper permitting more complex layouts. His original *Electric Express* car was gussied up with brass

American Flyer, operating out of Chicago, offered cast-iron wind-up locomotives like this No. 328 built in 1907. Eventually, Flyer engineers stuffed an electric motor into one of its cast-iron steamers to compete with Lionel in the lower cost O-gauge market. *Train Collectors Association Toy Train Museum, Strasburg, Pennsylvania*

strips at the corners, stirrup steps, and link-and-pin couplers for attaching a non-motored "trail car" creating a little train that, according to Cohen's words, ". . . will afford the user much greater pleasure than the trolley car, as it may be unloaded and loaded. Six miniature barrels are supplied with each outfit." His original box-on-wheels would last until 1905, eventually being offered in stamped metal and painted either olive or maroon with the name *Lake Shore* or—very rare—"B&O" rubber-stamped on its sides.

In Lionel's 1903 catalog, the *Electric Express* was now made of metal and had link-and-pin couplers. An unpowered trailer car was added to create a little train. Lionel was moving toward creating a line of rolling stock for more realistic railroading. *Train Collectors Association Toy Train Museum, Strasburg, Pennsylvania*

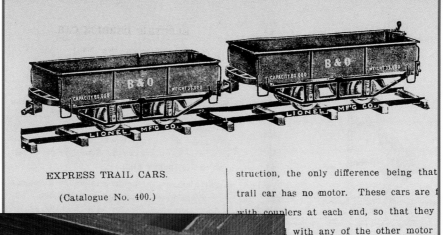

EXPRESS TRAIL CARS.

(Catalogue No. 400.)

struction, the only difference being that trail car has no motor. These cars are f with couplers at each end, so that they d with any of the other motor

n ....

Attached to this locomotive in the catalog illustration was an operating crane car offered either as an unpowered trailer or mounted on the motorized cast-iron frame used with the *Electric Express*. The crane itself operated with a hand-turned crank, but the motorized four-wheel truck version, when coupled to the No. 5 locomotive, created a double-headed powerhouse that could pull considerable rolling stock—and suck a stack of batteries dry in half their rated time. In 1904, an odd-looking "boxcar" that looked more like a passenger car with barred windows (ultimately referred to as the "jail car") was added, again in both unpowered and riding atop the *Electric Express* power truck. The venerable little power plant provided the motive power in 1904 when he introduced the Model 800 powered "passenger car" and its unpowered Model 900 trailer. These would be the last offerings using the 2⅞-inch-wide track.

By 1903, Cohen was still testing the merchandising waters. His trolley car appeared for sale on the pages of the Montgomery Ward catalog, and it was not until 1906 that Cohen even used the term "trains" in advertising copy. That was the year he made what must have been a rather agonizing marketing and manufacturing decision: he decided to forego the realism of two-rail track and abandon all his previous products. He dumped his original and unique 2⅞-inch-wide track for the more compatible "toy train" gauge of 2⅛ inches between the outside rails. This new Lionel track also had a center power rail.

Three-rail track was not realistic (three-rail track was and remains common on some commuter lines, but the third rail—the power rail—sits outside the two running rails, not between them), but it was electrically more simple with the center rail always being positive and the outside rails always being negative. This allowed more complex layouts without special wiring, as is required by two-rail track when track configuration included reversing loops. Insulating the locomotives was easier, and power pickup for both running the electric motors and illuminating the passenger cars was also simpler. In Lionel's 1906 catalog, Cohen announced with an illustration showing an outside-third-rail

This close-up shows the use of a link-and-pin coupler on the *Electric Express*. Joshua Cohen was a stickler for realistic details. Real railroads used link-and-pin couplers into the early twentieth century, although the Janney "clasping hands" safety coupler had been introduced in 1873. Railroads were not forced to begin employing the Janney coupler until 1893. *Train Collectors Association Toy Train Museum, Strasburg, Pennsylvania*

Cohen's first true locomotive was featured in the 1903 catalog. The No. 100 "No. 5" was modeled after a 40-ton Baltimore & Ohio electric locomotive that hauled trains through tunnels under the city of Baltimore. The prototype had eight wheels in articulated sets of four while Cohen's model got along with four wheels. As usual, the catalog text blared forth that the Lionel version was "an exact reproduction" and went on to add two phantom inches to the length of the 10-inch-long locomotive.

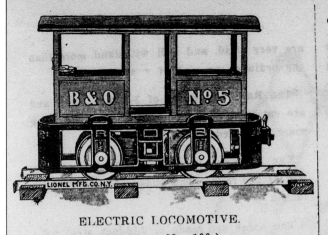

ELECTRIC LOCOMOTIVE.
(Catalogue No. 100.)

(Actual size, 12 inches long.)

This is a faithful reproduction of the 1,800 horse power electric locomotives used by the B. & O. R. R. for hauling trains through the tunnels of Baltimore. Every line is carried out to the proper proportions. The trucks, buffers and couplers are cast iron, perfectly constructed and reinforced to withstand more than the ordinary amount of usage. The cab is constructed of sheet steel. All parts are japanned and lettered in harmonious colors.

A full description of the other parts follows:

The CONTROLLER in front, which starts, stops and reverses the car is an exact reproduction of those ordinarily used on large cars. It is cast and nicely finished.

The MOTOR is designed to attain high speed and hauling power, and at the same time consume a minimum amount of current. The armature is laminated and drum wound. To those conversant with electricity the merits of this will be readily appreciated.

The first locomotive produced by Lionel was pictured in the 1903 catalog. It was a foot long and resembled a Baltimore & Ohio prototype electric "motor" used to haul trains, smoke-free, through Baltimore tunnels. *Train Collectors Association Toy Train Museum, Strasburg, Pennsylvania*

track leading from an electric railway commuter station: "Look Out for the Third Rail."

This was a watershed year for the Lionel Manufacturing Company, admitting to the world that it was a full-fledged toymaker. His new three-rail track, advertised as "Two-Inch Gauge," allowed less bulky locomotives and rolling stock to be offered. Three trolleys rolled off the production line along with two steam-type locomotives that could haul a new line of passenger cars and seven freight cars. For added play value, the roof of the caboose slid off so that young conductors could look inside and see if any crewmen were napping on the seats.

The No. 5 steam switch engine was a big hit and compared favorably in details and workmanship with any import of the time. It was a "tank" engine that carried its imaginary coal on board in a bunker rather in a separate tender. The No. 5 "Special" had a red-trimmed tender and no bunker. Resplendent in "japanned" black enamel on stamped steel with red-trimmed windows and a red pilot ("cow-catcher") riding above four nickel-plated, spoked drive wheels, it established the "Lionel" steam-engine look that would be further developed through the next few decades.

Another roadblock to be overcome was also dealt with in 1906: getting power to the rails. All this new rolling stock and motive power required stacks of batteries to get through the holiday season. Up to now, the alternative was that ghastly sulfuric acid/water wet-cell or another neat device Cohen offered using a light bulb as a power shunt from the house electric mains. It worked as long as the track didn't come in contact with a ground such as a radiator or other pipe

in which case Little Billy might end his play time doing an odd little dance while his hair smoked. To avoid hospitalizing his customers and also provide a continuing power source, Cohen's people came up with a transformer that "transformed" 110-volt house current into the 20 watts of power needed by the toy trains. The current entered from a screw plug into an empty light bulb socket and was sent to a soft iron core wrapped with wire. This wrapping bled off the current to a workable trickle. Taps into the wire fed different

Lionel abandoned its original two-rail track with this announcement in its 1906 catalog for easier-to-set-up three-rail track. Some prototype electric railroads also used three-rail track (though with third rail outside—not center), so Joshua Lionel felt justified. *Train Collectors Association Toy Train Museum, Strasburg, Pennsylvania*

Ives—Sixty Years of Superior Quality

Most major American toy train manufacturers had their start during the first decade of the twentieth century, but Ives predated them by over thirty years and survived well into the twentieth century. Edward Ives founded the Ives Manufacturing Company in 1868. In 1876, Ives constructed its own special "depot" at the Philadelphia Centennial, where it displayed Ives toys for sale. Between that year and 1900, the toy trains in Ives' product line were tin and cast-iron pull-toys. Eventually, Edward brought out Ives' own line of the wind-up types that ran on the floor. During this period, Ives was one of the leaders in creative devices to enhance his product line. One of these was the "smoking locomotive." A lit cigarette was concealed inside the engine's smokestack. A working piston attached to the drive wheel forced air through a tube between an airtight cylinder and the bottom of the stack, pushing smoke up and out of the stack while the train chugged around the floor. (In today's "smoke-free" society, this device would hardly be politically correct.) Still another Ives device that might not play so well today was the locomotive with the cap-firing "feature." A locomotive could chug along on the rug or floor until it struck an immovable object, causing the cap to explode. This forced the engine to detonate into pieces, as though its boiler had exploded. The "hand of God" would put everything back in order until the next "disaster."

When the plant was destroyed by fire in 1900, the insurance money provided a means of retooling. Now, Ives could offer a windup train with a smoother ride thanks to the addition of sectional two-rail track.

Strangely enough, although Ives had distributed Beggs steam-powered track-running trains and had sold electric motors during the late nineteenth and early twentieth centuries, Edward Ives himself didn't venture into electric-powered track-running trains until 1910. Although he had been manufacturing in the European No. 1 gauge and continued to do so until 1920, his first electric was built in O-gauge (running rails 1¼ inches apart) to run on three-rail tinplate track; a No. 1 gauge electric model followed in 1912.

Ives Toys
MAKE HAPPY BOYS

1868 · · · 1927

"Ives Toys Make Happy Boys" became a standard line for Ives advertising. This beaming lad from 1927 dressed as befitting a future captain of industry only concedes a bit of unruly hair to reality. *Train Collectors Association Toy Train Museum, Strasburg, Pennsylvania*

The early decades of the twentieth century were heady ones for American toy train entrepreneurs. Lionel Manufacturing Company began production in 1901; Voltamp followed in 1903, Howard in 1904, and Knapp in 1905. American Flyer, under the leadership of William Coleman and William Hafner, debuted in 1907. Obviously, Ives faced heavy competition. Even two of his former employees, William Haberlin and Timothy Hayes, formed the American Miniature Railway Company. Ives realized that he could stay competitive only if he got on the electric toy train bandwagon. His son Harry was now working for the company and helped design a range of electrically powered products that included a steam engine, a trolley, and a model of the New York Central S-type electric locomotive.

It must have been quite a challenge in those days to keep abreast of toy-train innovations, especially any product designed to appeal to a young man's creativity and imagination. In 1913, Ives came out with its Struktiron construction set, mimicking those of Gilbert, Meccano, and American Builder. Unfortunately, Ives' product apparently was unprofitable and was discontinued in 1917.

But Ives was not just following the crowd when it came to innovations within his product line. In 1915, he brought out a device called the Controlophone, designed to stop or start a train with a voice command, but again, the device had a short shelf life since it was not offered in the 1916 catalog. Ives also experienced problems from a new competitor when Lionel introduced its line of O-gauge electric trains in 1913. Then, in 1915 Lionel published ads attacking Ives' quality and durability. The steel-constructed locomotive that Lionel manufactured was far superior, Lionel claimed, to Ives' cast-iron product. Lionel even showed photos of an Ives locomotive and Lionel locomotive being dropped from a table with disastrous results for Ives, but not so for Lionel. Though Ives' name was never used, Lionel ragged on the "unknown" maker for everything from inferior track to using cheap lithography on rolling stock instead of the baked-on enamel Lionel favored. At one point, Ives asked Cowen to lighten up with the abusive advertising and, for a while anyway, Joshua assented.

This 3243 Ives electric in wide gauge represents the top of the line from 1921 through 1928. The 4-4-4-4 locomotive was every bit Lionel's rival for the diminishing dollars available in the large electric-train market. To many collectors, Ives' products were better built and more realistic than either Lionel or Dorfan. But, the Depression and some bad marketing and production calls sunk both companies while Lionel soldiered on.

Prior to 1921, Ives had manufactured its larger trains in No. 1 gauge (1³/₄ inches between the rails), the same as Electoy. Then, as a result of low profitability in the No. 1-gauge market, especially since German imports were making a comeback and were considerably cheaper, Ives moved to a 2¹/₈-inch gauge, now known as Standard Gauge when referring to a Lionel product. The term "Standard Gauge" had been trademarked by Lionel, so Ives, after tangling once with Lionel's lawyers, carefully avoided use of the word "standard" and instead marketed his locomotives as "No. 2" or "wide" gauge. Although Ives' No. 1 gauge 1920 motors had been better constructed than Lionel's Standard Gauge, Ives apparently didn't feel this gave them enough of an edge in the large-train market. This led the company to retool to wide gauge, and the trains sold very well during the 1920s, proven by the number of collectible Ives wide-gauge locomotives and rolling stock available today.

The same year that Ives introduced wide gauge marked the dramatic increase in Germany's inflation rate. Buyers returned from Europe with no orders; meanwhile, American manufacturers also commanded higher prices for their goods, forcing the buyers to delay placing orders, since they felt the prices might drop later. Eventually, the atmosphere calmed and buyers began placing orders for American-made goods.

An Ives No. 3237 electric precedes a 3245R model in an attractive double-headed passenger run. Both locomotives were produced in 1928 just before Ives succumbed to bad bookkeeping and even worse marketing. Based on the Milwaukee Road's "bi-polar" electric locomotive prototype, the 3245 was the last top-of-the-line product for the beleaguered company It was 18 inches long and had Ives" famous automatic-sequencing reverse mechanism that Lionel coveted.

Three years later, Ives came out with the three-position reverse unit, giving the "engineer" a means of controlling the direction of his train. Using a set of rotating electrical contacts, the device allowed the engine to go into pause mode whenever current flow was interrupted. When it was restarted, the locomotive went in the opposite direction. Children of the 1920s and their parents were also amazed to note that the headlights stayed lit while the engine was stopped. This innovation certainly helped to increase sales for Ives, but, not to be outdone, Lionel lost no time in offering a similar feature without infringing on Ives' patent. However, Lionel's reverse unit did not feature a neutral pause between directional changes—an inferior solution that could cause a train to suddenly reverse at speed at any brief interruption of track power.

It appears that Ives did its best to be a viable force in the toy train market. Its designs were more accurate, and the company offered more heraldry than any other manufacturer, but since it also used smaller pieces joined together to give greater detail, manufacturing costs were higher, making the Ives product less competitive in the marketplace. Ives was less aggressive in its advertising program, and its distribution was more limited than Lionel's and with their bookkeeping in total disarray, Ives continued to operate at a loss. In 1926 Ives applied for a capital loan to retool and pay off some of its debts. The remaining creditors probably became impatient. One of these, Blanchard Press who printed its catalogs, sued Ives in 1928. Others soon followed, and in 1928 Ives filed for bankruptcy. Shortly thereafter, Lionel and American Flyer bought up Ives property, machinery, and unsold inventory.

In 1929, Lionel and American Flyer made several changes in the Ives line, eliminating many of the company's tooling and dies and replacing Ives accessories with Lionel's, and Ives wide-gauge freight cars with American Flyer's. The new owners even discarded the heraldry that was a distinctive Ives feature and simply stamped "Ives" on the car sides. Such was the sad end to a company whose mission was to provide quality, accurately detailed products that would give pleasure to generations of children. But, if nothing else, the name lives on. In 1959, the Standard Gauge Association donated a memorial plaque to be placed on the building that once housed Ives Manufacturing. The plaque stated in part that, "This plaque commemorates Edward R. Ives and his son, Harry C, Ives and all their co-workers whose inspired efforts brought into reality the famous slogan: 'IVES TOYS MAKE HAPPY BOYS.'"

This somewhat battered model of the Lionel No. 8 trolley, sold between 1908 and 1914, is compared to a Carlisle & Finch passenger coach from the early teens. These big toys required a lot of handwork to fit the stamped brass pieces into place. Cowen offered a number of trolleys in his early lines, but they faded away in favor of steam and electric trains which required the purchase of new cars. *Train Collectors Association Toy Train Museum, Strasburg, Pennsylvania*

The Standard Gauge Lionel No. 5 engine (at left in photo) is compared with a contemporary from Germany, a 1913 model Marklin. This first Lionel steam locomotive was offered in 1906 and stayed in the line until 1926. It is shown as a tank engine—carrying its own coal and water—but it was also offered with a separate coal tender. The Marklin was comparable in craftsmanship—a quality American manufacturers had pursued. Note how it has been "Americanized" with a cow-catcher bolted onto the front for the U. S. market. World War 1 ended German toy train domination. *Train Collectors Association Toy Train Museum, Strasburg, Pennsylvania*

wattage to brass studs on the outside of the transformer box. A lever touched each of the arc of studs increasing or decreasing the locomotive's speed just like a real throttle. The trade-off for this control was heat. The 1906 transformer was made to look like a small slab of marble and designed to hang on a wall. Since most toy trains were seasonal toys, this semi-permanent fixture is a dubious solution—especially when it heated up enough to serve nicely as a small hotplate for an evening cocoa cup. However, in these

still-early days when electricity was feared by most and understood by few, a marble hand-warmer was better than acid scarring and electrocution during playtime.

Between 1906 and 1910 the line of Lionel trains had grown to include 13 different trolleys, some of them peopled with figures that could be moved about. The trolleys featured miniature electric lamps that shown down stretches of three-rail track, and they were realistically lettered to represent actual trolley railways. Cohen's steam locomotives now boasted No. 6, a 4-4-0 American-type steam engine, along with variations of the No. 5 switcher. This high-stepping 4-4-0 locomotive was even offered with a polished brass boiler and nickel-plated fittings at a whopping $22.50 to spiff up a window display for a merchant with deep pockets.

Always putting quality before anything else, Cohen continued to rage in print at his competitors who pandered to the marketplace with cheaper offerings. "Cheap goods are dear in the long run," he cautioned. However, he was not above soliciting at least one of his competitors for accessories such as brightly litho-graphed train stations stamped out by Edward Ives. The Ives company had been making toy trains since 1868, eventually adding key-wind locomotives in 1891 and

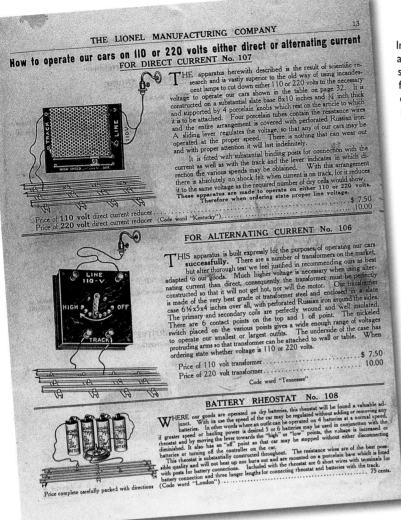

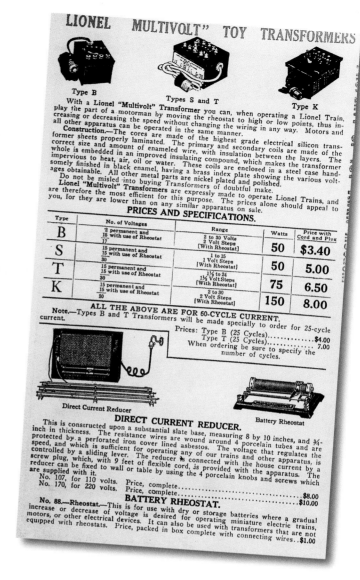

In 1906 Lionel created a transformer to squeeze direct current from the house mains down to the few watts needed to run their train motors. The power-reduction process, wrapping iron wire around a core, caused the marble-look box to heat up. The control lever traveled over an arc of brass studs, each one raising or lowering the speed. Besides controlling the train, the box could heat an evening cup of cocoa. *Toy Train Museum, Strasburg, Pennsylvania*

Lionel's early "Multivolt transformers" and "current reducers" were equipped with plugs that fitted a light-bulb socket rather than a wall plug because most homes were wired to use electricity for lighting only. A central ceiling light fixture could look like a may pole with all the cords reaching down from its sockets. *Train Collectors Association Toy Train Museum, Strasburg, Pennsylvania*

finally stepping into the twentieth century with electric-powered toy trains in 1910 (sidebar). As with many of Cohen's competitors, Edward Ives probably did not consider this upstart window dresser as much of a threat. This suggested attitude is bolstered by Ives' treatment of the young man a bit later when Joshua went calling on the elder gentleman with a deal in mind that Edward Ives rejected. About 20 years later, Ives would live to regret this decision.

Having accepted the mantle of toy manufacturer, Cohen did not ease his company into the competitive waters; he dove in head first, thrashing about with sharp elbows. Since 1905 and his harangue against "unscrupulous manufacturers [who] have endeavored to duplicate our outfits and sell goods at lower prices . . .," he lashed out with uncompromising text that exclaimed, "If you want an electric miniature train to work satisfactorily and for all time, YOU MUST GET A LIONEL."

With his line revamped to three-rail track, in 1909 he put his copyright where his mouth was. The slogan for that year was "Lionel—Standard of the World." After calling his track "Two-Inch Gauge" for a while, inspiration struck and he gleefully copyrighted the word "Standard" to apply to his track, and "Standard Gauge" was born. In fact, as standard gauges went, Lionel's was odd gauge out. Its width of 2 1/8 inches between the outside rails was nowhere near the two inches of established Carlisle & Finch nor the European two-inch gauges. Nor did it match the smaller No. 1 gauge that was 1 3/4 inches. But the use of Standard Gauge was a winner in advertising which, to public perception, made all other gauges "non-standard." Eventually, the other manufacturers would adopt the 2 1/8-inch gauge but would call it "wide" gauge, or "No. 1 gauge" to avoid Cohen's snide letters followed by a phalanx of lawyers (Ives sidebar). Voltamp's version was called "slab track" since its

Hafner—He Found the Key to Success

Hafner catalogs are rare enough. The manufacturer stayed with wind-up trains until production shut down in the mid-1950s. Notice the basic 0-4-0 wheel configuration. Marx followed the same pattern: a basic wheelset and many lithographed tin shells.
Toy Train Museum, Strasburg, Pennsylvania

About the same time that Joshua Cohen began manufacturing his little electric gondola, William Hafner launched the William Hafner Company, later known as the Toy Auto Company. One of his most popular products was the "Roundabout," an open-air key-wind toy auto which can still be found in collections today, and many of these still work because of the durable key-wind motor.

In 1905 he used this motor to propel his originally designed cast-iron locomotive. Some Hafner manufacturing was slowed down in 1905 while Hafner battled with typhoid fever. Nevertheless, he was eager to expand his manufacturing capabilities and approached William Ogden Coleman to form a partnership. Coleman was at that time involved with the Edmonds-Metzel hardware manufacturing company and agreed after Hafner secured a $15,000 toy train order (a healthy sum for the time) from a New York toy distributor.

Production started in full force in 1907 and proved so successful that Coleman shifted all production to toy trains. With William Hafner running the train business and Coleman handling finances, the firm now was known as the American Flyer Manufacturing Company.

Hafner left the company in 1914 after a dispute with Coleman regarding an agreement they'd made by which Hafner would receive an equal share of the business after a certain point. Hafner then formed the Hafner Manufacturing Company in Chicago. During the next several years, it grew beyond anything he had dared hope. Fueled by the onset of World War I and the laws restricting the purchase of German exports, Hafner enjoyed several years of healthy profits. His *Overland Flyer* engine sold very well due to the appearance of his products in general—bright colors with gleaming brass trim.

Unlike its competitors—mainly Lionel, Ives, American Flyer—Hafner's advertising budget was quite low and its catalogs are a rarity today. The trains were successfully displayed at the New York Toy Fair, which was limited to those in the toy industry. And yet, it was probably Hafner's dedication to quality that kept the company going through the

1920s, the Depression, and World War II. Hafner also expanded its product line to include auto accessories, lawn chairs, and Christmas tree holders.

Hafner was known for its high quality lithography, especially during the years 1914 to the early 1930s. Although the Depression forced many toy train manufacturers such as Ives, Dorfan, and Boucher to close their doors, Hafner continued to grow, moving twice between 1919 and 1931, both times to larger quarters.

Hafner offered its own colorful versions of real streamliners, such as its rendition of Union Pacific's M-10000, which came out in 1935, followed by a Burlington *Zephyr* replica a few years later. Prior to World War II, Lionel Corporation distributed Hafner trains overseas. Lionel no longer made clockwork trains (and Hafner never produced electric trains), but Cowen saw a way to make money from them in European countries where electricity was still at a premium.

With the onset of World War II, toy train manufacturing came to a halt. Hafner's tinplate was not strong enough for military applications, so Hafner made bottle caps for Fox Brewing Company, occasionally taking on some subcontracting work during the war years. William Hafner retired in 1942, passing the presidency on to his son John. Two years later, William passed away. In the postwar years, Hafner, in an effort to re-tool and possibly begin using plastic for its train wheels, merged operations with Wallace Erickson, a plastics manufacturer. Nothing resulted from this merger and, in fact, Hafner was sold to the All Metal Company in 1951. All Metal made Wyandotte Toys until 1956 when it filed for bankruptcy. The tools and dies were purchased by Louis Marx who shipped them to his plants in Mexico.

William Hafner never produced electric trains, believing they weren't "real" toys. Nevertheless, the Hafner line lasted far longer than one might expect, due to its dedication to quality, attractive colors, and William Hafner's philosophy of "shoot straight, keep your word, pay your debts, and speak ill of no man."

rolled brass rails fitted with pins to join sections was fastened down to lengths of solid wood roadbed.

Of all the events that marked the Lionel Manufacturing Company 10 years into the new century, one of the most significant was Joshua Lionel Cohen changing his last name to "Cowen." Joshua was brought up in a Kosher home with his spiritual education closely supervised by his mother, Rebecca. His father, Hyman, was a Talmudic scholar and president of his synagogue. However, throughout the family's history, the attention to business was a dominant theme. His father's hat business had provided the capital to extend into both real estate and the jewelry trade while his mother had started up a piecework shop of her own. But at no time had there been any denial of their Jewish roots. In 1904, Joshua had married Cecelia Liberman, a charming young woman who had captured his heart after their chance meeting on an uptown trolley. By 1910, they had two children, Lawrence and Isabel, and had settled into their own home on 114th Street near Central Park.

He must have agonized over the change of name, but "Cowen"—with Gaelic antecedents—was a less Jewish name than Cohen. The majority of toymakers in 1910 had Protestant roots, and anti-Semitism was not unknown in the board rooms of the movers and shakers of the time. Any handicap to his growing business must have been considered. Once he became "Americanized," he never denied his religion but participated in Jewish holidays, supported his synagogue, and made donations to Jewish charities.

Cowen also made another major decision in 1910. The State of Connecticut was offering tax breaks to new industries, so Cowen packed up his New York operation and moved into a four-story factory on Winchester Avenue in New Haven. This major leap would be managed by another young man who had been hired by Joshua back in 1905. Mario Caruso had come to America from Messina in Sicily as a graduate of Italy's naval academy. His arrival was less than auspicious, as he jumped ship and lost himself in the crowds of New York. He made his way to Brooklyn's Italian Settlement House and was recommended to Cowen as a diligent worker by a social worker. His first job with Lionel was as a solderer, but his dedication and hard-work ethic was rewarded with a fast rise through Lionel to become the head of manufacturing, a job he held—and expanded—for decades. He also became the first of an Italian strain of administrators,

salesmen, managers, and workers that drove Lionel's success throughout the company's future growth and its rocky stops and starts.

From a cheese box on rails sold for $4 in 1900, Lionel's profits had grown to $57,000 by 1910. He had a factory in New Haven and a line-up of trolleys, steam locomotives, freight, and passenger cars that ran on his copyrighted Standard Gauge track. His work force was recruited from the Italian neighborhoods of Newark, New Jersey, and he took nepotism to a whole new level as relatives from his own family and those of Mario Caruso's filled key jobs on the

Ives used prototype-like illustrations in its catalogs to sell its line of key-wind locomotives and sets as well as its more expensive electric trains. Harry Ives took a long time to realize that electric trains were not just a passing fad, so he gave his wind-up trains the full marketing sell even at their lower price range. *Train Collectors Association Toy Train Museum, Strasburg, Pennsylvania*

A comparison between a Voltamp two-inch-wide "slab track" attached to a wood roadbed and a Lionel 2⅞-inch strip track with separate wood ties. Note the Voltamp track already uses tubular rails and joiner pins—a design Lionel would later adopt when it created its "Standard-Gauge" track.

manufacturing floor and in the board room. At this time in history, Italian immigrants were low in the working-class food chain. With good jobs requiring skills above common labor offered by Lionel—a good worker could earn over $20 a week for piece-work—sons and cousins of Lionel's Italian managers filled employment list to the point where, as the joke goes, there were 100 employees and only 10 last names. To Cowen, Lionel was one big family, and he was the patriarch—a river to his people. A Lionel train was "... more than a toy ...," it was "... an electric achievement."

As he must have reflected on that busy year that marked a major watershed in both his life and his company, Joshua was aware that a competitor he had dismissed as hopelessly out-of-date suddenly upped the ante. Ives key-wind train line had been harried by competition since Lionel's tepid, but electrified, entry in 1901; then, between 1903 and 1905, Voltamp, Howard, and Knapp had marketed electric trains, and, in 1910, Elektoy introduced an electric train set that ran on the European 1-gauge (1¾-inch wide) track. While the senior Edward Ives viewed electric toys as a fad, his son, Harry, was far more sanguine about America's electrified future. In 1910, *Playthings* magazine, the flack publication of the toy industry, published an announcement most likely cribbed from an Ives' press release.

> "The Ives Mfg. Corp. is now showing for the first time their new Ives miniature electrical railway system. A great deal of time and money has been spent perfecting this new line, and the manufacturer is justly enthusiastic over the results obtained. "

With this subdued announcement, Ives not only threw its weight as volume toy sales leader behind its

electric line, but also introduced O gauge three-rail track (1¾ inches wide)—a low-cost American gauge that directly challenged European models and America's expensive big-train manufacturers elbowing each other aside for buyers' attention.

After four years at the New Haven plant, Joshua looked for a site closer to home—and closer to the source of his work force. He had 150 employees, and sales were climbing up the charts. Mario Caruso began searching the countryside and came across the small town of Irvington, New Jersey. Land was cheap and the factory was only a short trolley ride from Newark, which itself was in sight of New York City. Over the next few years, one factory led to another and, eventually, a large Lionel manufacturing complex emerged.

Lionel's Standard Gauge products were high-ticket items and Cowen's main competitors were the Germans with sophisticated trains and lines of accessories that far out-shown American offerings. Added to the overseas competition, Ives lower-cost electric trains had become a direct challenge. War broke out among the European powers in 1914, and America's sympathies were officially neutral but unofficially anti-German. Then, in 1915 a German submarine sank the oceanliner *Lusitania*, drowning a number of Americans. A communication from Germany to Mexico suggesting a beneficial alliance was made public by President Wilson on January 28, 1917, moving the U.S. closer to the conflict and virtually halting the import of all German goods.

On the toy train front, Lionel countered Ives with a line of O-gauge electric trains in 1913. Adopting the smaller track and less costly rolling stock and locomotives, Lionel's first O-gauge motive power was the No. 700, modeled after a prototype electric locomotive on the New York Central: the S-class "motors" that worked the electrified district into the new Grand Central Terminal. These locomotives would represent Lionel's O-gauge motive power until the 1930s when the first steamers were introduced.

The opening guns in 1914 had signaled the beginning of the end of Germany's toy market in the U.S. for the duration. Both sides of the conflict turned their attention to tooling up for war production. Though toy train manufacture in the U.S. was not halted, it was curtailed by material, manpower, and machinery shortages. In 1916, an organization called The Toy Manufacturers of the U.S.A. was formed by 68 toy-makers to act as a trade association for its members.

Among toy train manufacturers who were invited to join this "Old Boy" establishment were Lionel competitors Harry Ives and William Ogden Coleman, head of American Flyer. The association's first president was a Yale-educated doctor from old Yankee stock and champion pole vaulter from the 1908 Olympic team who turned toymaker in 1909 with a line of magic trick sets. Alfred Carleton Gilbert invented the Erector Set in 1913, and it wasn't long until he rose to the top of the industry. He would eventually face off against Joshua in the post-World War II era as owner of American Flyer. Among those not invited to join was Joshua Lionel Cowen.

This rather obvious slight that only pointed up his status as an outsider in the toy industry could account for the vitriolic zeal with which Cowen rapped his competition in print from then on. Not content to trumpet the virtues of Lionel at the expense of "cheap goods," he positively raked Ives in Lionel's 1917 catalog. He shows photographs of Ives lowest-cost equipment—without mentioning the name—compared to Lionel's top-of-the-line offerings while and denouncing the "flaky . . . cheap" lithographed paintwork and the crumble-at-the-touch fragility of dumpy cast-iron locomotives. He berates bait-and-switch dealers who unscrupulously lure buyers into the store by showing Lionel trains in the window, then peddle these sleazy competing models that will ". . . soon be a wreck in the ash box." This slashing tone would remain throughout the next three decades.

Cowen went on to set himself up as the Pied Piper of toy train play with an invitation to visit his manufacturing headquarters, which he described with a more-colorful term. . .

"Fun Factory! That's a splendid name for this big place. Hurrah for that magic word, 'fun.' I've been a boy and know what boys like! . . . Twenty years ago I started to make electric trains for you boys to play with—and NOW—over 500,000 sets have been sold. I hope you will be one of the thousands that owns one . . ."

Cowen's dark, balding, and serious face looks back at the reader fused to the word "fun" in big red type.

By the time President Wilson declared war on Germany on April 6, 1917, Cowen's blood was really up. Patriotic zeal had swept the country as its puny army—ranked 17th by international standards—mobilized

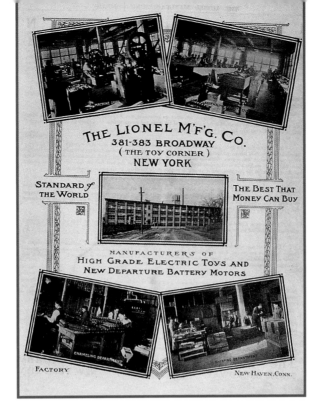

The huge success of Lionel trains was evident in this photo montage of Cowen's factory in New Haven, Connecticut. The State was offering tax breaks for new industries, so Joshua expanded to the new plant in 1910. A young man named Mario Caruso, who had risen from solderer to plant manager, ran the new facility and would become a driving force in Lionel's future. *Train Collectors Association Toy Train Museum, Strasburg, Pennsylvania*

Lionel's Irvington, New Jersey, plant sprawls in this artist's rendition of the campus on the back cover of the 1924 catalog. As Lionel outgrew its New Haven plant, Mario Caruso discovered the cheap plot of New Jersey land just a trolley ride from Newark—Lionel's labor resource. It was purchased in 1914 and gradually occupied over the next few years as Lionel grew into a major force. *Train Collectors Association Toy Train Museum, Strasburg, Pennsylvania*

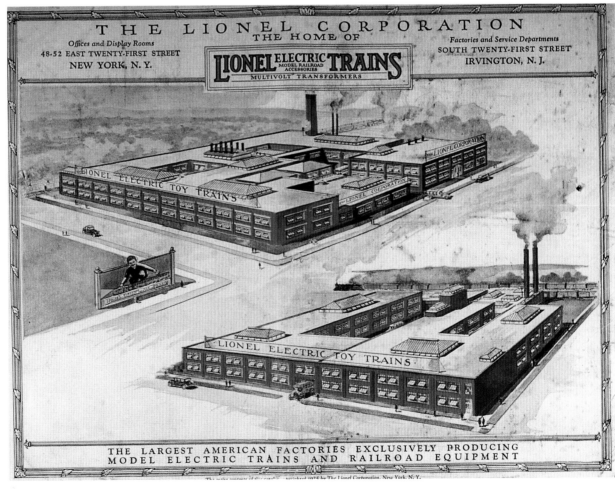

and puffed up its ranks with draftees and eager volunteers. While Lionel plunged into the war effort manufacturing navigational instruments, Cowen also hammered together the Model 203 "Armored Battle Car" and two ammunition cars. "Play War!" his 1917 catalog trumpeted. "Bring up siege guns on tracks!... Now there's bushels of fun ahead." With his usual breathless bombast, Cowen claimed the little gray train with its two guns in a rotating turret was "...a wonderful reproduction of the original." There probably was no "original," or at least no prototype roamed rail lines in France, but patriotic rhetoric of the time fueled youthful passions to be a part of the great adventure. "You can be a general just like the soldiers in Europe," copywriters promised, and Lionel went to war.

In July 1918, Cowen's original Lionel Manufacturing Company became the Lionel Corporation. At the conclusion of The Great War—the "War to End All Wars"—Lionel emerged cash rich by about $500,000 from government contracts. The two-man company that started on its present course by dipping cheese boxes into red paint in a Manhattan loft now had 500 shares of capital stock valued at $50,000. The new corporation offered both Standard Gauge and smaller O-gauge toy trains and accessories to postwar buyers who were caught up in a significantly changed world. Women had won the vote, and the Volstead Act made alcoholic beverages illegal. The economy was struggling to return from war footing to business as usual, and America's railroads had been severely mauled by wartime demands and their takeover by the government for the duration of the conflict. Material shortages and rationing had also severely cut back toy-train manufacture while a printers' strike in 1919 had stopped production of Lionel's color catalog. This forced Cowen to send out flyers that were: "An apology from the man who makes Lionel Trains to his millions of boy friends" explaining about the strike and promising to do better next year.

The calendar ticked over into 1920, and America, as it had in 1900, looked toward a rosy future. Joshua Cowen, however, must have had more on his mind than cranking out his next catalog. Carlisle & Finch had dropped out of the toy-train business and were now

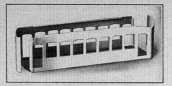

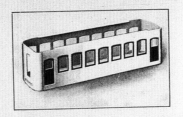

All Aboard, Boys! For a Trip Thru My Factory

Fun F A C - TORY!" that's a splendid name for this big place. Hurrah for that magic word "fun!" I've been a boy and know what boys like.

I can't imagine anything with more fun in it than to operate an electric train that rushes pell-mell around a steel track with its live third rail. Just think—having one all your own with electric locomotive operated from the third rail like trains on the New York Central; New York, New Haven and Hartford; or the Pennsylvania Lines. Boys everywhere like things that move when electricity is switched on. How fascinating!

Twenty Years Ago I Started to Make Electric Trains

for you boys to play with—and NOW—over 500,000 sets have been sold.

I hope you will be one of the thousands that owns one.

If you lived near Irvington, New Jersey, you would be welcome to visit my big factory and see just how Lionel trains are made from the smallest piece of metal to the finished trains. But since thousands of you boys write me every year and live hundreds—some thousands of miles away, I'm going to take you on a "word and picture journey" thru the Lionel Factory.

I have a big fireproof factory near Newark, N. J. where hundreds of expert workmen turn

Fig. 1—Tool Making Room—Here high-priced die and toolmakers produce expensive tools to cut out the hundreds of separate parts of Lionel trains, motors, etc. Here our experimental work is carried on.

Joshua Lionel Cowen looks out soberly from the page of this catalog next to the word FUN in red. His "Welcome Boys to My Factory!" message was an ebullient bit of fluff explaining that he was once a kid and how all kids "like things to move when electricity is switched on." He was actually a jolly person as long as things were going well. But he did not suffer fools, contradiction, or competition. *Train Collectors Association Toy Train Museum, Strasburg, Pennsylvania*

making electric motors as well as searchlights and other marine hardware for the military. Ives had wandered off into a dubious line of overpriced wind-up tin boats at the patriotic behest of the United States Shipping Board. Harry Ives might have seen these boats as a hedge to bolster summer sales since toy trains were expected to be holiday gifts. However, Ives' low-priced O-gauge electric trains were still competition against Lionel. In the Midwest, William Coleman's American Flyer chose 1918 to cram an electric motor into the boiler of its largest key-wind steam locomotive and brought out its first electric line of toy trains.

Joshua Cowen saw his low-end line being threatened by Ives and American Flyer and, like the dual guns of his military locomotive, pivoted both his manufacturing and marketing efforts in that direction while feeling secure that his line of big Standard Gauge train sets were on target for the emerging class of upscale consumers. What he could not see were attacks developing on his flanks: a Jewish sergeant returning home from the war who had an idea or two about how to sell toys, a sleeping giant waking up, and two brothers from Nuremberg, Germany, with some radical plans of their own.

The American public, meanwhile, was racing into what would be called the "Roaring Twenties" and the "jazz age" armed with a new concept called "buying on credit" and fueled by the soaring stock market. For toy train manufacturers—and Lionel in particular—this would be called the "classic period" and they rushed forward with throttles tied down and whistles wailing.

The Lionel armored war train of 1917 was trumpeted in patriotic advertising as the real thing used by our doughboys in France. In reality, U.S. troops didn't rely on armored trains, but that didn't stop Lionel from trotting out its flag-waving hooplah: "Bring Up the Siege Guns on Tracks! Best fun yet, boys! Now, there's bushels of fun ahead!" *Train Collectors Association Toy Train Museum, Strasburg, Pennsylvania*

LIONEL ELECTRIC TRAINS

THE TRAINS THAT RAILROAD MEN BUY FOR THEIR BOYS

"Just Like Mine", SAYS BOB BUTTERFIELD, ENGINEER OF THE "20TH CENTURY LIMITED" (See Page 3)

The 1931 catalog cover exclaims "Lionel Electric Trains—The Trains That Railroad Men Buy For Their Boys." The cover features Bob Butterfield talking to his grandsons visiting the railroad yards in improbable white suits with Lord Fauntleroy collars. "Just Like Mine," says New York Central engineer Bob, who was a "hogger" on the famous *20th Century Limited* passenger train, and the 400E he holds was supposed to be a model of "his" Hudson locomotive, which powered the train west of Harmon, New York. Butterfield would become a regular Lionel spokesperson. *Train Collectors Association Toy Train Museum, Strasburg, Pennsylvania*

chapter 2

Struggle to Triumph
Lionel Climbs to the Top: 1920–1940

". . . the nervous temperament of the average American child and the rapidity with which it tires of things (ensures) a continuous outlet in this country."—Playthings magazine, 1913

"Take Your Dad into partnership . . . Make him your pal."—Lionel advertisement copy, 1910

Joshua Lionel Cowen plunged into the Roaring Twenties as owner of a growing toy train business and "Friend of the Boys" of America, as he signed his ads. He had dragooned his son, Lawrence, into posing for advertising photographs as the "Happy Lionel Boy" and whose smiling face and outspread arms were worked over by an illustrator to become the familiar "Kneeling Boy" that was the Lionel advertising icon of the 1920s. But Lionel's rushing success wasn't due to just the blue smoke and mirrors of advertising. The company was producing the finest toy electric trains ever constructed in America.

By the close of 1920, Lionel had sales totaling over one million dollars and Cowen was anticipating even more growth to come. Both his Standard Gauge and O-gauge lines were selling well with models of prototype electric locomotives doing the hauling. These engines, like the fairly prototypical Model 1912 in Standard and the 150 and Model 700 series in O-gauge

were cheaper to build with their boxy bodies and simple wheel arrangements than the more complex steam locomotives. The only steamer still in the line was the Standard Gauge No. 6 4-4-0 patterned after the famous New York Central & Hudson River No. 999 speed record breaker of 20 years earlier. Lionel continued to sell this venerable model until 1923.

The toy industry sailed into 1921 ready for another big year—and it didn't happen. A prophetic few lines at the end of an article written in the *Literary Digest* in 1918 entitled "German Toys Not Wanted" suggested:

"The real test will come in those products of which Germany is still able to maintain a monopoly, or in which she is able to undersell our own manufacturers . . ."

At war's end, galloping inflation overtook the German economy, reducing the value of a single Deutschmark note to a wheelbarrow full of paper, all bearing many zeros and commas. As manufacturing costs soared and profit margins disintegrated, German manufacturers refused to commit to shipping orders on which they would lose money to American buyers. In the U.S., American manufacturers had raised prices. The nervous buyers, fearing they would be stuck with expensive merchandise when the price eventually dropped, shut down purchasing of American toys.

The crowning glory in Lionel's Standard Gauge stable of steamers was the Model 400E shown here in black and brass (on trestle) and its more showy *Blue Comet* 400E in blue with nickel trim. The model is supposed to be a "homage" to New York Central's famed Hudson-type locomotives, but looks nothing like the prototype. It made use of Lionel's ubiquitous four-wheel drive chassis, which translated to an obscure prototype 4-4-4 wheel configuration. *Train Collectors Association Toy Train Museum, Strasburg, Pennsylvania*

ABOVE LEFT: For some 70 years beginning during the first decade of the twentieth century, New York Central's S-series electric locomotives lived in relative obscurity, working the confines of Grand Central Terminal in Manhattan. In the world of toy trains, though, this locomotive type was in the spotlight for many years. S-1 No. 100 is at Mott Haven Yard in New York City in 1961. *Richard J. Solomon*

ABOVE: In 1910, Lionel introduced a line of locomotives modeled on New York Central's bidirectional S-series electric locomotives. Lionel model No. 1912 in Standard Gauge was 15½ inches long with an 0-4-4-0 simplified wheel configuration (the real locomotives had a 2-D-2 wheel arrangement: two pony wheels, four powered wheels, and two pony wheels). This engine was the precursor of a line that ended with the immortal 408E. Shown on the trestle is Ives' model of the same prototype, No. 3242, offered in wide gauge and built as the top of the line for the period from 1921 to 1925. *Train Collectors Association Toy Train Museum, Strasburg, Pennsylvania*

LEFT: The Lionel No. 42 electric is a minor classic. The side-rod-equipped locomotive was first introduced in 1912 with a single motor. In 1913, the frame was revised to accommodate a second motor. Finally, in 1921, that second motor was added, considerably increasing the 42's pulling power—all you had to do was wait nine years! *Train Collectors Association Toy Train Museum, Strasburg, Pennsylvania*

Cowen proved canny as ever. At the first sign of falling orders and price-cutting by the competition, he stopped selling and slowed manufacturing while he bought raw materials in bulk at market-reduced prices. He also pegged the price of future deliveries as a condition of his purchase. Cash-rich Lionel managed to weather the down-market and even kept employees' salaries stable, although overtime pay was cut.

At this time, in New Haven, Connecticut, the sleeping-giant Ives had been studying Lionel's pricing for Standard Gauge equipment and prognosticated that it could slightly undersell Lionel and still make a profit. Harry Ives had been selling large No. 1 gauge (1³/₄-inch width track that originated overseas) trains since 1904 but had not made much profit. With postwar Europeans returning to the No. 1 gauge market with cheaper production costs, Ives decided to bail and go head-to-head with Lionel. In January 1921, Ives announced its new line of "wide gauge" train sets running on three-rail sectional track 2¹/₈ inches wide. The well-proportioned and detailed No. 3242 electric-type is typical of these locomotives, but Ives also offered a chunky, wide-gauge, cast-iron steamer, the 1132, a modest 0-4-0 steam switcher that scooped Lionel's all-electric line-up (except for the wheezy old No. 6 puffer from 1904).

"Oh boy! You talk about fun—Lionel electric trains may now be had for as low as $5" boasted this ad from the December 1917 issue of *American Boy Magazine*. In 1917, $5 represented a significant amount of money. As Joshua knew, the train was only the hook. Next, you needed a new Lionel Multivolt transformer for $3.40 and then some new cars, and on and on. *Train Collectors Association Toy Train Museum, Strasburg, Pennsylvania*

The Lionel Electric Trains catalog of 1928 also featured "Lionel Electrically-controlled accessories. Boys! See the lights flash on and off. See the gates go up and down. Hear the warning bells ring. The action is automatic." Accessories were a big money-maker and manufacturers often would buy pieces from each other to hold down costs. *Train Collectors Association Toy Train Museum, Strasburg, Pennsylvania*

No. 384—Hand-Control Locomotive for "Lionel Standard" track—A fine steam type locomotive with the famous "Bild-a-Loco" motor. Equipped with hand reverse.
Length of locomotive, 12 inches, height 4½ inches. Tender, 8¼ inches long, 4½ inches high. Complete with headlight bulb and flags.
Code Word "PUFF." Price, $22.50

No. 384E—Same as No. 384 but with "Distant-Control" mechanism and No. 81 controlling rheostat.
Code Word "PURSE." Price, $27.50

No. 390E Steam Type Locomotive—One of the finest Steam type locomotives in the Lionel Fleet. Equipped with the Famous "Bild-a-Loco" motor and with "Distant-Control" unit. It has four driving wheels and front and rear pilot trucks. Copper exhaust and steam pipes, brass hand rails, and headlight mounted on front boiler suggest realism. The finish is a beautiful black enamel baked at high temperature.
At any distance from the track, it can be started, stopped, reversed and operated at any speed. Complete with No. 81 controlling rheostat, headlight bulb and flags.
Locomotive—14 inches long, 5 inches high. Tender—8¼ inches long, 4½ inches high. Length over-all 22¼ inches.
Code word "TONE." Price, $32.50

[*Page Eleven*]

A pair of "dandy" Lionel Standard Gauge locomotives, Nos. 384 and 390 all decked out in copper and brass trim, look like European locomotives in the 1931 catalog. Equipped with the Bild-a-Locomotive motor, a Distant Control reversing unit, and running on Lionel's ubiquitous four-wheel drivers, the locomotives are typical of Lionel's flashy offerings when money was tight during the depths of the Great Depression. *Train Collectors Association Toy Train Museum, Strasburg, Pennsylvania*

With a typical Cowen-esque move, Lionel spun around and stuffed a second motor into its No. 42 electric locomotive, and once again Lionel advertising painted single-motor engines like the Ives 3242 as cheap and cheesy. This advertising was spread over an impressive collection of American reading material from *Boy's World* and *Youth's Companion* to *Popular Mechanics* and *Colliers*, spreading Lionel's message over seven million copies. Adding to this drum beat was Lionel's innovative capture of a large piece of the Sunday newspapers' color funnies. Right beneath the laughs of Maggie and Jiggs, Gasoline Alley, or the Toonerville Trolley, boys and dads—with mom and sis looking on in admiration—were urged to become railroadin' pals over a busy stretch of Lionel track.

As the Lionel empire expanded with locomotives, passenger cars, freight cars, stations, bridges, and other accessories, new dies had to be in constant production. These industrial cookie-cutters that punched out the pieces of tinplate that were assembled into Lionel products were expensive to design and machine. Lionel drew from an island of high-paid, precision-minded German and Swedish toolmakers who existed in the general sea of Italian labor. Cowen

and his designers were sticklers for high quality, but labor and material costs were cutting into profit margins.

Mario Caruso was now second in charge at Lionel, and after a visit to his hometown of Naples, Italy, he suggested to Cowen that Italy might be just the place to set up a factory. In the early 1920s, American companies were taking advantage of Italy's eager desire for new industrial infusion. During World War I, the country had been one of the Allies against Germany and Austria and had suffered for that alliance. In March 1922, Joshua accompanied Caruso to Italy on a fact-finding mission. Mario wined and dined his boss in big cars/big cigars fashion, pointing out the antique glories, cheap real estate, and cheaper skilled labor available in Naples.

The Societa Meccanica La Precisa was founded by Lionel under the supervision of Mario Caruso who promptly moved his family to Naples and took up palatial residence. Besides saving considerable cost on creating Lionel's next generation of products, the move had a stylistic effect on the trains that would last until just before World War II when life under the Fascist bureaucracy and posturing of Mussolini's regime eventually put an end to the off-shore production.

The locomotives produced during the 1920s were colorful, boxy models of the New York Central S-class electric locomotives. The pinnacle of these designs was the dual-motored Model 402 brought out in 1923, an 0-4-4-0 electric that was only eclipsed by the 408E with upgraded trim. They came in Lionel's proprietary paint shades of red, green, tan, orange, maroon, blue, and small batches in experimental colors. Cowen's theory about color was based on the concept that women often influenced the purchase and preferred bright colors. This was not a unique vision as attested to by the dazzling rainbow of locomotives and freight cars sold by Lionel's competition.

The 408E, launched in 1927, is a tarted-up version of the 402E—the "E" referring to a reversing control—adding folding pantographs and additional lights and brass trim. The eight-wheeled electric-type locomotive boasting dual motors was a massive chunk of box-cab design with considerable pulling power. It was primarily assigned to pulling Lionel's medium-weight passenger sets and sold well. As with all Lionel electric-prototype locomotives since 1910, it represented the NYC S-class. In 1923, however, there was a change in this policy, adding a rounded-hood No. 380 "bi-polar" locomotive representing a prototype built by General Electric to pull the Milwaukee Road passenger trains over Western mountain ranges.

Lionel's show-stopper design in its bi-polar line was the massive 381E. This elegantly detailed and finished brute was 18 inches long—the largest locomotive built by the company up to that time. It came in "State" green with either an apple green or red sub frame and was paired to the top-of-the-line designs in Lionel's passenger car line—the State car set. These cars were each 21½ inches long, named for states such as Colorado, California, and Illinois and were beautifully painted in glistening enamel. Besides their exquisite outside finish, each car had a removable roof that revealed complete interior detailing including passenger seats and two washrooms complete with toilets and sinks as well as doors that opened and closed. These were heavyweight passenger cars in every sense of the word.

In their rush of enthusiasm to mate their biggest and most prestigious locomotive—the 381E—with these stately cars, the designers at Lionel made one miscalculation. Though their 381E was modeled after a brutish prototype that could (and did, in a publicity-stunt tug-of-war) drag a pair of smoke-blasting steam locomotives kicking and thrashing down a track, Lionel had only installed a single motor. When coupled to the State car set, there was a spinning of wheels and a bad smell in the air as the 381E labored forward wheezing and straining.

Caught with its pants down, Lionel marketing went into overdrive as the letters and phone calls came in from disgruntled customers. The dual-motored 408E was snatched from its medium-weight passenger duties and backed into the State car set. With a shrug, it rolled on down the line with the majestic passenger cars trailing obediently behind. Racing at full torque, Lionel's marketing spin doctors offered any owner of an exhausted 381E an even swap for a 408E in the same green color. The 408E became a Lionel catalog celebrity and a best seller while the elegant 381E became enshrined as the ultimate expression of toy train modeling in Lionel collectors' lore. Curiously, Lionel did create a really, really big 381E in Italy designed to run on 3¼-inch track as an experiment, but as a

When the Chicago, Milwaukee, St. Paul & Pacific (Milwaukee Road) took delivery of its five impressive EP-2-class "bi-polar" electrics in 1919–20, the event provided toy-train manufacturers with yet another electric-locomotive prototype. Bi-polar No. E-3 is shown in 1949. *Milwaukee Road Historical Association Archives*

Lionel's No. 381E bi-polar electric was the largest locomotive built by Lionel for the general public (Lionel did make an even larger version—but only one), but it was handicapped by only having one motor. It remains today a collector's prize and many are still running with that motor. The 381 was offered both as an "E" model (381E), with an automatic reversing unit and ringing bell, and as a "U" model—a kit version complete with assembly tools and parts to use the motor as a stationary power source. This wide-gauge electric was called the "Shasta" in 1928—a misnomer, as the prototype was found roaming the Cascade Mountains of the Pacific Northwest, not in the Shastas. *Train Collectors Association Toy Train Museum, Strasburg, Pennsylvania*

child's toy, the concept had little sales appeal and only one hand-built model was made.

When it came to launching Standard- and O-gauge steam locomotives, the drab countenance of American locomotives posed a problem. The early Lionel O-gauge steam-type engines were low-cost 2-4-2 engines —the rare "Columbia"-type wheel configuration only seen on an engine built by the Chicago, Burlington & Quincy Railroad in 1895. Lionel's initial O-gauge steam offerings were drab black-and-gray stamped-steel engines but were very popular with O-gauge buyers after years of electric-type locomotives. The steamers began with the Model 248 in 1926 and lasted until the first die-cast locomotives arrived at the end of the 1930s. They were the dowdy exception.

Cowen chose 1929 to pop for a seat on the Wall Street exchange for his son, Lawrence, to the tune of $585,000. In the catalog for that auspicious year, Lionel's big Standard Gauge steamers were flashy showpieces. If Cowen was aware of the coming stock

market crash, the Lionel line for 1929 did not show it. Forty-eight pages with fold-outs trumpeted a huge line-up of electric trains.

A four-wheel motor was used for economy sake producing a 2-4-0 (no listed prototype), the 2-4-2 Columbia type, and the famous 4-4-4 Model 400E—an obscure prototype built in 1915 by the Philadelphia & Reading based on a Bavarian locomotive design and revived by the Canadian Pacific (which called it the "Jubilee" type) in 1936. It is highly doubtful that any of these Lionel designs were consciously patterned after any real locomotives since none of them were typical of any locomotives that could be seen on the tracks that ran near the Lionel plant. They were also tarted up with red cowcatchers, nickel-plated and red-spoked wheels, copper and nickel piping, and brass plaques. They looked . . . well, Italian.

Mention of this fact was offered to Mario Caruso in Naples by Joe Bonanno, a consultant who arrived at Lionel in 1928. The Italian designers were seeing these

Dwarfed by its prospective train, a Lionel No. 9 engine with a single-motor Bild-A-Locomotive from 1928 roosts above two of the huge and highly detailed—both inside and out—State-series passenger cars circa 1929. These 21-inch beauties contained so much detail, they posed a hauling problem for any but the heaviest dual-motor locomotives. The little No. 9 would just polish the track with spinning wheels if it tried to make off with a set of State cars. *Train Collectors Association Toy Train Museum, Strasburg, Pennsylvania*

painted and polished locomotives every day clattering over Neapolitan tracks and the gaudy results were translated to America's toy train market. Of course, Cowen was loathe to comment on their design since it fit in so well with his own flashy concepts. On the cover of the 1931 catalog, veteran railroad engineer Bob Butterfield is posed in front of his *20th Century Limited* 4-6-4 "Hudson"-type locomotive showing a model 400E Lionel steamer to his two grandsons—both dressed in immaculate white outfits. "Just Like Mine," he assures the two slack-jawed youths.

The 400E was 31 inches long, trimmed in either copper or nickel piping and was the flagship Lionel Standard Gauge steamer. It was meant to represent the famous New York Central System Hudsons built by the American Locomotive Company; never mind that the 400E was a 4-4-4. The prototype was a passenger engine riding on either 75- or 79-inch drivers and was named after the river NYC tracks followed between

New York and Albany. By 1938, the NYC had built up its fleet to 275 Hudsons plying NYC rails and those of subsidiary Boston & Albany. While the 400E didn't look anything like the actual Hudson, it was a "homage" to the original as well as being the largest toy Standard Gauge steam engine then offered by any manufacturer. One model, the *Blue Comet*, represented a Jersey Central train that traveled a three-hour run between New York and Atlantic City. Cowen rode the all-coach train a number of times and lobbied for its inclusion in Lionel's lineup. The resulting two-tone blue passenger train included overnight Pullman cars which were not part of the real *Blue Comet*'s short-haul consist, but the result was a beautiful and impressive sight rushing down a stretch of three-rail track.

Another star of this period was an accessory, the beautiful Hell Gate Bridge. Offered in 1928, this 28-inch-long model was based on a span that crosses New York City's East River joining Long Island and

On the Toy Train Museum's Standard Gauge Layout, a 385E 2-4-2 steamer rounds the turn towing freight consist that includes a 515 tank car, 220 spotlight car, 211 flatcar with a lumber load, a 514 refrigerator car and 516 coal hopper. These cars lasted in Lionel's Standard Gauge line until it was scrapped in 1940. The 385E made it until 1939. *Train Collectors Association Toy Train Museum, Strasburg, Pennsylvania*

Die casting was a major leap forward for Lionel. While the 1937 700E overshadows the prewar models, small gems followed like the Lionel 226 (on trestle) built in 1938. In comparison is a stamped-metal 260E from 1932 that is brass-trimmed and toylike with its gaudy European touches. *Train Collectors Association Toy Train Museum, Strasburg, Pennsylvania*

STEAM TYPE PASSENGER AND FREIGHT TRAIN OUTFITS
for "Lionel Standard" Track—2¼ Inches Wide.

No. 391 and 391E OUTFITS

No. 391 Hand Control Freight Train Outfit for "Lionel Standard" Track. Comprises 1 No. 390 Steam-Type Locomotive and Tender, 1 No. 511 lumber car with load of lumber, 1 No. 512 gondola car, 1 No. 517 illuminated caboose, 8 sections C curved track, 4 sections S straight track, 1 STC "Lockon" connection. Track forms an oval 69 by 42 inches. The entire train is 62 inches long. Complete with headlight, lamp for caboose, and flags.
Code Word "TOSCA."

No. 391E "Distant-Control" Freight Train Outfit for "Lionel Standard" Track. This is in every way similar to No. 391 outfit described in the opposite column, but locomotive is equipped with "Distant-Control" mechanism, enabling the user to start, stop, reverse or operate train at any speed at any distance from the track. Complete with No. 81 controlling rheostat, headlight, lamp for caboose, and flags.
Code Word "TOAST."

No. 392 and 392E OUTFITS

No. 392 Hand Control Passenger Train Outfit for "Lionel Standard" Track. Comprises 1 No. 390 Steam-Type Locomotive and Tender, 1 No. 332 illuminated baggage car, 1 No. 339 illuminated Pullman car, 1 No. 341 illuminated observation car, 8 sections C curved track, 6 sections S straight track and 1 STC "Lockon" connection. Track forms an oval 88 by 42 inches. The entire train is 63 inches long. Complete with headlight, lamps for cars, and flags.
Code Word "TWINE."

No. 392E "Distant-Control" Passenger Train Outfit for "Lionel Standard" Track. This is in every way similar to No. 392 outfit described in the opposite column, but locomotive is equipped with "Distant-Control" mechanism, enabling the user to start, stop, reverse or operate train at any speed at any distance from the track. Complete with No. 81 controlling rheostat, headlight, lamps for cars, and flags.
Code Word "TROT."

No. 393 and 393E OUTFITS

No. 393 Hand Control Coal Train Outfit for "Lionel Standard" Track. Comprises 1 No. 390 Steam-Type Locomotive and Tender, 3 No. 516 coal cars, 1 No. 517 illuminated caboose, 8 sections C curved track, 6 sections S straight track, 1 STC "Lockon" connection. Track forms an oval 88 by 42 inches. The entire train is 74 inches long. Complete with headlight, lamp for caboose, and flags.
Code Word "TROOP."

No. 393E "Distant-Control" Coal Train Outfit for "Lionel Standard" Track. This is in every way similar to No. 393 outfit described in the opposite column, but locomotive is equipped with "Distant-Control" mechanism, enabling the user to start, stop, reverse or operate train at any speed at any distance from the track. Complete with No. 81 controlling rheostat, headlight, lamp in caboose, and flags.
Code Word "TWIST."

No. 394E OUTFIT

No. 394E "Distant-Control" Passenger Train Outfit for "Lionel Standard" Track. Comprises 1 No. 390E "Distant-Control" Steam-Type Locomotive and Tender, 1 No. 310 illuminated baggage car, 2 No. 309 illuminated Pullman Cars, 1 No. 312 illuminated observation car, 8 sections C curved track, 8 sections S straight track, 1 STC "Lockon" connection and 1 No. 81 controlling rheostat. This train can be started, stopped, reversed or operated at any speed at any distance from the track. Track forms an oval 102 by 42 inches. The entire train is 81 inches long. Complete with headlight, lamps in cars, and flags.
Code Word "TALE."

Prices are Listed on Page 45

19

The 1929 Standard Gauge 2-4-2 steam passenger and freight sets featuring locomotives Nos. 391 to 394 were printed in black and white; the catalog for that year only had a color cover. The locomotives with "Distant Control" offered the reverse mechanism Lionel came up with to counter the Ives' unit that was much superior. *Train Collectors Association Toy Train Museum, Strasburg, Pennsylvania*

New York's mainland. It was built by the Pennsylvania and New Haven railroads through a joint company known as the New York Connecting Railroad, a 10-mile line. Now owned by Amtrak, the four-track bridge spans what was once a treacherous channel formed by the juncture of the East River and Long Island Sound that was tamed by the U. S. Army Corps of Engineers in 1876. Due to heavy maritime traffic through the widened channel, Gustav Lindenthal, who designed the bridge, could not use support piers in the center of the span, hence the massive supports at either end that resulted in an elegant design that still looks good after 83 years.

While Lionel's version is a typically "compressed" impression of the actual bridge, its twin towers and the arch of its center span clearly resemble the prototype. Designed as a "rug-level" accessory, there was no need to ramp the track up to the start of the structure nor down from the other side. Once again, the enamel hues employed are unique, but the design reflects its colorful Italian origin, constructed from photographs—all in all a superb bit of modeling.

Lionel's big-shouldered, chunky locomotives and accompanying rolling stock, all in fancy dress, were introduced just as the bottom fell out of America's economy when the stock market imploded in 1929. While apples were being peddled for five cents each by out-of-work victims of the financial crash and stockbrokers were taking swan dives from the upper stories of their brokerages, Lionel released its most beautiful and most expensive line of trains, cars, and accessories. At about the same time three other things happened. Ives went broke, the Forchheimer brothers had showed up, and Louis Marx, a veteran of World War I and a super toy salesman, began selling toy wind-up trains for the Girard Model Works.

Back in 1910, Joshua Cowen had experienced a pang of doubt about Lionel's ability to compete. Ives was the toy giant of the time. At only 29, Cowen possessed a profitable company and had a world of opportunities in front of him. He wrote Edward Ives, the company's 71-year-old patriarch, for an appointment. At their meeting, Cowen proposed that Ives buy Lionel for cash. Old man Ives, who still considered electric trains a passing fad, turned down the upstart window dresser and Cowen left with his deal still in his pocket.

All through the 1920s, Ives had been a thorn in Lionel's side. Ives wide-gauge trains, introduced in 1921, were well-built, beautiful in design, and had been well-received, lopping off a chunk of Lionel's big-train market share. Ives had beaten Lionel to the market with low-cost O-gauge trains. In 1924, Ives hammered Lionel with a revolutionary innovation, an automatic reversing mechanism that could be initiated from the transformer. Until then, reversing a locomotive required the engineer to scoot across the carpet and flip a switch on the locomotive. The new device, invented by two gentlemen, H. P. Sparks and B. A. Smith, provided a three-step sequence of forward/neutral/reverse at the transformer throttle control. Lionel had nothing like it.

Cowen laid the lash to his engineers, and in 1926 they produced an electro-mechanical reverse mechanism that skirted Ives' patent, but left out the neutral step. Though better than the manual system, this two-step arrangement had a serious drawback in that it allowed the possibility of watching your Lionel version of the *New York Midnight Express* from Chicago thunder down the main line, experience an inadvertant power interruption, and then suddenly reverse, becoming the *Chicago Cadaver Express* as its motor thrashed and trashed.

With Lionel's usual fast-handed bombast, its upbeat advertising copy told kids, ". . . the Lionel 'Distant Control' system of electrical operation puts genuine excitement into model railroading—and it is a thrill you can experience only if your train is a Lionel. Boys, don't forget that!" For prudence sake, Lionel also offered ". . . an additional lever for disconnecting the 'distant control' mechanism."

Ives trains generally were more realistic than Lionel's and had more prototype details hand-soldered into place, but by 1928, Ives' management, burdened with shabby bookkeeping and out-of-control cost accounting, faced bankruptcy. They juggled plans for re-introducing a cheap wind-up set for $1 as well as bigger, better, more realistic wide-gauge sets, but Ives' unpaid vendors wanted settlement of money owed since 1926. On July 31, 1928, a public sale was held. Lionel partnered with William Coleman's American Flyer to buy Ives for the tragically small sum of $73,250.

Lionel continued the Ives line, producing interesting "transition pieces" such as the rare 1764E Standard

In the 1935 catalog, Lionel touted its famous 400E locomotive hauling passengers as part of the *Blue Comet* set and as a freight engine pulling the 358W (whistle) set. At a cost of $70 and $65 respectively, these sets were very expensive for Americans mired in the Depression. *Train Collectors Association Toy Train Museum, Strasburg, Pennsylvania*

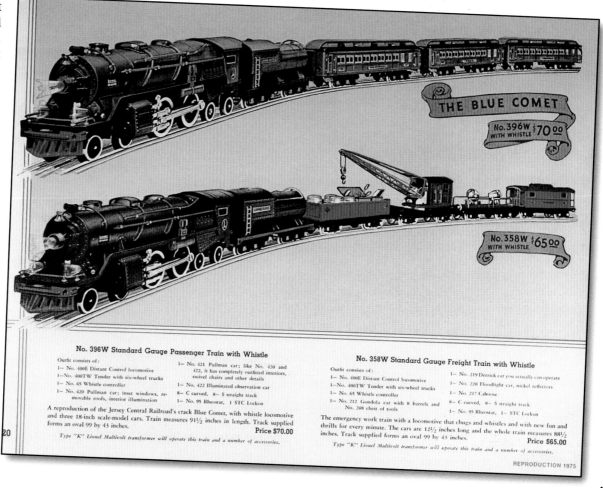

THE BLUE COMET

No. 396W WITH WHISTLE $70.00

No. 358W WITH WHISTLE $65.00

No. 396W Standard Gauge Passenger Train with Whistle

Outfit consists of:
1— No. 400E Distant Control locomotive
1—No. 400TW Tender with six-wheel trucks
1— No. 65 Whistle controller
1— No. 420 Pullman car; inset windows, removable roofs, interior illumination

1— No. 421 Pullman car; like No. 420 and 422, it has completely outfitted interiors, swivel chairs and other details
1— No. 422 Illuminated observation car
8— C curved, 8— S straight track
1— No. 95 Rheostat, 1 STC Lockon

A reproduction of the Jersey Central Railroad's crack Blue Comet, with whistle locomotive and three 18-inch scale-model cars. Train measures 91½ inches in length. Track supplied forms an oval 99 by 43 inches.
Price $70.00

Type "K" Lionel Multivolt transformer will operate this train and a number of accessories.

No. 358W Standard Gauge Freight Train with Whistle

Outfit consists of:
1— No. 400E Distant Control locomotive
1—No. 400TW Tender with six-wheel trucks
1— No. 65 Whistle controller
1— No. 212 Gondola car with 8 barrels and No. 208 chest of tools

1— No. 219 Derrick car you actually can operate
1— No. 220 Floodlight car, nickel reflectors
1— No. 217 Caboose
8— C curved, 8— S straight track
1— No. 95 Rheostat, 1— STC Lockon

The emergency work train with a locomotive that chugs and whistles and with new fun and thrills for every minute. The cars are 12½ inches long and the whole train measures 88½ inches. Track supplied forms an oval 99 by 43 inches.
Price $65.00

Type "K" Lionel Multivolt transformer will operate this train and a number of accessories.

American Flyer—The Chicago Original

"Its a Bear!" booked the ads announcing American Flyer's leap into wide-gauge trains to challenge Lionel's Standard Gauge line. AF's first effort, the model 4019 brought out in 1925, is shown with one of the passenger cars offered with it. American Flyer's timing was lousy. Production of the new line drained its resources and then the stockmarket crash in 1929 further damaged the company. *Train Collectors Association Toy Train Museum, Strasburg, Pennsylvania*

American Flyer has a colorful history, dating from approximately 1907. The first American Flyer trains were manufactured by the Edmonds-Metzel Manufacturing Company, which was founded by William Ogden Coleman and joined later by William Hafner, who struck out on his own in 1914 with his Hafner line of wind-up trains. By 1910, the company was known as the American Flyer Manufacturing Company of Chicago, Illinois, producers of wind-up toy trains. Up until that time, the company had featured only O-gauge passenger sets in its catalog. (These were known as "Chicago cars" since they had no number, only the "Chicago" name stamped on the side.) Then in 1910, AF introduced a line of freight cars. During the next several years AF offered a wide variety of freight and passenger cars, including its low-end Hummer line (although the name "American Flyer" was never mentioned in the Hummer catalogs), but didn't venture into electric-powered trains until 1918, long after Lionel and Ives began exploring the possibilities of electricity and scrapping with each other over market share.

Flyer's first electric O-gauge steam locomotives, produced in 1918 and 1919, were made of cast iron and were toylike in appearance; it wasn't until the 1930s that proportions became more accurate. In 1920 AF produced models of prototype electric locomotives, and from that year until 1934, the company could boast of a variety of models made of lithographed steel, enameled steel, and cast-iron resembling trains that operated in New York State and New England.

In 1925, American Flyer also brought out its premium wide-gauge line to match Ives, Lionel, and Dorfan. These electric-locomotive models were touted as "Wonder Trains." They were colorful, shiny, and even patriotic. The trains' eye-catching names, such as *American Legion*, *President's Special*, and *Mayflower*, didn't come cheap. The *Mayflower* set was cadmium-plated and priced at $100—that could

buy a lot of groceries in the mid 1920s. Freight cars came a year later, a hybrid collection of Lionel bodies on American Flyer trucks. In 1929 and 1930, after Lionel and American Flyer jointly bought out the Ives line, the products became an amalgamation of parts from the three companies and offered under the three different trade names. By 1931 Lionel had bought out American Flyer's ownership in Ives, and AF now manufactured its own line of freight cars along with its passenger line.

Near the end of the 1930s, Coleman's health and company were in a bad way. But even in bad health, the wiley Coleman turned his company over to the aggressive entrepreneur Alfred C. Gilbert who had already become a successful toy- and appliance-maker. Gilbert was also a toy train buff and had meticulously studied the industry looking for a way to get in. Coleman worked out a deal whereby Gilbert would take over American Flyer by paying a small royalty to Coleman for each product sold. By that time Coleman needed someone with high standards and the ability to turn around the morass of bad debt that hung over his company.

American Flyer had weathered the greater part of the Depression, but its sales suffered, especially in the wide-gauge line. After significantly paring down the line, manufacturing in wide gauge ended in 1932, but the company continued to sell off inventories until 1936. Thereafter, AF concentrated on low-end O-gauge products. In that year, AF produced a die-cast Hudson that surprised buyers, but that was a last gasp before A. C. Gilbert took over. The Chicago plant was closed, and everything was moved to Gilbert's plant in New Haven, Connecticut.

Unfortunately, William Ogden Coleman never had time to enjoy his royalty deal. In 1939, his chronic health problems followed him on vacation down to Guatemala where he dropped dead. So ended the original American Flyer—the electric train maker from Chicago.

Gauge electric locomotive and O-gauge steamers that carried both Ives and Lionel logo plaques. Bits and pieces of Ives rolling stock found their way into Lionel and American Flyer freight trains, but American Flyer eventually bailed and was not around when Lionel, with its own books hemorrhaging red ink, scuttled the Ives name in 1932.

For Lionel, watching its greatest competitor self-destruct was a diluted triumph. Two brothers from Nuremberg, Germany, had just blown into town and set up shop in Newark with a line of trains and a line of politically correct patter that must have given Joshua Lionel Cowen more than a few sleepless nights.

Milton and Julius Forchheimer had established their Newark toy train factory at 137 Jackson Street in 1924. By 1925, their marketing plan for Dorfan Electric Trains was established and their challenge to the other toy train manufacturers was clear. On the cover of their first catalog, beneath a looming photograph of a bi-polar-type electric locomotive and passenger train, is a small grinning boy—as usual dressed in suit and tie, the apparent favored costume of small boys who ran trains in the prewar period—and he is digging into the innards of a disassembled Dorfan locomotive with a screwdriver. The copy reads, "Dorfan Electric Trains With the New Locomotive-Builder Engine . . . Fascinating—Instructive—'Twice as much Fun.'"

At this time, educational toys commanded a major slice of the overall toy market. Wooden Tinker Toys introduced in 1919 now came with a motor and instructions for building a radio. Sears offered the "U-Make-M" Home Toymaker kit with its own scroll saw and blueprints. Toy innovator—and later a player in the toy train market—A. C. Gilbert had delivered the ever popular Erector Set in 1913 and now sold radio kits as well as construction sets that featured a real soldering iron so the young engineer could also mend mom's pots when not dabbing hot solder on electrical circuits. Even Ives jumped on the education bandwagon in 1926 claiming kids who once operated Ives trains had graduated ". . . to the manly love for mechanical and electric things which help the world do its work." They also boasted that ". . . regular electrical

Here is a big Standard Gauge train that would brighten the heart of any kid on Christmas morning: a brutish 400E steamer at the head end of a Lionel 200-series train of freight cars including the 215 tanker, 216 Hopper, 214 searchlight car, and 217 caboose. Hopefully, Daddy didn't have to hock the set when the stock market crashed in 1929. *Train Collectors Association Toy Train Museum, Strasburg, Pennsylvania*

rails to independently control the train's direction. Our engineer could run, stop, and then go forward again without having to override a reversing mechanism that wanted to shoot his locomotive back to Chicago.

When the Forchheimer boys took tours through their factory, they enjoyed selecting a random casting and hurling it at the floor, and then presenting the undamaged shell to one of their guests as a remembrance. Dorfan's passenger cars used lithography for the low-end cars and glistening painted enamel for the deluxe class that competed directly with Lionel. Each example of high-end Dorfan rolling stock was built like a bank vault, with some cars having as many as 117 parts. Passenger cars in the more expensive lines even had die-cast passengers in the windows. While these cars were expensive to make, the low cost of the die-cast locomotives helped balanced the scale.

With Dorfan, Lionel faced a challenge to its entire line of trains. Lionel offered two sizes of passenger and freight cars in both Standard and O-gauge as well as lower-cost locomotives to reach the broadest possible market. Lionel marketed a line of wind-up trains in 1931, made mostly of cheap bits under the defunct Ives name for the lowest market segment, but Cowen hated them and they were withdrawn. Ives, American Flyer, Hafner, and the Joy Line trains from Girard Model Works fought over that cheap end of the market until Dorfan elbowed its way in. There was little Cowen could do with combative advertising as he had done putting down Ives' brittle, cast-iron locomotives. However, Lionel could be as educational as the next guy.

engineers design these sets," implying the god-like status of the engineering profession. Manufacturers created contests for clever boys to show off their creations and encouraged "graduating" from simple sets to complex crates of girders, pulleys, wheels, nuts, bolts, and springs whose construction possibilities were virtually limitless.

Dorfan came to this party with its Locomotive-Builder kit and another innovation, die-cast locomotive shells that simplified the manufacturing process and offered exquisite detail at the same time. Its top-of-the-line trains cost less, pulled more, and looked as good as—or better than—comparable Lionel's lines. The only exception was Dorfan steam locomotives, which were more toylike than Lionel's juggernauts. But even these small O-gauge steamers were a cut above the cast-iron offerings of Ives and American Flyer. Milton and Julius attacked the market with a wide choice of products from wind-up to narrow gauge (O-gauge) to wide gauge (i.e., Lionel Standard Gauge) trains for every pocketbook.

Dorfan engines had a built-in "Distance Remote Control" that reversed the locomotive safely. While Lionel used an electromechanical process that set the reversing sequence to the opposite direction whenever the power was cut, Dorfan used DC power through the

Three years after Dorfan hit the market, Lionel pushed its "Bild-A-Locomotive" kits out the door in both Standard and O-gauge. With the Lionel kit, an aspiring young engineer could not only assemble and take apart his electric-type locomotive, he could use the motor as a stand-alone reversible power source for other construction projects. Its lifting power was ". . . 20 times its own weight." The copy also acknowledges that the Bild-A-Locomotive was first introduced in 1919, but ". . . was ahead of its time."

Lionel made another thrust into the low-end market in 1931—again using recycled Ives parts—by spinning off a new company called Winner. Ads ballyhooed, "And now! A Real Electric Train for Little Brother!" The 0-4-0 locomotive, three cars, a circle of track, and a small transformer hidden in a tin station with a removable roof cost $3.25. Cowen hated this cheap set as much as he despised the wind-up trains, but the Depression was tightening and something had to be done to keep sales alive.

Lionel was in financial trouble. In 1930, Cowen had been caught in a bank scandal when the Bank of the United States failed. He was one of the directors and his brother, Joseph Marcus Cohen, was president. Marcus—father of Roy Cohen, the legal council to Senator Joseph McCarthy during the infamous 1950s Communist hunt—was sued for almost one million dollars. Auditors also discovered Joshua had received an unsecured loan of $500,000. Together with $700,000 he lost because of his brother's fast and loose money manipulations, Cowen ended up paying back $850,000 over the next three years. Only a penalty payment of $5,000 kept him out of the $60 million lawsuit brought by the State Superintendent of Banks.

Cowen dropped the Winner line in 1932, but simple economics forced the cheap trains back under the "Lionel Jr." name in 1933. Lionel stubbornly continued to make high-quality trains even as it was hemorrhaging red ink. Banks that had been free and easy revolving doors to loan requests were now padlocking those doors. Thousands of companies were ruined and many of their presidents chose suicide over financial disgrace. For Joshua Lionel Cowen, the only ray of sunshine was the devastating effect the Depression was having on his competitors—that and the self-destruction of Dorfan in the mid-1930s.

Ives had disappeared a few years earlier, absorbed in 1929 and finally dissolved completely in 1933. In Italy, Mussolini was applying heat to Lionel's La Precisa to add military goods to the electric-train line as the cost of tools and dies was becoming expensive. Meanwhile, wages in America had dropped 60 per cent from 1929. The Italian operation was sold to

ABOVE: Modeled after an actual New York span, Lionel's Hell Gate Bridge typifies Lionel's credo of color and action over accuracy that marked its period of ascendance just before and after World War II. The bridge could be used with Standard Gauge trains, but looked better on O-gauge layouts. *Train Collectors Association Toy Train Museum, Strasburg, Pennsylvania*

LEFT: Massive Hell Gate Bridge has been a landmark in New York City's east side borough of Queens since early in the twentieth century. The four-track span was built by the New York Connecting Railroad to gain New Haven trains easy access to Manhattan. Today it serves as a conduit for Amtrak's high-speed Boston–New York–Washington services as well as limited freight operations. In this 1996 scene, a Conrail freight heads across the majestic structure. *Joe Greenstein*

Dorfan: Terrific Trains—Too Short a Time

While most U.S. toy manufacturers were American born and bred, the Dorfan company's origins were in the pre-World War I toy capital of the world, Nuremberg, Germany. In 1910, two employees of the Joseph Kraus & Company were Kraus' cousins, Milton and Julius Forchheimer. The brothers Forchheimer created the Fandor toy train line as a tribute to their mother's sisters, Fanny and Dora. Following the war, Milton and Julius fled the German depression and arrived in the U.S. in 1923. They re-established their toy train line, this time giving Dora top billing with the new name, Dorfan.

Although the Forchheimers were relatively late bloomers in the American toy train market—Lionel, American Flyer, Hafner, and Ives were already well-established—the brothers managed to have their factory in Newark, New Jersey, up and running by 1924. Joshua Cowen was busy pursuing the high-end train markets as he fended off Ives and took no notice of the three-story building opening in his home turf.

At that time, American toy train manufacturers used stamped-steel pieces soldered and tabbed together or cast iron as materials for their products. Dorfan saw a more economical solution: zinc alloy die-casting for making large parts. In the process, locomotive shells were produced in two halves that screwed together, which reduced manufacturing costs considerably. According to the Forchheimers, playthings should be first and foremost "educational," and to that end they even created a kit from which a kid could create his own locomotive using only a screwdriver. Dorfan also invented its own copper-zinc alloy formula known as the

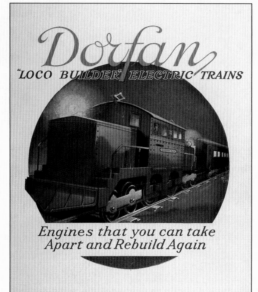

To Dorfan, toys were not to be just playthings, but also taught life lessons. *Train Collectors Association Toy Train Museum, Strasburg, Pennsylvania*

3930 locomotive even featured "Dorfan Dan the Engine Man" sitting in the engine's cab. Some passenger cars had as many as 117 parts to be hand-assembled by the company's 150 workers. Dorfan's locomotives were not only strikingly detailed, they possessed a power unlike other engines of the day. An O-gauge locomotive could pull a load up a 25 per cent grade—the maximum recommended grade is at best 4 per cent!

But, the Dorfan alloy proved to be the company's Achilles heel. Within a few years of its introduction, cracks and expansion began to appear in the die-cast locomotives due to impurities in the alloys. Where shafts passed through the castings, they jammed as the halves warped and became mismatched. That catastrophe coupled with thin profit margins caused by heavy production costs and the financial pinch of the early Depression years started Dorfan's rapid decline.

In 1931 Dorfan's Jackson Street showroom became the home of an experimental wide-gauge 4-6-0 locomotive. The advantages of the beautifully proportioned engine were touted by the brothers and salesmen in the showroom who continually reminded people of the locomotive's superiority to the Lionel 400E of that same year. The brothers rhapsodized on the 4-6-0's innovative features: directional reverse, die-cast boiler, detailed valve gear, and working headlight. But Lionel's locomotive was a money-making reality and the Dorfan 4-6-0 was a one-of-a-kind prototype.

Although Dorfan existed a short time in the U.S., the company was known for its manufacturing innovations and dedication to quality while providing an educational toy. The Take-Apart Locomotive introduced in 1925 showed a boy how the engine worked, yet simplified the process of putting it back together after the parts were scattered on the parlor floor. The company also came out with its "Distance Remote Control," which allowed the "engineer" to determine direction in an efficient way that skirted both Ives' and Lionel's patents.

"Dorfan alloy," which was so solid that they claimed a tempermental child could throw his locomotive on a concrete floor without any damage to the toy. The material was also naturally "slick," eliminating the need for bearings where shafts ran though the castings.

Dorfan's line consisted of several price ranges. The small O-gauge—or "narrow" gauge in Dorfan parlance—passenger cars were cheapest to manufacture since they came from a single sheet of tinplate that incorporated the hook coupler on one end and the ring on the other. At the top of the line were the deeply detailed, hand assembled wide-gauge sets with their brass trim, bright colors, and realism that appealed to the more affluent and competed directly with Lionel's Standard Gauge trains. Dorfan is especially known for its cars showing die-cast passengers with hand-painted features in each window. The

It's not surprising that Dorfan experienced several years of growth and prosperity and gave the industry a run for its money. Dorfan was forced to close its doors in 1934, although it continued to sell off inventory up to 1936. The Unique Art Manufacturing Company bought the Dorfan dies, but most were never used. Although Dorfan's existence was relatively brief, the Forchheimer brothers made contributions to the toy train industry that will never be forgotten.

Mario Caruso for $110,000 although Caruso continued to work for Lionel in the States while his son took over the presidency of La Precisa. Now, Dorfan was gone and American Flyer in Chicago was limping along, having dropped its wide-gauge trains in 1932, then cutting its electric-type locomotives in 1934. Only cast-iron steam and wind-up trains clicked along until even the cast-iron engines were dropped in favor of cheap stamped steel puffers in 1935. The health of American Flyer's president, William Ogden Coleman, was also waning as his company searched for salvation.

Nevertheless, there was little joy at Lionel. By 1934, the company owed $296,000 with only $62,000 in pocket. All Lionel had going for it was its reputation for reliable products and a valuable name. Cowen was able to parlay this combination into what was euphemistically called a "friendly" receivership which, though flinty-eyed bankers examined every decision, giving the company a financial breather to develop a plan for climbing out of their financial hole.

The toy train market reflected the plight of America's railroads. Caught in a muddle during World War I, their inefficiency at getting war materiel to the East Coast ports was an excuse for the government to take over their operation. The USRA—United States Railroad Administration—not only took over and operated the railroads but directed traffic and told locomotive and car manufacturers what kind of motive power and rolling stock could be built. Interstate trade regulations dictated who could ship what to where; meanwhile, the automobile had matured into a long-distance travel machine as paved roads began to branch out from cities and towns. By the time the Depression had scourged America's economy for four

years, the railroads were over-regulated, under-funded, and under-appreciated. Rolling stock bought for the war emergency rusted away on sidings while short-haul freight and passenger runs disappeared as people stayed home and banks turned clapped-out steamers into more profitable scrap. The railroads as well as the toy train market needed a shot in the arm.

The shot in the arm came in the form of two diminutive new trains introduced by rivals Union Pacific and Chicago, Burlington & Quincy. Both roads had been looking for a way to entice people back to the rails and yet accommodate these travelers with something less

Comparing Lionel Standard Gauge Series 19 yellow baggage, parlor, and observation cars built in 1906 and continued through 1925 with Ives 187 buffet and 189 observation car first offered in 1921 and 1922 shows how close in quality the two companies were. The Series 19 basic design held up for almost 20 years—a rarity for Lionel. *Train Collectors Association Toy Train Museum, Strasburg, Pennsylvania*

This rare Ives 1764E was a transitional model in wide gauge from Lionel. It was a 4-4-4 electric locomotive, about 17 inches long sporting Lionel latch couplers. Lionel kept the Ives name alive after the company was bought out. *Train Collectors Association Toy Train Museum, Strasburg, Pennsylvania*

costly to operate than a full-fledged, conventional, steam-powered passenger train. The answer was the lightweight, streamlined train.

Union Pacific worked with Pullman Car & Manufacturing and Electro-Motive Corporation to develop its streamliner, identified as the M-10000. Meanwhile, Burlington worked with the Edward G. Budd Manufacturing Company and Electro-Motive for its train, which was the *Zephyr* 9900. Pullman and Budd supplied carbodies while EMC provided power plants.

UP introduced its M-10000 in February 1934, making it the world's first lightweight, streamlined train. Burlington's *Zephyr* arrived in April 1934, becoming the first lightweight *diesel-powered* streamliner (the M-10000 was powered by a spark-ignition distillate engine—a dying technology in railroading). UP's all-aluminum, three-car train weighed in at about 124 tons—not much less than one of the several heavyweight sleeping cars that could be found within UP's Chicago–West Coast *Pacific Limited*. All three cars of the M-10000 were semi-permanently coupled to operate as a single unit in "articulated" fashion; that is, with

each car pair sharing a single four-wheel truck (wheel assembly). She was built with a low center of gravity, her 204 feet hugging the rails for maximum stability at high speeds. The power car housed not only the train's engine, but also a mail-handling area. The second car accommodated 60 passengers while the third held 56 passengers and housed a kitchen-buffet. The M-10000's biggest selling point was her speed. Passengers could munch a B.L.T. sandwich while cruising along at a smooth 110 MPH.

While the M-10000 was still testing before it entered scheduled service in 1935, Joe Bonanno, Lionel's chief engineer who had remarked to Mario Caruso back in the 1920s that designs coming out of La Precisa in Italy didn't look like American trains, was alerted by the public relations-hungry Union Pacific. He visited the UP and was presented with a copy of the M-10000's plans. Under the rules of the receivership, Lionel was permitted to create new train models if they had the promise of success. Even through the dusty eyepiece of a tight-fisted banker, the M-10000 looked like a winner. One problem arose. Though the M-10000 model

The Lionel Junior set was introduced in 1934. It was a low-priced set "for little brother" marketed to take advantage of Ives equipment inherited during the take-over and those made for the Lionel-Ives line thereafter. The lithographed tin cars and stamped locomotives evolved into the O-27 line in 1935. *Train Collectors Association Toy Train Museum, Strasburg, Pennsylvania*

In 1930, the Lionel "Winner" train set was announced with a gray, four-page folder as a complete train set with transformer for $3.95 by the "Winner Toy Corporation." Lionel treated this low cost O-27 train set like a poor relation, not even giving it the Lionel name. This was an "Electric Train for Little Brother" in the advertising, but Joshua hated it like he hated wind-up trains. *Train Collectors Association Toy Train Museum, Strasburg, Pennsylvania*

would be a featured offering—even claiming the cover of the proposed 1934 catalog—she was too expensive to build in Standard Gauge. The Union Pacific plans were reduced to 1/45th the size of the original, and the M-10000 was released in O-gauge. Another problem surfaced, however. The sharp curves of O-gauge could not accommodate the articulated train, so 20 pieces of wider-radius sectional track—called O-72 for its 72-inch radius—was packaged with the train for $19.50. This was a democratic price, putting the Lionel M-10000 within the reach of Depression-era kids who could not afford even a single locomotive in the "rich boy's" Standard Gauge. The era of the big trains was coming to an end.

On February 12, 1934, UP's M-10000 embarked on a 68-city tour, including a stop at the Century of Progress Exposition in Chicago. She was cheered all along her route by Depression-weary Americans

clamoring for a glimpse of hope. At Lionel, as the presses began churning out the 1934 catalog, there were also cheers in the board room. The M-10000 was the hot ticket of her time, and her success rocketed Lionel's profit column into the highest sales numbers of any December in the company's history.

In that same 1934 catalog was a wind-up toy that sold for a dollar. Around its sales success grew a myth that fired the media and added thousands of those dollars to Lionel's coffers.

Mickey Mouse Saves Jersey Toy Concern; Carries It Back Into Solvency on His Railway
—special to the New York Times, Jan. 21, 1935

Mickey and Minnie Mouse, pumping a red-painted hand car around a circular track before 253,000 Christmas Trees this Winter pulled the Lionel Corporation, Irvington toy manufacturers, back into the black, Federal Judge Guy L. Fake was told today.

After hearing the success story of the widely exploited cartoon characters, Judge Fake discharged equity receivers and turned assets of $1.9 million back to the company . . .

> "...As this big, $2,000,000 corporation lay struggling in the coils of bankruptcy, out came Mickey and Minnie, nibbled away at the cords and set the prisoner free..."
>
> —*New York Times, January 26, 1935*

And so the myth was born that the wind-up handcar licensed from Walt Disney saved Lionel. True, the $253,000 earned by the peripatetic rodents paid off considerable claims against the company, but it was actually the huge popularity of the M-10000 that rolled Lionel into the black.

Another M-10000 toy train was marketed at this time—a key-wind model made in the Girard Model Works in Albion and Girard, Pennsylvania. Though the colorful streamliner sold briskly, the financial bell had already tolled for Girard, and it skidded toward bankruptcy. In a flurry of cost-cutting efforts, Girard management broke relations with their top salesman. In doing so, they saved their company, but not in the way they could have possibly imagined. That salesman was Louis Marx, and he wasn't about to let go of a good thing.

Marx, born in Brooklyn of German parentage, had climbed from private to sergeant in World War I and resumed his job as a toy salesman in 1918, then incorporated himself as Louis Marx & Co, Inc., in 1919. His former employer, Ferdinand Strauss, went broke and Marx bought the tools and dies for two of Strauss' most popular mechanical toys, "Zippo the Climbing Monkey" and the "Alabama Minstrel Dancer." By 1922, he

A high-speed triumvirate of Union Pacific M-10000 "yellow caterpillars" comparing a Marx wind-up version on the trestle to the Lionel 1934 dollar winner that helped pull Lionel out of a financial hole. Next to the Lionel is a tiny No. 10 lithographed HO version from Marx that ran in channel track. *Jim Flynn collection*

had sold eight million of each of these toys and, added to other successes, he became a millionaire by age 26.

His great gift was being a shrewd, cost-conscious designer with marketing savvy. Where other manufacturers shaved pennies from a design, Marx shaved mils. By the mid-to-late 1920s, he abandoned heavy plant investment by giving commissions to other manufacturers, and his logo was soon appearing in Sears catalogs. In 1928 he produced the toy success story for the ages—the yo-yo—and he became very interested in toy trains.

Joy Line trains, built by Girard Model Works since 1927, seemed to have high sales potential, so he bought the dies and lithography. He continued to sell the trains as a commissioned agent and received an 8–10 per cent commission for each train that went out the factory door. As Girard's economic future sagged in the face of the Depression, they cut him loose, paying him off with shares of common stock. Louis shrugged, and through deals with shareholders of preferred stock—suggestions like, if he dropped his considerable shares of common on the market, their preferred shares could be used to patch the holes in their shoes—and other manipulations, he emerged as owner of the company. He designated his new holding as the Girard Manufacturing Company to keep it separate from his other plants in Erie, Pennsylvania, but for ever after he referred to it as his "train factory."

Once Louis Marx took over, the Joy Line of toy trains became electrified in greater numbers. He also justified some research and development in 1930 to produce a better transformer and electric motor. As

Union Pacific's M-10000 streamliner, manufactured by Pullman Car & Manufacturing Company and the Electro-Motive Corporation, turned out to be one of the most significant trains in U.S. history: it was the world's first lightweight streamliner. It is shown on display at Chicago's Century of Progress Exposition in 1934 shortly after the train debuted. The caterpillarlike speedster inspired many model interpretations. *Union Pacific Museum collection*

thousands of cheap electric train sets began rolling out the back door of Marx's train factory, Louis' presence in the marketplace fell under the double-barreled scrutiny of Joshua Lionel Cowen.

Lionel had achieved a modest miracle, pulling itself out of receivership in the middle of the Depression with the help of a mouse and a yellow train. Sales of Lionel's big Standard Gauge trains were steadily falling as the company continued to build on its lower-cost O-gauge while pushing it hard in its catalogs. The lower end of the market was Lionel's salvation if it were to keep up the sales momentum. Now, here was Marx, hacking away at low-end market share.

American Flyer was phasing out its wind-up locomotives and had matched Lionel by getting the plans to Burlington's high-speed, diesel-electric *Zephyr* 9900. Flyer was now going full electric with low-cost stamped steel and cast-iron locomotives—some of which rivaled Lionel's O-gauge trains in looks and features. Hafner was contentedly punching out key-wind trains with no apparent intention of going electric. But this Marx guy had electrified the tinny Joy Line key-wind creations and sold them as sets complete with track at prices that wouldn't buy a Lionel transformer. While Lionel sold its lines through "authorized dealerships," Marx peddled thousands of these tin cans on

wheels through Sears—soup labeling could be found inside early Marx cars when he bought cheap surplus tinned steel. He sold sets through Woolworth dime stores and even muscled into Gimbles department store and the May Company, allowing them to make up their own sets sold under their own logos. He was naming passenger cars after the towns where store buyers lived in order to promote sales.

Every time Cowen would bark a threat that Lionel would design a really really cheap set, Louis Marx put a story out that he was designing an really expensive set, packing it with more cars, track, switches and accessories shooting the price up to a resounding $35. This shouting over the fence relationship continued for years without change.

Regardless of Marx chewing away at the low-end market and American Flyer gearing up its electric lines, the year 1935 was a good one for Lionel. Its designers streamlined a pair of steamers, cranked out more key-winders, countered a coup, and gave Lionel locomotives a voice.

Following the streamlining trend started by Union Pacific's M-10000 and Burlington's *Zephyr* 9900, a number of railroads took a less radical approach by adding streamlined shrouding to existing steam locomotives. The first railroad to do this was the New York Central, which debuted its *Commodore Vanderbilt* 4-6-4 in December 1934, the work of Central's West Albany (New York) Shops. Although the prototype cut through the air in dark gray livery, powering the esteemed *20th Century Limited*, Lionel issued its Vanderbilt-style steam locomotive in a virtual rainbow of colors, from silver and blue to bright red, all running on regular O-gauge track. Both articulated and standard passenger sets rode behind her. Even Mickey Mouse got to ride behind a *Vanderbilt* when a circus train was added to the little handcar he shared with Minnie. That first key-winder now headed a collection of the cars piloted by Santa Claus, Donald Duck, and other critters pottering around the track.

Another interesting item about Lionel's *Vanderbilt* was its combination of die-cast cab and stamped sheet-metal boiler. In its next iteration issued in 1936, the *Vanderbilt* would be all die-cast construction. Literally, the die was cast for stamped-steel locomotives and rolling stock. For Lionel (and rival American Flyer), die-casting was the way of the future

Streamlining continued to spread throughout American life like a rash. Everything from airplanes to automobiles to toasters took on a sleek look. With the M-10000 in regular service as the *Streamliner* between Kansas City and Salinas, Kansas, in 1935 still dazzling

These wind-up handcars became popular after the 1100 Mickey and Minnie model was credited with helping Lionel emerge from receivership in 1934. Santa with Mickey in his sack was added to the line in 1935 and a quacking Donald Duck with Pluto followed in 1936. They cost young railroaders $1. *Train Collectors Association Toy Train Museum, Strasburg, Pennsylvania*

folks, the Chicago, Milwaukee, St. Paul & Pacific stepped up with its magnificent steam-powered *Hiawatha* "Speedliners" also in 1935. Though based on an outdated wheel configuration—the 4-4-2 Atlantic type—the orange-and-gray, streamstyled steamers' 84-inch drivers could sail the *Hiawatha* along easily at 100 MPH with a top speed of 120. Engines 1 and 2 were delivered in the spring of 1935, and Lionel's toy train version appeared in the catalog of that same year. This suggests that, as with many locomotive builders of the period, plans had been sent to Lionel well in advance of the prototypes' debut.

At last, Lionel could finally use its four-wheel drive motor and have the correct wheel configuration as the prototype. The 250E *Hiawatha* required the same O-72-radius track as the M-10000, and it used a similar orange-and-gray color scheme, but on the head end was a red and blue Lionel "L" logo. Its smooth flowing shroud was achieved though die-casting. Lionel had long been using die-cast parts and frames in its locomotives, but the *Hiawatha* locomotive took the process to an aesthetic level that was a tribute to the innovative work of the long-gone Forchheimer Brothers. A non-prototypical articulated passenger-car set was created with a matching color scheme and "Milwaukee Road" lettered on the cars. This flashy steamer lasted until 1942 and was very popular.

Cowen also responded to the coup American Flyer had perpetrated when Flyer got its hands on the plans of Burlington's *Zephyr* 9900 in 1934. The prototype *Zephyr* had been as successful as UP's M-10000, obliterating a dawn-to-dusk speed record over specially cleared tracks. Her Winton diesel engine in the power car and the passengers in the two articulated cars behind were sheathed in welded stainless-steel panels shot-welded together by the Budd Company to form a strong, rivet-free cocoon resembling the fuselage of the DC-3 aircraft. She bucketed along easily at 100 MPH, often pushing beyond that mark in her record-breaking run.

While American Flyer (and Burlington) flogged the *Zephyr* as theirs and theirs alone, Budd sold the *Zephyr* design to two other roads with short-haul passenger needs: the Boston & Maine and neighbor Maine Central. Jointly they took delivery of a *Zephyr* twin, but called it the *Flying Yankee* while operating it between their two lines. Lionel seized upon this prototype. Lionel's O-gauge version had a black die-cast top as part of the sheet-metal power car and, unlike the M-10000 model, the Lionel *Yankee* could run on O-gauge track. For the kids playing with low-end Lionel Jr. O-27 gauge, Lionel made up a copy of the

Zephyr-type streamliner designed by Otto Kuhler for the Gulf, Mobile & Northern Railroad, the *Rebel*. It was painted bright orange with gray trim not unlike the *Hiawatha*. Even farther down the price column was the "Silver Streak," a key-wind version of the *Rebel* but with a reversed color scheme favoring gray on the cars and silver on the shovel-nose locomotive—with a bell and a battery-powered light. Take that, Louis Marx.

The huge event of 1935, however, was Lionel's steam whistle. The clatter of tinplate locomotives and tinplate cars over tin track with the whine of the motor and rattle of the valve gear on Lionel trains was a tonic to most toy train operators, but there was that missing element, that wail of the lonesome whistle in the night, or the combination of long and short blasts that signaled every grade crossing. Posting your little brother next to the gates and having him bellow "woo-wooo" every time the *Limited* swept past lost its charm and besides, he required either threats or candy.

In 1933, Lionel had introduced the "Chugger" to its Standard Gauge steamers. This mechanical device was activated by electricity from the third rail that caused a coil to shake some metal discs. A contact attached to

Two versions of the same crane car offered by Lionel from 1938 to 1942 show the size difference between large and small O-gauge cars. Specialized rolling stock like this, as well as operating accessories such as the coal loader in the background, were promoted as having extra "play value." *Don Roth collection*

A Lionel *Commodore Vanderbilt* streamlined steam locomotive—model 264E—from 1935–36. This O-gauge steamer is a 2-4-2 design modeled on the actual 4-6-4 J-1 Hudson that pulled New York Central passenger trains. *Don Roth collection*

MICKEY MOUSE CIRCUS TRAIN OUTFIT

Mickey Mouse and his tribe of movie stars are in the circus now. The whole Walt Disney family is on this decorated circus train that's hauled by the wind-up Commodore Vanderbilt and stoked by Master Mickey Mouse himself. And what a stoker he is! As the train whizzes around the track, his shovel goes up and down and bingo—right toward the firebox. And look at the tent that comes with the train. A set-up, made of heavy cardboard, 20 inches long, 14 inches high to the top of the flagpole. Outside is a moulded Mickey Mouse barker. Inside is an arena of fun and a flying trapeze. There are regulation circus tickets, a commissary auto, gas station and other cardboard accessories. Band car, dining car and animal car are made of steel, gilded and lithographed in many colors. Train measures 32 inches. Track supplied forms oval 27 by 35 inches. No. 1536, complete, $2.00

Mickey Mouse Circus page from 1935 catalog showing complete circus train, Tent set up, hand car and Santa hand car. Mickey was part of a complete circus outfit featuring a wind-up *Commodore Vanderbilt* locomotive fired and driven by the mouse. "And what a stoker he is!" credits the copy. How true that was for Lionel's financial fortunes. Notice that Santa Claus has been thrust into the breech as well.*Train Collectors Association Toy Train Museum, Strasburg, Pennsylvania*

Lionel's famous Mickey Mouse handcar with Mickey and Minnie at the handle-bars. Loaded with fun and a thousand thrills, they scoot around the track ten times or more at a single winding, bending back and forth, pumping up and down. Handcar measures 7¾ inches long. Eight sections of curved track supplied form a 27 inch circle. No. 1100 Price $1.00 (Price slightly higher in far west)

Santa's taken to the handcar. A Mickey Mouse doll peers out of the pack he is carrying on his back. The figure, the tree and the pack are moulded and hand painted. Santa and his Christmas tree handcar measure 10½ inches in length, 6 inches to the crown of the head. Complete with 8 sections of MWC curved track forming a 27 inch circle. No. 1105 Price $1.00 (Price slightly higher in far west)

REPRODUCTION

40

the piston rod broke and re-connected the contact in time with the turning of the wheels, or a cam was located on the front driver axle, synchronizing the "chug." But Little Brother or a helpful friend was still needed for the *woo-wooo*. In 1935, the locomotive was given its own *woo-wooo*.

The mechanism was located in the coal tender and was activated by a DC current surge initiated by a button on the transformer and piggybacked over the AC power in the track. A small fan was switched on, causing air to be blown over tuned resonating chambers that gave the unmatched breathy quality of a real steam whistle. Its inventor, Charles Giaimo, worked with engineer Joe Bonanno to perfect both the sound and the triggering relay. For those who had older locomotives, "whistle tenders" were sold to update their silent trains.

Lionel's P.R. flacks wanted Cowen to be the father of the steam whistle, so the two inventors obediently knuckled their forelocks and stepped aside. A fictitious story was circulated that has Joshua dashing into the engineering room, wide-eyed and breathless, calling for a halt to all activity until they could gather all manner of recording equipment and follow him down to the New York Central tracks to capture the whistle sound of an NYC steamer. Everybody leaped to their feet and followed their leader with microphones, wire recorders, and oscilloscopes to cling to the grassy banks at trackside, recording the perfect pitch of the passing steamer in the key of F. Actually, according to Ron Hollander's account in his book, *All Aboard*, the tests were made by Bonanno and his staff, but the site was the Lehigh Valley yards near the Irvington plant and Joshua was nowhere to be seen.

The whistle was a real coup. Lionel patented the tender-born mechanism with airtight specifications and later, when American Flyer attempted to provide a similar on-board whistle using an impeller fan in its K-5 locomotive, Lionel sued for infringement and won. Lionel's chief competitor in the years to come had to settle for steam locomotives that emitted an adenoidal squawk that never came near the real thing. After that, any realistic steam toots came from stationary "whistling billboards" spotted along the Flyer layout to be activated by the young engineer when the steamer passed on by.

Lionel's fortunes really gathered steam in 1935 as the country was beginning to see light at the end of the Depression's long dark tunnel. Roosevelt's shotgun efforts to jump-start the economy were having a positive effect in some quarters and the perception that at least something was being done revived many flagging spirits. Cowen's designers and engineers were as unflagging in their enthusiasm as their new little gateman that popped out of its trackside house every time

a whistling locomotive sped past. Lionel's profit for that year was $154,000.

Realism was the guiding principle as railroads routinely sent their plans for new locomotives and rolling stock to Lionel (and American Flyer) headquarters. Die-casting allowed precise sculpting of metal to produce very accurate models—although Lionel had to compress dimensions so that locomotives and cars could negotiate the tight turns of three-rail track.

Continued on page 60

Lionel's *Hiawatha* rounds a curve hauling its articulated passenger car set. Manufactured in 1935 following the debut of the prototype train (below), this so-called "scale model" was designed to run on O-72 wide-radius track and was pricey for its time. The train was very popular and graced the cover of the 1935 catalog. *Chris Rohlfing collection*

Although the 4-4-2 wheel arrangement had largely been replaced by the 4-6-2 (Pacific) on most U.S. railroads by the 1930s, Milwaukee Road chose the Atlantic type to power its new "Speedliner" *Hiawatha* trains. *Hiawatha* engine No. I is shown in 1937. *Ken Zurn, William Raia collection*

Louis Marx and His Tin Trains

arx trains occupy a unique niche in the toy train industry. The products were cheap, attractive, and fun, and—unlike his competitors—Louis Marx sold his product in dime stores as well as Sears and Macy's.

He started out in 1912 as an errand boy for the legendary Ferdinand Strauss, known as the "Founder of the American Mechanical Toy Industry." Strauss said of Marx, "He was a boy with the brain of a man of forty." The elder Strauss took Marx under his wing, but eventually they came to a parting of the ways in 1917 when Louis was 21.

Sergeant Louis Marx returned from World War 1 and picked up where he left off—founding Louis Marx & Co. with his brother, Dave. Without sufficient capital to lease or buy a toy factory, Marx started out working as a middleman between dime stores and toy manufacturers. After establishing himself with his customers, he decided to take a chance on manufacturing the toys he sold. While contracting the C. E. Carter Company to produce cheap tin toys for the mass market, Marx also started selling Joy Line trains produced by Girard Model Works in 1928.

The relationship between Louis Marx and Girard was somewhat unusual. Joy Line Trains were shown next to Marx's products in the 1928 Sears Catalog. In 1928 Marx bought Joy Line materials and yet kept his commission arrangement with Girard. In 1934 they ended their agreement since Girard had been paying Marx commission to sell the trains after Girard had manufactured and shipped them.

Shortly after Louis left, Girard filed for bankruptcy. Marx lost little time in using the common stock they had given him as part of their severance deal as leverage to purchase the company, but kept the Girard name at the plant's location. The Joy Line trains thereafter became electrified and the Girard plant became Marx's train factory while his other locations concentrated on the rest of his toy line.

Even though Lionel was noted for its expensive, high-quality products and Marx for its low-priced electric and key-wind train sets, rumors persisted each year that Lionel would offer cheap sets to challenge Marx and that Marx was going to offer a higher priced line with more accessories to beat up on Lionel's low end offerings. But buyers shrugged at the breast-beating and continued to support Lionel for upscale products and Marx for more economical trains.

Besides having an uncanny gift for knowing what toys would sell, Louis Marx was a whiz at sales promotion and marketing. When Marx dealt with the larger chains such as Sears, Woolworths, or Macy's he allowed each chain to order its own set marketed under their own name. For example, Sears' trains sported the "Happy Time" label. Different colored and detailed sets also meant that he could negotiate different prices for each chain.

Apparently the Depression and World War II had little effect on Marx Manufacturing. Perhaps this was because Louis Marx was always concerned with holding costs down and yet quality was always foremost in his mind, so that each customer got the most for his money. Following the war, the government sent Louis on a tour of German industrial plants to determine their future weapons-making capability. From contacts made during this tour, he expanded his foreign production capacity. As of 1946, the closely held Louis Marx & Co., Inc. released a "financial report" that simply stated, ". . . the company has increased its earnings every year since its inception in 1919."

Variety of product was a Marx standard. It was not uncommon for his plants to blow out 275 toy products in a year. In his train line, Louis believed (as Joshua Lionel Cowen had believed back in the early 1900s) that flatcars

This Honeymoon Express train by Louis Marx provided a lot of action for a couple of bucks including a streamlined articulated train running on a circle of channel track, operating semaphores, tunnels, and bridges plus a surprise action at the center building. This building was often an airplane hangar with a plane circling on a wire or a garage with a car that popped out—all with a single key-wind mechanism. *Don Roth collection*

This is an example of Louis Marx pre-World War II arsenal. All lithographed pieces include wind-up tanks, spring-action guns that shot little bullets, airplanes, trucks, and two prototypes: a war department gondola and a "staff car" that is a war-time version of Marx's "Tricky Taxi" tin toy. The engine is the wind-up 897 in olive drab with a wedge-type tender. After the war, battle toys dropped considerably in popularity until missiles and outer space rockets came along in the late 1950s. *Jim Flynn collection*

and gondolas had more play value than any other type of rolling stock. A child could pile on the cargo, start the engine and off it went. Marx offered ready-made loads, including cars and trucks and military pieces from his own line. Even the passengers on a Marx train had certain personalities. Unlike the anonymous silhouettes on the Lionel cars, Marx passengers included some of his VIP friends along with radio and TV stars such as Jack Benny and Rochester. Marx also negotiated with manufacturers of consumer products to use their logos on the little boxes that would be used as loads on Marx gondolas. His biggest cash savings each year was in sales and advertising. Each year's ad budget was about $2,400 and he employed no outside salesmen. Customers came to Marx, not the other way around. Dime-store chains such as Woolworth and Kresge could be counted on for annual orders of $1 million or more providing Louis with an average profit on each toy of about 10 per cent.

Marx trains halted production in November 1975 when the company was sold to Quaker Oats. Thereafter, the Erie and Girard plants manufactured "Marx Toys," but the metal-lithograph era ended the following year when the company switched to all-plastic sets thanks to new Federal rules on toy materials. From then on freight cars were made of plastic, although Marx Toys still carried some Marx accessories. But Quaker Oats' efforts

were not enough to save the operation. In 1975, the company ended Marx toy manufacturing in Erie and Girard. The country was in the midst of a recession, and disappointing pre-Christmas sales plus heavy competition from Fisher-Price's high quality products were more than Marx could handle. The last toy produced at the Girard plant was the 428C crossing gate.

For the next four years, Marx struggled under new ownership when Quaker Oats sold the operation to the London-based trading firm of Dunbee-Combx-Marx Ltd. DCM only purchased certain assets and personnel, but the struggle continued and in 1980 the Louis Marx & Co. filed for protection under Chapter 11 bankruptcy, after which the assets were scattered among Mego Corporation which took tooling and rights to certain products, Amigo Toy Products, and Empire Products of Atlanta. A real-estate broker handled the dissolution of the facilities at the Girard plant. Only the name remained when a new company was formed in 1983 under the title Louis Marx Toys International Ltd., which now owned the rights to the Marx brand name. Louis Marx died on February 5, 1982, at the age of 85. The company he had built died with him. Years later, that indomitable Marx trademark rose again, reviving its brightly-colored, often whimsical, toy trains, thanks to two enterprising people who believed in the spirit of Marx toys.

The *Flying Yankee*, shown in a colorized postcard scene at Old Orchard Beach, near Portland, Maine, was a virtual twin to Burlington's famous *Zephyr* 9900 of 1934. It was jointly purchased in 1935 from Budd Company and Electro-Motive by the Maine Central and Boston & Maine. Because Burlington had laid claim to the *Zephyr* name, B&M and MEC chose the *Flying Yankee* name for their new streamliner. Later it was rechristened as the *Minute Man* and *Cheshire* when transferred to other runs. *Mike Schafer collection*

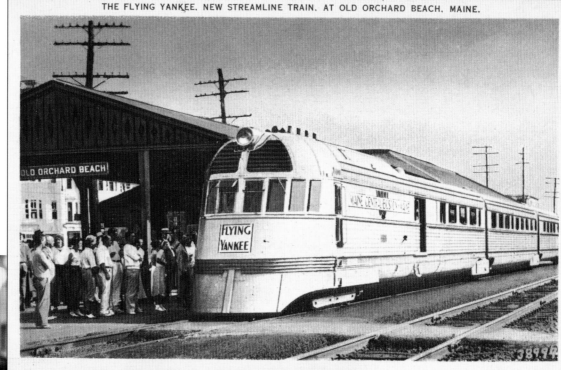

THE FLYING YANKEE, NEW STREAMLINE TRAIN, AT OLD ORCHARD BEACH, MAINE.

The 1936 Lionel *Flying Yankee* was fabricated with a cast nose section grafted onto a stamped metal carbody. The prototype for this train, shown at top of page, ran between Boston, Massachusetts, and Portland, Maine. In response to American Flyer snapping up the plans for the original Burlington *Zephyr*, Lionel produced this version of a *Zephyr* cousin. *Don Roth collection*

Continued from page 57

Specific model prototyping spread to all the toy train manufacturers. When the Union Pacific's diesel-powered M-10005 streamliner, the *City of Denver*, was placed in service in 1936, Marx received a set of plans and by Christmas of that same year put out a model of its own in colorful lithographed tin. American Flyer, following in Lionel's wake with die-cast *Hiawatha* locomotives and *City of Denver* models of

its own, jumped out with a die-cast 4-6-4 Hudson steamer in 1936. It was a good-looking engine with six drivers and two departures from the prototype—the front truck had only two wheels instead of four and the rear truck looked like a it had four wheels but only had two. Lionel's die-cast No. 1688 Pennsylvania Railroad streamlined "torpedo" K4-class steamer was featured on the cover of Lionel's catalog when the aerodynamically cowled prototype made its debut. The Pennsy locomotive saw brief assignment to the *Broadway Limited* in 1938, but maintenance was found to be too costly and the shrouding eventually was removed. Lionel's streamlined K4 made its debut as a Lionel Jr. product and remained a popular model for the low-end market the following year when the Lionel Jr. name was dropped in favor of "O-27 gauge." The torpedo continued in the line with variations in both O-27 and O-gauge until 1940.

In 1937, Lionel scooped the entire industry. The scale model No. 700E 4-6-4 Hudson showed that if

Lionel wanted to flex its design muscle, it was still the big dog on the block. The Toy Fair held in New York every spring offered buyers a preview of proposed models to be brought out later in the year. Of course, some of these models were experimental or were shown to test the waters for reaction. Among its other offerings, Lionel displayed a pair of bombshells. One was a handmade brass model of a Hudson created by a Swedish firm in New York. It was exquisite with every detail of piping, valve gear, pop valves, pumps, reverse gear, and rivet detail from the prototype's plans. The wheel rims were not the usual wide flanges needed to circumnavigate tubular tinplate three-rail track; rather, they were scale size in correct proportion to the drive wheels. Next to the brass model was a plaster replica of another variation of the Hudson, this one with a Vanderbilt-style tender and slightly less detail with wheel flanges designed for tinplate track.

Buyers and dealers looked to see if they had wandered into the wrong booth. Lionel had upped the quality of its designs with die-casting, but the four-wheel drive motor still provided the power. This six-wheel beauty was no "homage" to the real thing like

the 400E or any of the other stamped-steel locomotives in Lionel's roster. This was a 1:48 scale model appealing to real hobbyists who had long disdained Lionel's best efforts, hobbyists who expected to pay several hundred dollars for such craftsmanship. Had Joshua finally gone soft under the strain of bootstrapping his company out of the red?

Joshua Lionel Cowen could do something neither Louis Marx, nor William Ogden Coleman, nor Harry Ives, nor even the hotshot toy entrepreneur of the time, A. C. Gilbert, could do. He could see a real opportunity, back his hunch to the hilt, and turn the market on its ear. Cowen had recognized that there was a growing segment of adult males who were building accurate reproduction layouts that were more than toys. Lionel had never been considered for this market because of its "cartoonlike" locomotives and rolling stock. Although some small startup companies were serving these more sophisticated customers, none had the resources commanded by Lionel. Also, the extreme detailing allowed by modern zinc-alloy die-casting would begin showing up in the rest of Lionel's trains as employees in the American

The Model 238 K-4 "Torpedo" was offered by Lionel in gray from 1936 to 1938. It is a streamlined shrouded 4-4-2 steam engine built for the Pennsylvania Railroad that should have a Pacific-type 4-6-2 wheel configuration. The prototype was designed by Raymond Loewy and wind-tunnel tested. *Chris Rohlfing collection*

plants became more skillful with the process. This model represented more than an announcement of a product—it was a challenge.

The cost to build the first 700E was somewhere between $45,000 and $75,000, requiring Lionel's sales staff to peddle at least 1,500 of them to break even. Customers could buy it to run or to show it off on a special walnut stand. To run it required a special track called "T-rail" whose edges were prototypically sharp to accommodate the narrow driver flanges. Cost to the customer for the locomotive and tender alone was $75—a huge sum for a toy train in 1937—but then again, this was no toy. Back at Lionel headquarters, a special passenger train, the *Rail Chief,* was designed to ride behind the Hudson: four cars including a combine, two coaches, and an observation car—all for $97.50 including enough T-rail track for a 100 x 72-inch oval. While potential buyers patted the sweat from their brows and called their home offices, the brass model was shipped to Italy to have the dies made. When the 1937 catalog arrived, the 700E Hudson—exactly as seen at the Toy Fair—the 763 Hudson, priced at $37.50 and designed for tubular O-72 track, and the *Rail Chief* train set were all a reality. The 700E locomotive and tender were 24 inches long and weighed more than 15 pounds. Complex Baker valve gear was connected to open-spoked drive wheels. Its tender contained Lionel's whistle and rode on trucks with Timken bearings. Hobbyists took out their magnifying glasses and counted 1,600 separate rivets on its shell—just three short of the prototype. For hardcore O-gauge scale modelers who ran two-rail track and an outside third rail for power, a pick-up shoe

was included with the 700E with directions for its attachment. Its introduction hit the media and the toy train market like a grenade.

That same year, Lionel went public for the first time with an offering of 77,000 shares at $12 a share. Also, the boy in the knickers seen in early Lionel ads spreading his arms wide over a Lionel train set was being lured into the business. Lawrence Cowen was taking time off from his brokerage firm to attend board meetings. The grooming of Lawrence to eventually take over the growing enterprise had begun in earnest. This reeling in of Lawrence must have made Joshua feel as proud as Lionel's first strike made him feel bitter.

The strike was more of a slap against Mario Caruso than against Cowen. Caruso had assumed Cowen's mantel of *paterfamilias* to the work force—a stern pater to be sure, but he felt the workers owed him their absolute dedication. He wouldn't even listen to their demands for unionization and better working standards, plus a raise in the base pay. After two weeks, they knuckled under accepting less of a raise and no union. But the rift had occurred and the "one big happy family" that had once been Lionel was scarred. By 1942, the Toyworkers' Union had become established in the plant and now grievances would be settled by arbitration rather than management's benevolence, or lack thereof.

In 1938, the run at the hobbyist market started by the 700E was kept on the boil with Lionel's leap into the OO-gauge market. This strictly hobby gauge was smaller than O and slightly larger than HO, the distance between its rails measuring 3/4 of an inch (compared to 7/8 of an inch of HO and 1 1/4 inches for O-gauge). Here again, the market was served by a few

The legendary New York Central System rostered hundreds of Hudsons—locomotives which came to symbolize the mighty NYC—and subsequently a number of toy and model train manufacturers have released models of NYC 4-6-4s. The railroad's Hudson fleet kept passengers moving throughout the reach of the NYC, from New York to Chicago and from Boston to St. Louis. NYC Hudson 5399 is leaving St. Louis Union Station circa 1950 with a train bound for the East Coast. *Jay Williams collection*

small companies that offered scale model kits for a discerning customer base interested in rivet-counter realism. Lionel's move to this market was following the trend of downsizing which in those days meant smaller homes, smaller paychecks, and less space for toy (or scale model) train layouts. Also, hobby buyers bought all year long. They were not a seasonal business, but assembled large, scenery-laden "pikes" in their basements and spare rooms.

The toy train manufacturers made their money in the fall and winter and gave it all back in the spring and summer with product development and advertising set-up for the seasonal push. Every manufacturer was searching for the year-round filler product. Lionel had added a tethered model airplane to its line and were always trying to crack American Flyer's Erector Set grip on the metal construction and chemistry set market. Farther back in its history, Lionel had offered race cars and even a working stove for girls, but neither caught on. The adult hobby market was growing. Germany had introduced HO back in 1924, and OO-gauge arrived in the 1930s. Like the days in 1913 when O-gauge was introduced by Ives, here was a market Lionel could make its own.

In *Standard Gauge*, a title in the series of Lionel books by Tom McComas and James Tuohy, an interview with Elliott Donnelley, founder of Scalecraft and a pioneer maker of OO-gauge kits, gives some insight into Lionel's high-handed entry into the market. There is no doubt that Lionel engineers produced an excellent offering of die-cast OO

locomotives and rolling stock, but while the rolling-stock dies were being made, Lionel was, apparently, not above salting the mine a bit by using a competitor's products.

Elliott Donnelley was passing the F. A. O. Schwartz toy store window in New York and saw a display of Lionel OO-gauge trains. The freight cars looked familiar so he went inside and buttonholed a buyer he knew who rhapsodized on the beauty of Lionel's trains. Donnelly led the buyer to the display and picked up one of the freight cars. Stamped on the bottom was the name Scalecraft. Lionel had bought Scalecraft OO kits, built them, and put on its own decals. The cast-metal cars, when they were produced, were dead ringers for the Scalecraft/Lionel samples. Fortunately, Donnelley had patented the miniature wheel suspensions and Lionel had copied those too. Thereafter, Lionel paid Donnelley a royalty on each car built. Unfortunately, when Lionel muscled into the OO market, its marketing and manufacturing horsepower forced Scalecraft out of OO production.

Lionel built an exquisite OO-gauge die-cast version of the O-gauge 700E for two-rail track and a "semi-scale" version—like the O-gauge No. 763—for OO three-rail track. Either locomotive could be had with or without a whistle. In 1939, both Hudsons were offered in two or three-rail versions, and the same freight cars were continued: box car, tank car, coal hopper, and caboose with variations in decals and road names. These ready-to-run models were expensive but were well-received by the hobby market and

The legendary Lionel 700E scale Hudson offered in 1937 stunned modelers both with its extensive die-cast detail and its $75 price tag. It ran on special T-rail track with a 72 inch radius curve. It is a valuable collectible today since it closely followed the prototype, capturing the flavor of New York Central's finest. *Chris Rohlfing collection*

were carried until 1942 when World War II shut down all toy train production. If they had been brought back after the war, who knows where Lionel might be today in a marketplace dominated by adult hobbyists? But Lionel had made a commitment to O and O-27 gauges as its market winners, and only later, in 1957, did Lionel make a desperate lunge at the HO market as its world was falling down around itself.

This commitment to what were once its "low end" gauges tolled the bell for Standard Gauge as well. The rich-boy's gauge was now too expensive to build, and sales had plummeted during the Depression years. When the financial crunch eased somewhat as the 1930s ended, those sales did not rebound. Lionel's beautiful big trains now looked old-fashioned and out-of-touch with a world of realism opened up by zinc-alloy die-casting and the real world of America's downsizing demographics. There were plans afoot to further expand Lionel Lines with electronic and modeling innovations that would only be possible in the smaller scale. There were no more big train competitors.

Joshua could take some comfort that he had outlasted them all with his glorious electrics, brawny steamers, hefty State passenger cars, and a rainbow of freight rolling stock—the stuff that made young pulses race faster as the metal wheels sped around impossibly tight curves with a clatter of noise and blur of brass and enameled steel. In 1939, Lionel discontinued Standard Gauge.

The end of the 1930s also brought to market two evolutionary developments that would mark Lionel's future until the present. When Lionel created its Distant Control locomotives back in the 1920s, the idea of controlling other parts of a train layout without leaving the transformer evolved into the new steam whistle and, ultimately, "remote control" of all manner of electro-mechanical accessories. A panel board had been designed by Joseph Bonanno that used knife switches to activate lighting and accessories, but push-button control was more modern, and the controls took up less space. In 1938, Lionel introduced the coal elevator that loaded coal dumped into a bin by a remote-controlled dump car standing on a magnet-activated track section. At another command, the full elevator bin dumped its contents into a car waiting on a parallel track. From this came the log loader, the magnetic crane, and an aluminum bascule bridge that, when raised, stopped an oncoming train. By 1940, these accessories were selling briskly, and designs for even more complex models were on the drawing boards.

The second development was a natural extension of the die-casting process using phenolic—trade name, Bakelite—plastic to make a fully detailed boxcar and magnesium alloy to create a tank car, coal hopper, and caboose designs. These cars were first built to run behind the 700E Hudson with scale couplers and shallow-flange wheels on T-rail track, but a second set was made with deep flanges and tinplate trucks with the new "box" couplers invented in 1936 and improved in 1938. The cars were introduced in 1940 both as ready-to-run and as kits and met with a good reception from the hobbyist community. Though their production was shut down in 1942, lessons learned in their construction would result in Lionel's most realistic and successful toy trains in the postwar period.

Over at American Flyer Manufacturing Company in Chicago, changes were also occurring that would profoundly affect that company's postwar market as well and put them on sound competitive footing against

Prewar (1938–42) Lionel automated accessories included this classic No. 97 Coal Elevator that accepted coal dumped into its rear bunker; a remote-control motor-driven conveyor then moved the coal up into the shelter. At the push of another button, the coal then spewed down into a waiting car on the front track. *Don Roth collection*

Lionel built a set of scale freight cars for the 700E scale Hudson to haul on T-rail scale track. The 1:48 proportion models were a huge leap forward for Lionel. The 714 box car was cast from "phenolic plastic" (Bakelite) while the tank car and hopper were cast from magnesium alloy. They only lasted until 1942 and then Lionel dropped the scale modeler hobbyist market. *Train Collectors Association Toy Train Museum, Strasburg, Pennsylvania*

For size comparison, a Lionel O-gauge 685 "small" Hudson built in 1953 is alongside a 5342 OO Scale Hudson from 1938. The OO scale came from Europe and was slightly larger than HO scale. This beautiful little engine represented Lionel's bid for the scale hobby market that was growing before World War II. Second guessing and second thoughts doomed the line and it disappeared in 1942 when all toy train production was shut down. *Train Collectors Association Toy Train Museum, Strasburg, Pennsylvania*

Lionel. In 1936, William Coleman produced a die-cast Hudson that was a quantum leap ahead of anything American Flyer had produced to that time, but it was not the magic bullet that could restore financial stability to the rocky company. At this time, toy entrepreneur A. C. Gilbert was looking for a way to expand from his Erector Sets, chemistry sets, and magic kits into the toy train business. He struck a deal with Coleman and bought the company with the idea that Coleman would stay on to manage the operation. Coleman's untimely death in 1939 put A. C. Gilbert in full charge.

Letting no grass grow under his feet, Gilbert packed up the entire American Flyer operation and moved it to New Haven, Connecticut. Being as sharp as Lionel's people, Gilbert embraced the realism concept, and in that same year he scrapped the toylike Flyer stock and had dies made of new scale model designs to be ready for both the 1939 catalog and the Toy Fair. These first locomotives—New York Central Hudsons—ran on O-gauge track but were built to $3/16$-inch scale. In this proportion, they were elegant models. Also part of the package was a "choo-choo" device that produced a similar effect to Lionel's "chugger" and an automatic link-type coupler that would last into the postwar period. To run behind the Hudsons, a line of die-cast freight cars plus a passenger car set was rushed into the market. They were long, low, and realistic.

By 1940, the scale American Flyer line fielded a full line of die-cast locomotives including a 4-8-4 ("Northern" type), a Pennsylvania K-5 Pacific (4-6-2), as well as a Reading 4-4-2 Atlantic, and a sleek streamline-shrouded locomotive that arrived as a 4-4-2 Atlantic, then evolved into a 4-6-2 patterned after the streamlined Pacific that pulled Baltimore & Ohio's *Royal Blue* between Jersey City and Washington, D.C.

Over at Lionel, as the American Flyer scale model trains made their startling appearance under the new A. C. Gilbert ownership, there must have been an uneasy feeling that the gauntlet had been taken up. Lionel's challenge had been met by an old competitor guided by a new Paladin no less driven and market-savvy than Joshua Cowen himself. And would Lawrence, the heir apparent to guide Lionel's hard-won pre-eminence, be up to the task of running with the likes of Gilbert and the canny Louis Marx?

Overseas, Hitler was spreading the stain of Nazism over Western Europe. In December 1939, a Roper poll determined that 67.4 percent of Americans interviewed favored neutrality. By May of 1940, that same poll noted 67.5 percent now favored aiding Britain in her lonely stand against the Nazis and Fascists. America was shifting into war production as the proclaimed "Arsenal of Democracy" and the Depression economy was fading fast.

Hearts must have beat faster at Lionel as Americans went to work churning out tanks, planes, and armaments earmarked for the war. Big overtime paychecks meant more disposable incomes for both hobbyist acquisitions and presents for little tikes as the holiday season of 1941 loomed. As "America First" champions railed against involvement in any foreign wars, plans moved forward at Lionel to meet American Flyer head to head in 1942. At the same time, old filing cabinet drawers were probably opened and plans stored in 1918 for wartime assembly line conversion were perhaps dusted off and re-opened—just in case.

The classic of all classic Lionel offerings, the Electro-Motive F3 in Santa Fe "warbonnet" colors. The O-gauge Santa Fe F3, Model 2333, arrived in 1948 and became the signature electric train locomotive for postwar Lionel. It offered kids in the Western U.S. a locomotive of their own complete with coil-cooperating couplers and a battery-driven horn. Released with a companion in New York Central livery, the F3 diesel's debut was not expected to be auspicious by Lionel's founder. Joshua Cowen expected to maybe sell 10,000, then yank the locomotive from the catalog. As the locomotive disappeared from dealers' shelves and manufacturing zoomed past the 100,000 mark, he gladly admitted he had been wrong as he wheelbarrowed F3 revenues to the bank. More than a half century later, you could still buy Lionel F-units. The famous Santa Fe livery would itself become an icon in American railroading, its image still seen in 2000. *Steve Esposito collection*

chapter 3
War and Postwar
The Enemy is Joined: 1941-1957

"President Roosevelt urges armament manufacturers to bring the production of planes up to 50,000 a year."
—New York Times, *April 1940*

"Unglaublich!" ["Unbelievable!"]
—Field Marshall Hermann Goering

"The Americans are so helpless that they fall back again and again upon boasting about their materiel . . ."
—Joseph Goebbels, Minister of Propaganda

"American aircraft production exceeded 290,000, naval ships, 71,000, tanks and self-propelled guns, 102,000 . . . at no time did armaments exceed more than 40 per cent of gross national product . . ."
—This Fabulous Century, *Time-Life Books, 1969*

"Lionel Always Leads"
—Lionel advertising copy

As Japan's brilliant tactician, Admiral Yamamoto, sat with his officers in the ward room of the battleship *Yamato*, basking in the success of his surprise aerial attack on the American fleet at Hawaii's Pearl Harbor anchorage, a note was brought to him. For the first time, he discovered his attack had been delivered before the diplomatic declaration of war had been made to the American government. He was thunderstruck. Gravely, he looked up from the sheet of paper and said, "We have awakened a sleeping giant . . ."

When that attack was made on December 7, 1941, America's army was rated 17th among the other nations of the world. Her air forces flew obsolete planes, and now her heavy-gun navy was virtually wiped out in a stroke. Yamamoto, having once been stationed in the U.S., understood what Hitler, Goering, and Goebbels did not. Although America had weak armed forces now, her war-production capacity could outstrip the combined Axis powers. To that immense capability was now added a cold-eyed, implacable resolve. And, as he feared, with a collective roar from millions of throats, the giant leaped.

Lionel had been on war footing before, during what was now called World War I. In 1940, it had already shifted parts of the plant to war production. Now, its toy train plans were shelved for the duration, and, like its competitors, Lionel converted all its machinery from stamping out track and trains to producing war materiel. Lionel returned to its World War I specialty—marine navigation instruments: magnetic compass binnacles, the pelorus for taking bearings on nearby shores, and the alidade, a telescopic version of the pelorus for taking bearings on distant shore points.

At the A. C. Gilbert Company in New Haven, Connectictut, workers that had been assembling American Flyer trains were now turning out piece parts for

A Lionel 3356 operating horse car unloads its nags into their corral where they mill about and re-enter the car—all at the push of a button. It took a careful hand at the throttle to align the car doors with the two ramps back in 1957. A fascinating array of operating accessories such as the corral and other gadgetry helped make the postwar electric train phenomenon the most fascinating of all to watch and operate. *Chris Rohlfing collection*

67

Model Builder magazine shows a 1934 M-10000 and a *Flying Yankee* diesel running on O-72 track with more ties and generous 72-inch radius curves. The war was approaching, and Lionel was already featuring past glories. *Toy Train Collectors Association Toy Train Museum, Strasburg, Pennsylvania*

An ad inside a war-era copy of the *Wonder Book of Railroading* announced that "Lionel has gone to sea." The copy explains how Lionel's engineering expertise was being put to use building navigational aids for the Navy. The photo shows one of the compass binnacles Lionel built, and below was a pennant for victory and the "M" flag for merit from the Maritime Commission. *Toy Train Collectors Association Toy Train Museum, Strasburg, Pennsylvania*

MODEL BUILDER

DECEMBER, 1941

10¢

LIONEL HAS GONE TO SEA

LIONEL has gone to sea! Which may explain why you couldn't get the equipment you wanted this year.

Yes, Lionel too, like almost everyone else these days, is working for Uncle Sam.

On any warship today you will find the kind of instruments that Lionel is now producing, such as: the compass compensating binnacle; the pelorus; the alidade, azimuth and bearing circles and taffrail logs.

Lionel's precision tools of hairline tolerances and its close, expert engineering supervision have been employed in producing these all-important marine instruments.

The compensating binnacle holds the ship's compass. The pelorus is an instrument used for obtaining bearings by stellar observation. The alidade is a calibrated sighting device. You can see that a ship—or lifeboat

—without these navigating aids would soon be a prey to those sharks of the underseas, the submarine, as well as to enemy planes and battleships.

The binnacle is equipped with inner and outer magnet trays mounted on riser rods helically geared and calibrated so that, by means of a crank, the magnets can be adjusted micrometrically. The compass itself is adjusted to an accuracy of ten minutes or less at all headings. The pelorus is made of parts so finely machined, clean cut and accurate that its use has really been simplified.

All of this goes to show that the talent Lionel has been bringing—for some 43 years—to the production of those highly intricate miniature locomotive parts is now being employed in full force for the United States Government. The precision and accuracy which has produced such true-to-life model trains is now producing instruments that not only safeguard the lives of our men and ships but are working to guarantee the peace and the freedom of the high seas and the open road!

In recognition of "outstanding achievement", the Lionel Corporation has been awarded the coveted "M" pennant and Victory Fleet flag of the Maritime Commission.

can's—that the Axis would be defeated. Once that was accomplished, kids would want trains again. And this time, not just kids would be the focus of sales efforts, but their dads as well—as hobby model builders. Lionel had seen the trend toward providing realistic kits to model builders grow during the late 1930s. The OO-gauge trains had a chance to gain a foothold after World War I, and the stir caused by Lionel's scale Hudson and freight cars had been exhilarating. The trick was to keep Lionel's name in front of current and future customers even as the new war raged overseas.

In 1937, Lionel had launched a magazine called *Model Builder*. This publication replaced *The Lionel Magazine*— "A Magazine of Railroading for Boys" introduced in 1930. The *Model Builder* more closely allied itself with a "hobby" readership that included not just model railroaders, but modelers interested in "Trains, Planes and Boats" as stated on the magazine's masthead. Since Lionel offered ready-to-run motorboats as well as a tethered-control airplane, Joshua Cowen wanted to move the company into a venue that offered year-round sales potential, not just a seasonal Christmas-tree train set rush at the end of the year. This resolve lasted for one year.

By 1938, *Model Builder*—its shortened name—was reclassified as "The Magazine of Model Railroading for Men and Boys," an admission of defeat in its effort to boost interest in boats and airplanes. Lionel was now a model railroad company and seeking to appeal to a broader spectrum of railroad aficionados. Between 1938 and 1941, editorial content wrestled between the "Men and Boys" market. More and more articles showed complex permanent layouts and scenery projects well beyond Little Billy squatting next to the Christmas tree watching his four-car freight whiz around the carpet. Dads and even grown-ups without kids were filling basements and corners of recreation rooms with scale miles of HO- and O-gauge tracks. Evenings were being spent listening to Fred Allen on the radio while laboring with sticks of wood, Ambroid cement, flash-filled castings, soggy decals, and barely decipherable mimeographed instructions on the dining room table spread with a newspaper that read, "Hitler Overruns France."

machine guns and land mines. Gilbert's design know-how was channeled into creating triggers for booby traps and other firing devices. Louis Marx's plants pushed weapons parts out the doors by the millions.

On the home front, ships that had taken months to build now were sent down the ways in a few weeks; auto manufacturers cranked out planes and tanks while B-24 bombers flew with engines made by Singer Sewing Machine Company. As men went off to fight, women filled their places on assembly lines. Retirees were called back to help run the railroads alongside kids who were below draft age while women went to work in the shops and yards.

As many old Lionel trains were collected in scrap drives and war materiel flowed out by the truck- and trainload, Lionel's marketing people understood—with the matter-of-fact confidence shared by most Ameri-

There were also cartoons, puzzles, and chatty pieces on "Railroad Jargon" and how real railroad brakemen and conductors signal engineers with hand signals. And, of course, new Lionel O-gauge trains and accessories were featured. With the economy climbing out of the Depression on the back of war production—President Roosevelt's "Arsenal for Democracy" was already shipping to threatened European nations—Lionel returned to the warm and fuzzy relationship with its customer base by changing its stated mission yet again in 1941. *Model Builder* was now "The Magazine of Model Railroading for Fathers and Sons."

The war stopped production of toy trains, and *Model Builder* magazine was Lionel's vehicle to keep its name afloat as its ads boomed, "Lionel Has Gone to War!" The magazine obeyed restrictions of the War Production Board and reduced its use of paper by 25 per cent and dumped color from its photos and illustrations, turning to stark, single-color pen and ink covers. Stories about prototype railroads and operation replaced new product fluff. Complex model railroads built by adults—and father-son projects—provided future dreams for kids who had no new additions to their train sets as the war rolled through 1942, 1943, and 1944.

With the successful D-Day landings in June 1944, and the Marines' bloody successes against the Japanese in the Pacific, the end of the war was actually in sight. *Model Builder*'s quality and content also improved and began to gear up expectations for postwar wonders to come. That changeable masthead finally lost its targeted message and now read simply, "Published by Lionel."

As the magazine struggled with its identity, another device was pushed out the marketing door in late 1943 that really puzzled everyone—the Paper Train. Here's the picture: Little Billy races downstairs Christmas morning, rips the paper off a thick and heavy box, sees the name "Lionel," lets out a whoop and spills colorful sheets of light cardboard out on the living-room rug. Silence. That same afternoon, Dad begins assembling a cardboard locomotive while Billy struggles with folding and tabbing together lengths of cardboard track. A brown bag of wood axles is opened, and they are pressed into nickel-thick cardboard wheels. At 2 P.M.

on New Year's day, Billy looks down at his completed Lionel cardboard train. Silence.

This lamentable effort was the product of fast-talking Samuel Gold, the self-styled "Premium King" who cranked out millions of cheap little toys and premiums stuffed into candy boxes. He convinced Joshua that a cardboard train was just the ticket to keep the little mites happy and keep Lionel in the public mind. He was wrong on both counts.

The year 1944 marked another high-water mark in the history of Lionel. Mario Caruso, the *capo de tutti capi*—boss of bosses—at Lionel's manufacturing plants resigned. Since 1904 when Caruso arrived at Lionel from an Italian settlement house, his rise through the organization had been swift. His obvious mechanical ability had been revealed when he became a solderer at age 19, and from then on Joshua had become his benefactor. What blossomed was Caruso's organizational ability and his willingness to extract the last ounce possible of efficiency from the production lines. Though nepotism was rampant at

During the war, Joshua Cowen was pressured to keep a train of some kind in kids' hands. Lionel came up with this paper train with 198 inches of O-gauge paper track, locomotive, tender, boxcar, gondola, and caboose rolling on flanged wheels and 22 wood axles. Also featured were self-locking couplers; a railroad crossing signal; railroad crossing gate; cut-out stand-up figures including an engineer, brakeman, and freight handler; freight; lumber; and packing case. The train ran around its oval track with a push of the hand—after dad recovered from his nervous breakdown caused by building the thing. *Toy Train Collectors Association Toy Train Museum, Strasburg, Pennsylvania*

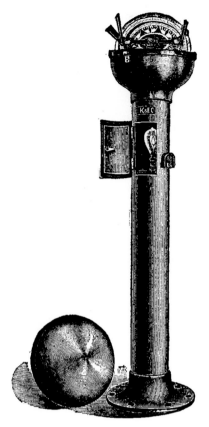

Lionel made navigational equipment for the Navy during both world wars. This pelorus was mounted on an outside bridge wing and was used to take bearings on a floating magnetic compass card from fixed objects on the near shore. *Blue Jacket Manual, U. S. Navy, 1939*

Lionel, and drafts of Italian immigrants from shelters in New Jersey swelled its work force, Caruso's heavy-handed touch of the lash was also relatively even-handed. Everyone, regardless of ties to the old soil, fell under his hard ascetic gaze at one time or another. As one former Lionel worker said, "When J. L. C. visited the plant, everyone smiled. When Caruso arrived, everyone hid."

The cycle of Lionel manufacturing, driven by the seasonal market, required that assembly and other production workers be laid off following Christmas and then re-hired in late March. The New York Toy Fair in March was the hunting ground for Lionel sales people, writing up orders as fast as they could. This resulted in a mad scramble to push the re-hires into their jobs and get production up to full steam. Outside vendors were frequently pressed into service, taking away from Lionel's bottom line.

Caruso's suggestion to move tooling and die-making to Italy in the 1920s saved Lionel a fortune in labor and material costs. The subsequent purchase of the Societa Meccanica La Precisa in Naples by Caruso in the 1930s and installation of his son as president also seemed wise as La Precisa continued to provide dies and designs for Lionel such as the 1937 Hudson scale model locomotive. That same year, Caruso had stared down the unions in Lionel's first strike, but by 1942, the United Paper, Novelty, and Toymakers Union had outflanked the boss, and Caruso lost control of the assembly lines to arbitration. That 1937 watershed also saw young Lawrence Cowen ascend to the Lionel board of directors blocking any chance for Caruso's son, Anthony, to accept the mantle when Joshua retired. Anthony had a considerable knowledge of the business through his management of La Precisa and having left school at age 14 with his sister, Lydia, to work at Lionel's assembly line. Also, Caruso, who had grown up with grease under his fingernails, did not get along with Lawrence, the Cornell-educated and pampered scion whose road in life had been paved with Joshua's money. To compound Mario's dilemmas, his La Precisa operation in Naples had been nationalized by Mussolini to produce Italian armaments and stood a good chance of being bombed to rubble. All of his and Lionel's investments in its facilities would be lost.

With Lawrence Cowen on one side and Benito Mussolini on the other, Caruso's future legacy and his family's fortunes were on precarious ground. He looked around for other possible opportunities in the wartime economy. He chose boxes. Lionel needed wooden boxes to ship its war materiel now and its trains later. The armed forces needed boxes to ship thousands of items overseas. After dispatching his overworked administrative assistant, Lawrence Parker, to scour the forest country of the Northeast for a manufacturing facility, Caruso settled on a dilapidated woodworking plant in West Paris, Maine, and a former shoe factory in Richmond, Maine.

Caruso spread his bets by creating "C-8 Laboratories" with a board of directors made up of himself, his wife, and their six kids as well as the "Oxford Wood and Plastics Company." Even though the long-suffering Parker discovered most of the forests in the area had prior claims on their lumber and the labor pool in the area was also committed, Caruso, oblivious to the problems, complained about costs and low production as Lionel waited for its contracted boxes. To further confuse matters, Caruso talked Joshua into producing a line of wooden, insipid-looking dog rockers with googly eyes for the kiddy trade. Cowen had already punched out the Paper Train flop in 1943, and the kiddy rockers, called "Lion-Eds," probably seemed like a good idea as Paper Train sets gathered spider nests on dealers' shelves.

By October 1944, Caruso resigned from Lionel. The Maine corporate entities, rebuilt in part with Lionel's money, passed into the Caruso family's hands. The box business eventually improved, and Lionel products continued to use Caruso's crates at least through 1949. Lion-Eds also died a deserved death in 1945, and with the end of the war, Lionel returned to making toy trains. Larry Parker, who was on Lionel's payroll while slaving for Caruso's private interests, quit to go to work for A. C. Gilbert. Joshua Lionel Cowen, who was no fool and could read a balance sheet with the best of them, had indulged Caruso's private manipulations as repayment for 40 years of unflinching loyalty and the establishment of Lionel's extremely high quality manufacturing capabilities.

World War II ground toward its degraded Wagnerian conclusion in Germany, and in the Pacific the Japanese were committing their young men to suicide tactics to stem the Allied tide. Even as tragic casualty lists appeared in America's newspapers in 1945, the march toward victory seemed inevitable. Also inevitable was the return to the business of business. For Lionel, this meant storming the toy train market with exciting innovations and an advertising blitz fueled with baskets of war contract cash. They must have known the folks over at A. C. Gilbert's American Flyer camp were supercharged with new products.

Louis Marx had not been idle wearing his millionaire industrialist hat, hobnobbing with friends in the military such as Supreme Commander Dwight Eisenhower,

Air Force General "Hap" Arnold, and Eisenhower's key man, General Walter Bedell Smith. Marx's postwar expansion plans were greased financially and politically. After the European victory, Eisenhower asked Louis to tour the surviving German toy plants to make sure they could not be reconverted to war production. This visit to 171 factories eventually led to Marx production being expanded to numerous foreign countries when the postwar "baby boom" hit.

The end of the war was a busy time for Lionel. First, some farm animals at the factory had to be ousted. A wonderful story in Ron Hollander's history of Joshua Lionel Cowen and the Lionel company, *All Aboard* (Workman Publishing, New York), tells about how fresh albumen was needed for an alcohol-resistant paint that coated the inside of marine compass binnacles. To obtain the freshest possible albumin, a chicken roost was built on the premises with a red light that signaled whenever an egg dropped. Catching farm fever, Mario Caruso installed a pair of pigs to eat up cafeteria garbage, make a family, and provide bacon and ham to the employees.

As the critters returned to New Jersey's rural farms, Lionel designers began to unleash a steady stream of innovative products that pushed the company to the top of toy train market. Stunning everybody—especially American Flyer—was the introduction of a realistic, remote-control knuckle coupler.

For decades, no one had created an operating toy train coupler that resembled the modern version of the Janney knuckle coupler. Everything from bent pieces of wire to Louis Caruso's "automatic" latch coupler had been tried, and while they managed to link the cars together, coupling and separating the cars required "hand-of-God" railroading manipulating them with the fingers. In 1938, Lionel had introduced a remote control "box" coupler that could be opened with the push of a button while crossing an electro-magnet-loaded section of track. The couplers worked, but did not even remotely resemble the prototype. In 1945, that all changed.

The first Lionel knuckle coupler had an electromagnet built in to the four-wheel truck. It was activated by a sliding shoe that passed over a rail on a special track section that could be energized to trip the magnet and open the coupler. Once open, simply backing one coupler into another produced a firm join like a pair of grasping hands. It had two basic flaws. There were too many parts, making it expensive to manufacture, and the sliding shoe would occasionally either derail or uncouple a car passing over a switch. Regardless of these problems, the coupler hit

Once Lionel assimilated Ives, a "transition" hook and latch coupler was designed to accommodate rolling stock from either line. *Toy Train Collectors Association Toy Train Museum, Strasburg, Pennsylvania*

Lionel's first manual box coupler was introduced in 1936 for the large O-gauge cars. Later on, it was dropped down into the smaller-series cars. In 1938, Lionel followed up its manual box coupler with an automatic version that opened when passing over an electro-magnet in a special track section. In that same year, different truck designs also dictated high and low coupler heights, adding to coupling problems when cars were intermixed. *Don Roth collection*

the toy train world with the same force as the remote-control steam whistle.

American Flyer had a few tricks up its sleeves as well. Flyer's big selling point for the postwar period was "Realism!" To achieve that end, it abandoned 40-year-old three-rail track and went to two-rail track. Flyer abandoned O-gauge and followed its prewar lead by staying with scale models but adopting S-gauge—smaller than O but larger than either OO or HO.

	O-gauge	S-gauge	HO-gauge
Proportion to prototype	1:48	1:64	1:87.1
Scale to prototype in feet	1:4	3:16	1:7.3
Distance between rails (inches)	1¼"	.875"	.65"

The leap to two-rail track flew in the face of convention, but real railroads did have two-rail track, and if the wiring for a loop of track that turned back on itself was a bit more complex to avoid a short circuit, Flyer (and hopefully its customers) could live with that. What saved American Flyer a ton of tooling dollars was being

ABOVE: In 1945, Lionel stunned its competition with an automatic knuckle coupler. It had an electro-magnet on board that was activated by a sliding shoe passing over a special rail section of an uncoupler track. All a young engineer had to do was press a button to uncouple the cars. The coupler had too many pieces, and the shoe often caused derailments, but Lionel was first, patented it, and trumped American Flyer who cared—and Marx who didn't. *Toy Train Collectors Association Toy Train Museum, Strasburg, Pennsylvania*

RIGHT: A top view of Lionel's 1945 automatic coupler. This coupler looked more realistic than American Flyer's link coupler and was fully automatic through its sliding shoe and uncoupler track section. American Flyer started airbrushing its link couplers out of catalog illustrations. *Toy Train Collectors Association Toy Train Museum, Strasburg, Pennsylvania*

able to use its prewar ³/₁₆-inch scale locomotive and car dies. To be sure, the prewar locomotives had been "fattened" a bit to run on wide O-gauge track and this chubbiness around the boiler did hang over the new, narrower S-gauge running gear, but considering the cost saving, so be it. The new scale-proportioned American Flyer trains looked great racing around their two rails. But the knuckle coupler really beat A. C. Gilbert over the head, and the patents on that innovation were made of cast iron.

On the heels of V-E Day in April 1945, Lawrence Cowen accepted the position of presidency from the Lionel board of directors while Joshua assumed the venerated seat of chairman. By August of that year, two atom bombs had devastated the Japanese and World War II was abruptly over. Even after giving back some money to the Navy for a bit of price gouging during the war—about $300,000 in 1942 and $325,000 in 1943—Lionel came out of the conflict with bags of cash. The company even received an "M" award for merit and the Fleet Victory flag after Lawrence Cowen petitioned the United States Maritime Commission in 1943. So, with patriotic honors and money, with die-casting and knuckle couplers, Lionel turned quickly to resume its leadership position.

Speed was everything. By Christmas of 1945, Lionel fielded a nice little freight train for $33.50—with track, but no transformer—headed by a die-cast No. 224 steam locomotive. Behind it rode three prewar stamped steel cars: a tank car, a boxcar, and a caboose. Also tucked into this consist was one unique car—a molded black plastic gondola in Pennsylvania Railroad livery—the shape of things to come. Every car wore a pair of the new knuckle couplers. Lionel people worked overtime to get their East 26th Street showroom in shape for the launching of this little train while the advertising department dropped $90,000 of Lionel's ready cash on a marketing blitz touting the new "Realism" of knuckle coupling on big O-gauge locomotives. In New Haven, American Flyer could only show off last year's locomotives on this year's smaller track waiting for a huge stampede of new buyers who never really showed up.

A casualty of the 1945 launch was OO-gauge and the push to reach adult scale model builders. As the end of the war neared, later copies of *Model Builder* magazine showed Lionel slowly regressing from its "year-round" adult hobby customers and returned to the market it knew—toy trains for kids. While OO-gauge was abandoned and miniature scale modeling was left to companies like Atlas Tool Works, Ambroid, Ulrich, Athearn, and Varney, the low-end Lionel "Scout" line was expanded. Scout sets became "O-27" sets and anything resembling "scale" cars was squeezed into foreshortened versions of their prototypes to get around the impossibly tight 27-inch radius curves. The search for the elusive year-round market would take curious twists and turns over the next 20 years.

The year 1946 really set the pattern for Lionel over the next decade. Innovation after innovation hit the tracks as Lionel's designers literally came out smoking. Buyers at the Toy Fair in New York City in March 1946 were treated to a Lionel steam locomotive rolling down the three-rail main line belching puffs of smoke. The noxious whiffs coming from the steamer's little stack were clouds of nitrogen oxide. They were produced by burning a pellet made of ammonium nitrate dropped through the engine's

continued on page 76

A collection of Lionel smoke pellets, from left to right: The latest version, with no label, was offered in postwar production; the labeled bottle was the most common; and the early unlabeled plastic case was made only in 1946. It is never found today with pellets inside since their noxious ingredients disintegrated over time. These early pills were dropped through the smokestack onto a dimpled hot light bulb used in locomotives such as the first 671 steam turbine. In 1947, Lionel went to the more efficient "heater" modules to make smoke. *Chris Rohfling collection*

Following the success of the operating milk car, an operating cattle car arrived in 1948. The car, its nine patient cattle, and the loading ramp could be had for $15. Little brushes on the cows' bases allowed a vibrating floor pad to move them along the caorral ramps and both into and out of the car. A touch of Vaseline on the edges of their bases smoothed the journey. The track was to position the car over the electromagnetic track section so the ramps lined up with the car's doors. It was pricey for $1,947 but sold well. *Stan Roy collection*

Competing forces: A. C. Gilbert's American Flyer

Yale-educated and former Olympic athlete Alfred Carleton Gilbert would prove to be a formidable competitor to Lionel's growing empire. He was a believer in the vigorous life which led him into sports as well as academic achievement. While studying for his medical degree at Yale, he became an expert pole-vaulter and broke the world's record at the 1908 Olympic Games in London. In 1909 when Gilbert graduated with a degree in medicine, he expanded his love of magic into the Mysto Magic Company, for which he and partner John Petrie rented a shed near New Haven, Connecticut, to assemble and box magic trick sets. In 1913 he invented his fabulously successful Erector Set, having been inspired by the construction of New Haven Railroad's electrification system. But sales of both products peaked only during Christmas, so Gilbert entered the appliance market.

Before America's entry into World War 1, a number of toy manufacturers got together to plead with the government for a stiff tariff against the importation of German toys. Spurred by the efforts of Gilbert, Henry Ives, and American Flyer's William Ogden Coleman, the Toy Manufacturer's Association was formed. After winning an even tougher tariff, Gilbert was made its first president in 1916. Joshua Lionel Cowen was not invited to join this elitist club.

After adding to his product line with toys and chemistry sets, A. C. Gilbert managed to survive the Depression and, seeing an opportunity in the toy train market, purchased the struggling American Flyer line from Coleman. AF's senior staff and all experienced employees who agreed to relocate were transferred from the Chicago plant to Gilbert's factory alongside the New Haven Railroad main line in New Haven.

During the short period between 1938 and the onset of World War II, the company concentrated on the hobby market with a series of 3/16-inch scale trains (about two thirds the size of Lionel's O-gauge trains) but running on three-rail O-gauge track. There was a dramatic shift in the quality of manufacture as Gilbert concentrated more on die-cast realism and detail in its products. Though a die-cast New York Central Hudson had been shopped out in 1936, it was Gilbert's 3/16-inch Union Pacific 4-8-4 "Challenger" (actually a Northern type) Model 806 that stunned buyers and led the product line in 1939. The following year, Gilbert came out with the Pennsylvania K-5 locomotive and the Baltimore & Ohio streamlined *Royal Blue* 4-6-2. These exquisite die-cast products had sheet-metal counterparts to appeal to the consumer with a limited budget; the Depression was not quite over. As 1941 drew to a close, Gilbert had virtually revamped the American Flyer O-gauge line with new dies and retooling. Then in 1942, Gilbert was forced to switch to wartime production, although about 5 percent of manufacturing was still devoted to toy trains.

After the war, it took Gilbert all of 1945 to regroup and get toy train production up and running, trailing behind Lionel's single train launch and all-important introduction of the realistic automatic knuckle coupler. Nevertheless, once AF hauled away its war production equipment and dusted off the Flyer machinery, Gilbert flexed his muscles and made ready to take on the competition—but with a new twist: in the name of realism, Gilbert kept its 3/16-inch trains but switched to S-gauge two-rail track. The new line was first offered in 1946, and though it did not take the toy train market by a storm, Flyer earned over $6 million from that year's sales.

A now-collectible postwar offering in the "new" two-rail American Flyer product line was the circus train, powered by none other than Flyer's prewar Baltimore & Ohio *Royal Blue* 4-6-2 dolled up in candy red (and with narrower wheelsets for the new S-gauge track). Gilbert touted its postwar trains to be more scalelike and realistic than those of three-rail competitors, but one area where Gilbert stumbled was in the realm of whistles. Although Flyer did have built-in whistles on some of its locomotives, its best-sounding whistles and horns were in the form of stationary, trackside "whistling billboards," as shown behind the circus train. *Mike McBride and Mike Schafer collections*

It wasn't long before AF and Lionel locked horns. The first spat was over couplers. Lionel had introduced its automatic knuckle coupler in 1945. Gilbert's people could only grind their teeth and keep saying their trains were more realistic though they were stuck with a very un-realistic (though mechanically very simple) link coupler. It took seven years before Gilbert was able to introduce its own version of the knuckle coupler to its Flyer line due to Lionel's cast-iron patent.

With S-gauge trains, AF had its own niche and developed a very loyal following in the market, offering cars with greater detail traveling on realistic two-rail track. Another battle that Gilbert never quite resolved was the on-board whistle patent owned by Lionel. AF could only offer trackside "whistling billboards" or an on-board raspy "Nathan air-chime" whistle, but never the built-in sound of a real steam whistle.

During World War II, in an effort to keep American Flyer's name before the public, the company had opened the Gilbert Hall of Science in New York. Other cities soon had their own scaled-down versions of the Hall, all offering a large train display and sales offices. Copying Lionel's idea, the New York version featured a huge layout 80 feet long with nine different lines wending their way through mountains, waterfalls, towns, crossings, and showcasing top of the line accessories for toy industry buyers. The other floors of the buildings were devoted to Erector toys, appliances, displays, and offices.

Following the war, A. C. Gilbert sought to expand his marketing program beyond the usual catalogs and print advertising. He followed Lionel's lead and sent showcase layouts to department stores for Christmas displays. A large layout was designed for television shows and appeared on Dave Garroway's popular program as well as *The Price is Right* game show and *American Bandstand* among others.

The late 1950s saw the advent of the shopping mall and the discount store—two trends that impacted heavily on the toy train market. Toy train manufacturers were told by the discount retailers such as the multi-store Korvettes chain to lower their prices and sell at a higher volume. As if this weren't enough, the public became enamored of other miniature forms of transportation such as slot cars, model airplanes, and rockets, manufactured

American Flyer's answer to Lionel's tremendously popular Electro-Motive Santa Fe F3 diesels was the Alco passenger diesel, a set of which splashes across the pages of AF's 1957 catalog. The locomotives proved popular for A. C. Gilbert and were still being manufactured (by Lionel, no less) as the twentieth century drew to a close. *Mike Schafer collection*

by new companies like Ideal, Aurora, and Revell. The 1958 recession didn't help either. By the early 1960s, the railroads themselves were in a steep decline, which was reflected in toy-train sales. AF saw where the toy industry was heading and began veering away from toy trains into other areas of toy manufacture.

A. C. Gilbert died in 1961 and his son, Alfred Jr., was at the helm a year later when Jack Wrather, producer of the *Lassie* TV show, purchased 52 per cent of the company. American Flyer experienced a modest peak in 1965, but finally faded and was, ironically purchased by Lionel in 1966, thus ending several decades of fierce competition.

Capitalizing on this small but loyal market, Lionel occasionally has offered bits and pieces of American Flyer rolling stock and a few locomotives—mostly the popular Alco PA and the Electro-Motive GP7—using original dies, but other companies such as Ron Bashista's American Models in South Lyon, Michigan, have provided more continuous and sophisticated support in the surprisingly tenacious world of S-gauge. American Flyer fans are still with us keeping alive the memory of A. C. Gilbert and his two-rail S-gauge trains.

ABOVE: The No. 224 steam locomotive was the first locomotive produced by Lionel after World War II. It pulled Lionel's first postwar freight set offered in 1945 as well as employing the first knuckle couplers. This unremarkable die-cast steamer led the way to Lionel's postwar roll-up of sales success. *Chris Rohlfing collection*

A close-up of the molded plastic Pennsylvania Railroad gondola offered with the 1945 Lionel freight set. This model predicted the postwar industry shift from tin to die-cast plastic rolling stock as an economy measure that also offered considerably more detail—if attention was paid to the dies. To the right of the gon stands one of Lionel's classic accessories, the ubiquitous highway crossing flasher. Though it towered out of proportion to the trains it protected at grade crossings, its alternately flashing lights added yet more pizazz to a young engineer's growing rail empire. *Jim Flynn collection*

Continued from page 73

stack on top of the heated light bulb that served as the locomotive's headlight. A dimple in the custom-made bulb served as a glass hot plate. Pill experiments had produced an earlier version whose fumes could drop a strong man in his tracks and another that was less toxic when sniffed, but lethal when swallowed. The gas produced by the chosen tiny pellet is known today as a "greenhouse-effect pollutant" and can induce a hacking cough and eye-watering if inhaled in heavy doses.

Compared to the joy registered on the buyers' faces and the flutter of pages in order books, this small side-effect was negligible. Moms and dads today would give pause before handing their Little Billy a bottle of smoke pellets that, if swallowed, produced dizziness, whooping heaves, and explosive diarrhea. Toy safety was not as strictly enforced in 1946.

Down the street at A. C. Gilbert's New York showroom, American Flyer's locomotives sent billows of smoke ceiling-ward as they not only smoked but "choo-chooed." A device in the steamer's tender accepted a few drops of paraffin-based, cedar-scented smoke solution—non toxic—and after heating the little puddle into smoke, pumped that smoke to the engine through a tube while a crank and bellows huffed "choo-choo"—though not in synchronization with the churning wheels, until a subsequent redesign put the smoke and choo-choo mechanism in the locomotive itself.

Later, Lionel replaced the expensive dimpled light bulb with a cup and hot-wire mechanism designed by engineer Frank Petit to perform the same task, and a faster-dissolving, less toxic pill was formulated by Mario Mazzone. The locomotives that were pumping this smoke into the overheated Toy Fair atmosphere were all winners.

Two steam engines that would become Lionel flag-bearers for years to come headed the parade. The first was a model of a Pennsylvania Railroad experiment rolled out of the Baldwin shops in 1944. The No. 6200, Class S2 prototype was powered by two steam turbine engines, a large one to move forward and a smaller one for reverse. A single pair of side rods connected the eight drive wheels of the 6-8-6 wheel configuration. Changing direction was achieved with a clutch and gears, not unlike an automobile, shifting forward power to the second set of drivers and reverse to the third set. Coupled to a string of heavyweight passenger cars, at a speed above 40 MPH, the S2 had the considerable equivalent pulling power of a 6,000-hp. diesel

Pennsylvania Railroad's one-of-a-kind steam turbine locomotive No. 6200 was sheer brute power for high-speed passenger service, but its arrival on the railroading scene came just as dieselization took hold in an unprecedented way. If nothing else, the hulking steam engine served as a worthy prototype for one of Lionel's most popular model offerings. *Paul Slager, William A. Raia collection*

Debuting in 1946, Lionel's model steam turbine became an instant hit. It looked huge and busy with all those 20 wheels churning away. There was whistle blowing, smoke spewing, and lights flashing. It became the guinea pig for the "Electronic Train" by concealing a radio receiver in its tender. The model shown is the 682 version built in 1954 with a fussy lubricator linkage that caused some sticking problems. It tows a 2046W-50 tender complete with water scoop for filling up at speed from water tanks set between the rails as on prototype railroads. Note the blind center drivers. *Mike Wilson collection*

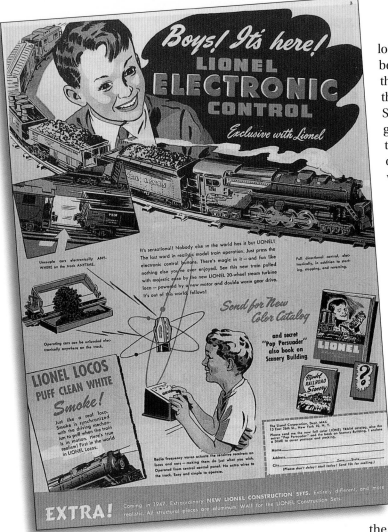

"Boys, it's here. Lionel Electronic Control—exclusive with Lionel." proclaims this 1946 ad featuring a radio-controlled train headed by the steam turbine locomotive and featuring operating cars that could also be uncoupled automatically anywhere on the track. The system worked well in theory, placing a radio receiver in each car and triggering responses at the push of a button from a central control. Unfortunately, it didn't work well in practice and, at $75 a set, cost too much. Computer chips would eventually make the idea work much better almost 50 years later. *Train Collectors Association Toy Train Museum, Strasburg, Pennsylvania*

locomotive today. However, below 40 MPH, trundling through the yard to get to the head end of its train, the S2 chowed down coal and gulped water at such a rate that it could only be used on short runs. Only one was built, and it usually ran on the PRR main line between Chicago and Crestline, Ohio, pulling Chicago–New York trains before being quietly scrapped. During its brief life, however—arriving at a time when the railroads were performing heroic service during the war—its brawny, 20-wheel presence served faithfully as America's big-shouldered railroad weapon against the evil Axis powers.

Lionel's version of the PRR S2 steam turbine was a semi-scale replica and was the very first to show off the new smoke unit. It survived for almost 10 years and was sold by the thousands undergoing some 18 variations. In 1985, 30 years after it was dropped from Lionel's roster, the S2 was revived by Fundimensions as a tarted-up version in Pennsylvania Brunswick green and silver complete with "Sound of Steam," smoke, whistle, Magne-traction, and whitewalls—a "what-if" homage to that magnificent 1944 failure that became a Lionel success story.

The 1946 S2 made its debut as No. 671 in O-gauge, as No. 2020 in O-27, and also as the 671R, a model more in keeping with the fate of its prototype. During the war, Lionel's designers had experimented with radio control of train operations. The 671R coupled to a special freight train made up of an operating coal dump car, a boxcar, gondola, and caboose was the result. Attached to each car and to the locomotive's tender was a radio receiver. A special push-button transformer—the ECU-1, with a function attached to each button—sent out radio frequencies tuned to each receiver. The cars could be uncoupled anywhere on

the layout, the dump car could unload at any point on the track, the whistle could be blown, and each start, stop, and reverse function had a button as well. This "Electronic Set" was heady stuff for 1946, long before today's wireless controls and computer chips perform similar functions. Sadly, this 1946 technology was expensive, driving the price of the set up to $75, and it was not reliable. The Electronic Set hung on through 1947 and, like its luckless Pennsylvania prototype, was quietly scrapped.

The other die-cast locomotive that arrived in the 1946 line was the 2-8-4 Berkshire. Unlike the 671, the 726 "Berk" never had an O-27 counterpart and remained on the Lionel roster for 20 years in one variation or another. The first 2-8-4 prototype showed up in 1925 as a demonstrator from Lima Locomotive Works' Lima, Ohio, shops rolling over trackage belonging to the New York Central subsidiary Boston & Albany. From that run, the B&A bought 45 locomotives, and word of this engine's hauling power and steaming efficiency spread until Berkshires were hauling trains on several different railroads across the Midwest and in the East. The prototype Berkshire had a more massive look than Lionel's version, peering, beetle-browed, from under an Elesco water heater with larger pistons and a much larger rear truck to support its huge fire box. But the prototype never had to negotiate 31-inch radius curves at full speed. Lima outshopped its last Berkshire in 1949 having built 611 locomotives. Lionel built millions by 1966, and then the model was, like the 671 turbine, resurrected by Fundimensions in 1980 in Nickel Plate livery.

For 1946, Lionel offered all its prewar operating accessories and an improved version of its "flying shoe" knuckle coupler. Having been rushed into production for 1945, the coupler's design had required numerous "fixes." To top off the line, Lionel also offered its "Chem Lab" chemistry set. Presenting a glittering array of test tubes, retorts, and other ominous-looking instruments, Lionel promised young chemists a list of awe-inspiring experiments including the Biblical equivalent of turning water into wine. Lionel was primed for production. It was ready for a sales blitz. It had no catalog.

A paper shortage had stopped the 1946 catalog in its tracks. With this order-book-busting lineup ready to go, Cowen the younger must have been upset while Cowen the elder was apoplectic. Marketing people scattered like a covey of quail until Joseph Hanson, the advertising manager, experienced an epiphany and called *Liberty* magazine to place a 16-page ad in its November 23, 1946, issue. The "ad" was in essence the

The Berkshire-type locomotive—the 2-8-4—was developed for New York Central's Boston & Albany subsidiary, and the wheel arrangement and the locomotive's "Super Power" technology eventually spread to other roads as well. One of B&A's Berkshires barrels out of a tunnel on the B&A main line circa 1940. Lionel, which had always seemingly been partial to NYC prototypes, adopted the "Berk" for its steam locomotive offerings. *H. W. Pontin, Andover Junction Publications collection*

Lionel's No. 726 Berkshire was released in 1948, two years after the first model was manufactured. The 2-8-4 locomotive was the workhorse of Lionel's steam fleet. It was beautifully proportioned and well-motored to work in either freight or passenger service. *Chris Rohlfing collection*

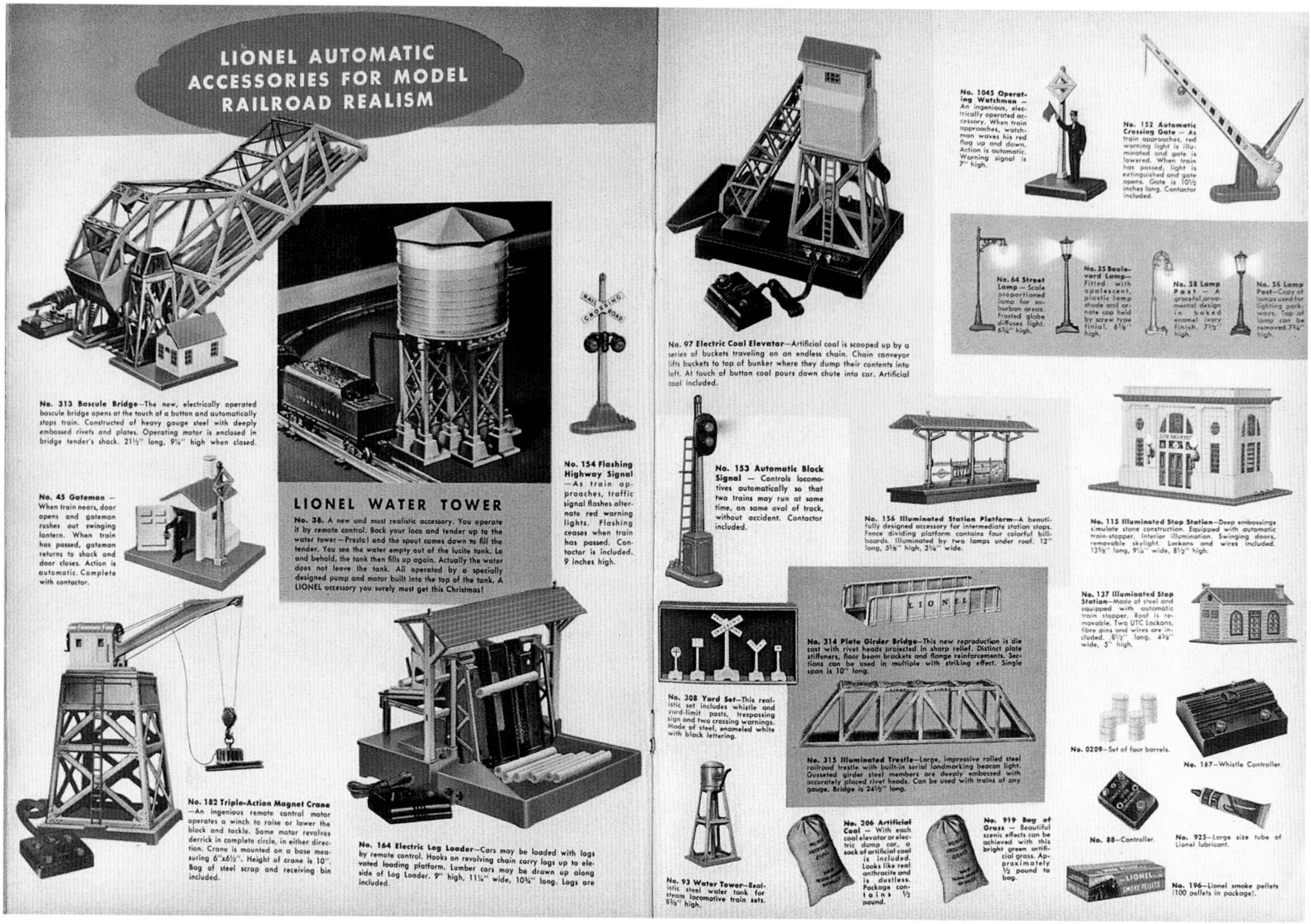

LIONEL AUTOMATIC ACCESSORIES FOR MODEL RAILROAD REALISM
No. 313 Bascule Bridge—The new, electrically operated bascule bridge opens at the touch of a button and automatically stops train. Constructed of heavy gauge steel with deeply embossed rivets and plates. Operating motor is enclosed in bridge tender's shack. 21½" long, 9¼" high when closed.
No. 45 Gateman — When train nears, door opens and gateman rushes out swinging lantern. When train has passed, gateman returns to shack and door closes. Action is automatic. Complete with contactor.
LIONEL WATER TOWER
No. 38. A new and most realistic accessory. You operate it by remote control. Back your loco and tender up to the water tower—Presto! and the spout comes down to fill the tender. You see the water empty out of the lucite tank. Lo and behold, the tank then fills up again. Actually the water does not leave the tank. All operated by a specially designed pump and motor built into the top of the tank. A LIONEL accessory you surely must get this Christmas!
No. 154 Flashing Highway Signal —As train approaches, traffic signal flashes alternate red warning lights. Flashing ceases when train has passed. Contactor is included. 9 inches high.
No. 182 Triple-Action Magnet Crane —An ingenious remote control motor operates a winch to raise or lower the block and tackle. Same motor revolves derrick in complete circle, in either direction. Crane is mounted on a base measuring 6"x6½". Height of crane is 10". Bag of steel scrap and receiving bin included.
No. 164 Electric Log Loader—Cars may be loaded with logs by remote control. Hooks on revolving chain carry logs up to elevated loading platform. Lumber cars may be drawn up along side of Log Loader. 9" high, 11¼" wide, 10¾" long. Logs are included.
No. 97 Electric Coal Elevator—Artificial coal is scooped up by a series of buckets traveling on an endless chain. Chain conveyor lifts buckets to top of bunker where they dump their contents into loft. At touch of button coal pours down chute into car. Artificial coal included.
No. 1045 Operating Watchman — An ingenious, electrically operated accessory. When train approaches, watchman waves his red flag up and down. Action is automatic. Warning signal is 7" high.
No. 152 Automatic Crossing Gate — As train approaches, red warning light is illuminated and gate is lowered. When train has passed, light is extinguished and gate opens. Gate is 10½ inches long. Contactor included.
No. 64 Street Lamp — Scale proportioned lamp for suburban areas. Frosted globe diffuses light. 6¾" high.
No. 35 Boulevard Lamp—Fitted with opalescent, plastic lamp shade and ornate cap held by screw type finial. 6⅛" high.
No. 58 Lamp Post — A graceful ornamental design in baked enamel ivory finish. 7½" high.
No. 56 Lamp Post—Copy of lamps used for lighting parkways. Top of lamp can be removed. 7¾" high.
No. 153 Automatic Block Signal — Controls locomotives automatically so that two trains may run at same time, on same oval of track, without accident. Contactor included.
No. 156 Illuminated Station Platform—A beautifully designed accessory for intermediate station stops. Fence dividing platform contains four colorful billboards. Illuminated by two lamps under roof. 12" long, 5⅛" high, 3¼" wide.
No. 115 Illuminated Stop Station—Deep embossings simulate stone construction. Equipped with automatic train-stopper. Interior illumination. Swinging doors, removable skylight. Lockons and wires included. 13⅝" long, 9¼" wide, 8½" high.
No. 137 Illuminated Stop Station—Made of steel and equipped with automatic train stopper. Roof is removable. Two UTC Lockons, fibre pins and wires are included. 8½" long, 4⅞" wide, 5" high.
LIONEL
No. 314 Plate Girder Bridge—This new reproduction is die cast with rivet heads projected in sharp relief. Distinct plate stiffeners, floor beam brackets and flange reinforcements. Sections can be used in multiple with striking effect. Single span is 10" long.
No. 308 Yard Set—This realistic set includes whistle and yard-limit posts, trespassing sign and two crossing warnings. Made of steel, enameled white with black lettering.
No. 315 Illuminated Trestle—Large, impressive rolled steel railroad trestle with built-in aerial landmarking beacon light. Gusseted girder steel members are deeply embossed with accurately placed rivet heads. Can be used with trains of any gauge. Bridge is 24½" long.
No. 0209—Set of four barrels.
No. 167—Whistle Controller.
No. 93 Water Tower—Realistic steel water tank for steam locomotive train sets. 8⅜" high.
No. 206 Artificial Coal — With each coal elevator or electric dump car, a sack of artificial coal is included. Looks like real anthracite and is dustless. Package contains ½ pound.
No. 919 Bag of Grass — Beautiful scenic effects can be achieved with this bright green artificial grass. Approximately ½ pound to bag.
No. 88—Controller.
No. 925—Large size tube of Lionel lubricant.
LIONEL SMOKE PELLETS
No. 196—Lionel smoke pellets (100 pellets in package).

A spread from the famous catalog-turned-magazine ad that appeared in *Liberty* Magazine in 1946 after Lionel was unable to get a regular catalog printed account of a paper shortage with its printer. "All new" for 1946 really meant prewar accessories. *Jim Flynn collection*

whole of Lionel's catalog. When the cheering and whooping settled down at *Liberty*'s offices, artist Percy Leason was commissioned to paint a cover entitled "Father takes Over." It shows a perplexed son watching his intrusive and happily oblivious if well-meaning dad fudge with the lad's Lionel train.

Two million subscribers and six million readers received Vol. 23, No. 47 of *Liberty* magazine. For Lionel, outflanking the paper shortage with this publishing *fate accompli* helped clear dealers' shelves and net $10 million in profits for a record year.

For Joshua Cowen, this resurrection of his struggling company should have been a fulfillment of his life's work, but he had lost his sweetheart after 42 years of marriage. Cecelia Liberman Cowen, the young girl he had met on a trolley car in 1902, succumbed to a heart attack on June 12, 1946. Friends, colleagues, and employees all stepped in to help him through this great sadness in his life.

American Flyer had waited out the paper shortage and published a giant 32-page, 10 x 29-inch full color catalog on October 11. Unfortunately, many of the items graphically illustrated inside were unavailable for sale and would trickle onto the market as they were punched out. The great two-rail revolution wasn't quite working out except for a growing core of contrarians who thought American Flyer's closer-to-scale proportions and track offered more realistic modeling possibilities and just plain looked better than the chunky Lionel toys.

Flushed with success, Lionel pushed into 1947 with many train sets built around its new locomotives and also expanded its line of automated accessories by offering the milk car with its unloading platform. Invented by inveterate tinkerer and designer of numerous Lionel accessories, Richard G. Smith, the No. 3462 Automatic Milk Car was such a hit that Lionel literally could not make them fast enough. Smith's past successes such as the log loader and log car were eclipsed in 1944 when his working model of the milk car came together. His early design called for an auto-mated "can pusher" to swing the milk cans onto the platform. However, Lionel people came up with the lit-tle man who popped out at the push of a button and did the deed—once for each push. Always somewhat pinch-penny in its dealings with outside inventors, Lionel offered Smith a 2 per cent royalty, figuring—at

tops—it would cost Lionel's bottom line maybe $1,200 a year. Accustomed to getting a flat fee, Smith had to be cajoled into accepting the "deal."

The milk car exploded all over the marketplace and as hundreds of thousands of milk cars flew off dealers' shelves, Smith's fortunes rose. In 1952 alone, his take was about $20,000 from the little men who threw out the milk cans.

Still trying to crack the year-round market, Lionel brought out its construction sets as companions to the Chem Labs competing against Gilbert's entrenched Erector sets and chemical mixing creations. However, no matter how hard Lionel pushed these lines, they never really got off the ground. By 1950, they were his-tory. Lionel had even bought Porter Chemical com-pany to resuscitate the line, but all it managed to do was run Porter's company into the ground.

The 1946 Lionel No. 221 New York Central 2-6-2 imitated NYC's famed streamlined Hudsons (4-6-4s) designed by Henry Dreyfuss for the 1938 *20th Century Limited*. The scene shows a corner of Mike Moore's "Lionel City" layout, which includes a number of operating accessories, including the popular operating milk car just beyond the train. The switch tower is a Marx tin model. *Mike Moore collection*

Decked out in Brunswick green with gold striping, a Lionel GG1 electric rounds a curve towing a string of *Irvington*, *Madison*, and *Manhattan* passenger cars. The GG1 was a signature Lionel model that could draw power from overhead wires as well as from the third rail. This model 2332 was made in 1948, and the design is offered today both as a popular replica from Lionel and as a scale model from Mike's Train House (MTH). *Chris Rohlfing collection*

The GG1 played prominently in this 1948 painting by noted artist Grif Teller, who painted a number of illustrations for the Pennsylvania Railroad, mostly for the railroad's calendar. *Mike Schafer collection*

The big deal of 1947 was Lionel's O-gauge model of a Pennsylvania Railroad GG1 electric locomotive. Lionel's model went on to become a toy train classic. The prototype GG1 was a child of the Depression—a bastard, actually, sired by the New York, New Haven & Hartford Railroad early in the 1930s. A New Haven articulated EP3a electric locomotive was leased by the PRR to compare with its own then-standard electric

locomotive, the boxy P5a model. The EP3a won hands down, so PRR included its best features in its GG1 prototype. The GG1 fleet—built by General Electric and PRR's Altoona (Pennsylvania) Shops with help from Baldwin and Westinghouse—would serve on Pennsy's newly electrified New York–Washington main line.

Famed industrial designer Raymond Loewy was called in to improve the GG1's rivet-covered carbody design. The result was a rakish, all-welded carbody with smooth, flowing lines. Dressed in solid Brunswick green paint with gold pinstripes and a command of up to 8,000 hp., the GG1 became, arguably, the most perfectly conceived electric locomotive ever built. Early in the 1950s, PRR introduced a Tuscan red scheme for some of its "Gs." Between 1934 and 1943, 139 GG1s were built, and the last of their breed served until October 29, 1983.

The Lionel design, though squeezed to accommodate the O-gauge curves, was accurate even to the "pans" (pantographs) atop the locomotive that could be wired to work off overhead catenary wires for more realistic operation. Loewy's five-stripe paint scheme was copied perfectly by Lionel artist, Louis Melchionne, and even the unique sound of the GG1 horn was reproduced using a vibrating metal rod in a plastic box. Eventually, over its 17-year design evolution, a second motor and Magne-traction were added, giving the locomotive tremendous pulling power. Like its prototype, the Lionel GG1 hauled everything from long freight drags to prestige passenger trains, making it a huge hit and staying in the product line until 1963, after which it experienced numerous resurrections.

Joshua Cowen was never a fan of diesel locomotives—they didn't have the "movement" of a steamer's flashing valve gear—but he loved the GG1 and the way it seemed to slide on down the track. Of all Lionel locomotives, when the GG1 is run at high speed, it looks just like its prototype. Its rush over the three-rail main line mimics the 100 MPH original that flashed along the high iron with a moan of electric motors that rose to feral howl and was gone in a blur of gold and green.

For Lionel, the successes of 1946 and 1947 were definitely a blur of gold and green as the money flowed in, products flowed out and there was cash for research and development that would grow the business even larger. A new demonstration layout was constructed that summer at a cost of $12,000 complete with bridges, towns, rivers, and a four-track main line. Salesmen took turns at shifts working the showroom to answer questions and steer potential customers to the latest additions to the Lionel Line. Ron Hollander, in his biography of Cowen and the company, *All Aboard*, sites a particular event. A customer came to the showroom complaining that he bought a train set that didn't work. As it happened, Joshua Cowen was on the floor and asked the man if he had connected the wires to the track using the provided clips. The man said he had placed the wires under the track expecting the weight of the train to provide the contact. Cowen exploded, "The reason your trains don't work is because you didn't read the instructions you damned fool!" While Cowen was considered a lovable curmudgeon to most people who knew him well, he did not suffer fools easily.

Beginning in 1948, a continuous string of amazing products flowed from Lionel's designers that lasted for more than a decade. Their mechanical ingenuity and marketing savvy served them well through this finest period of the company's history. In the post-war baby-boom market, almost everyone at Lionel sensed a real winner as the first fully assembled and painted Santa Fe Electro-Motive F3 diesel locomotive rolled down its three-rail test track. On that day in 1948, that "almost" referred to Joshua Lionel Cowen himself.

As mentioned earlier, Cowen was not a diesel man. To him, they were like a brick moving down the track; there was no "action." Lawrence Cowen, on the other hand, saw an opportunity. The Atchison, Topeka & Santa Fe had been running passenger diesels built by the Electro-Motive Division of General Motors between Chicago and Los Angeles since 1939. These locomotives made the run in a blistering 39.5 hours—14 hours faster than their quickest steamer—with the throttle cranked back to notch eight much of the time giving a speed of 90 MPH. General Motors artist Leland Knickerbocker had created a dazzling red, yellow, and black livery for the front end of the E- and F-type silver/stainless-steel Electro-Motive diesels that Santa Fe assigned to its *Super Chief* and other passenger runs out of Chicago to the West Coast. Lawrence Cowen recognized two possible sales opportunities.

Lionel had always featured models of East Coast prototype trains, mainly because of the company's location and familiarity with those types. Kids out West had no Lionel train that mimicked Western carriers. Second, the diesel revolution started by the *Zephyr* and M-10000 in 1934 was beginning to overtake steam as an efficient, cost-effective form of motive power.

The new F3 diesel in New York Central livery leaps from the comic page ad together with the message, "Oh boy! Oh boy! This is fun! Real railroading with Lionel." The ad appeared in the November 27, 1949, New York *Journal American. Train Collectors Association Toy Train Museum collection, Strasburg, Pennsylvania*

83

Lionel's Santa Fe version of the Electro-Motive F3 was destined to become the toy train locomotive most often associated with Lionel. Baby-boomers were more likely to be entranced by diesel locomotives than steam, if for no other reason than that railroads had embarked on a widespread dieselization program after World War II that would wipe out mainline steam on America's railroads by the end of the 1950s. Of course, the flashy Santa Fe "warbonnet" livery helped sell Lionel's model F3 as well—a paint scheme developed in the late 1930s by General Motors' stylist Leland Knickerbocker. Even today, this venerable, timeless paint scheme in generally regarded by railroad historians as the best ever. *Stan Roy collection*

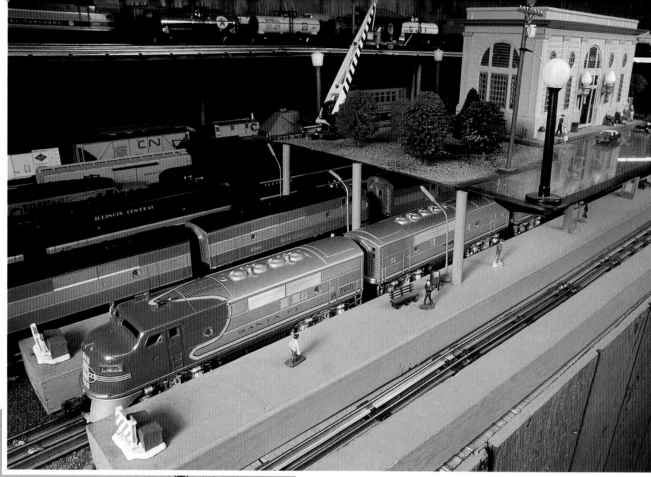

A cab-booster set of F7 diesels—the updated version of the F3—lead Santa Fe's *Grand Canyon* passenger train out of Chicagoland in the fall of 1967. F-units clad in Santa Fe's red, yellow, black and silver (or stainless-steel) color combination inspired many a toy and scale-model train manufacturer to produce models of Electro-Motive's F-series diesel in many different railroad paint schemes, including Santa Fe. *Mike Schafer*

World War II had prompted steam engine designs to accommodate long trains of vital materiel ending with the huge articulated locomotives such as the 4-6-6-4 Challengers, the Norfolk & Western Y-class coal drag steamers, and the ultimate 4-8-8-4 "Big Boy" types of the Union Pacific. But even the most efficient of these new breed of steam locomotives was eventually surpassed by the evolving and tireless diesel power plants. If Lionel was going to keep up with real railroad progress, it needed to move forward as well. What better way to accomplish this than with flashy Santa Fe "warbonnet" diesels.

Lawrence Cowen made a pitch to Santa Fe people, who were eager for the publicity that would result from having likenesses of their trains zipping around Lionel tracks in America's homes. General Motors was also keen, since its GM logo would appear on the locomotives. The elder Cowen added one proviso to his capitulation: kids on the East Coast also needed a diesel to call their own. Since the GG1 was already carrying the Pennsylvania logo, Lionel contacted the New York Central. In a financing coup—probably the best deal Lawrence ever made for Lionel—Santa Fe, General Motors, and New York Central all ponied up a quarter of the cost to make the dies —about $6,000 apiece.

Lionel's Executive Vice President Arthur M. Raphael, and Vice President Phillip Marfuggi gave the deal their sanction and chose the Beacon Tool & Die Company of Clifton, New Jersey, to make the dies for the F3 diesel locomotives.

The result was the twin-motored F3, available in two-unit, back-to-back "A-A" (two cab or "A" units) configuration complete with a battery-powered horn. The set could be had in either Santa Fe red, yellow, black, and silver or New York Central's understated two-tone gray. And thus was born the most famous Lionel motive power ever to come down the three-rail track. The Santa Fe and NYC models were cautiously featured on page 20 of the 1948 catalog while the PRR steam turbine captured the cover belching smoke and looking massive. Cowen did not expect the diesel pair to make a big splash. He was gloriously wrong.

For 18 years, the Santa Fe diesel pair, in subtle variations, was a sales champ followed by the NYC model, which lasted for eight years. Over that time, additional road names were added to the F3 bodies to become a colorful fleet of locomotives hauling both passenger and freight trains. But for 1948, the big diesels virtually flew out the door, selling as fast as they could be stocked on dealers' shelves. Joshua

Cowen was, of course, quite happy to have been proven so wrong as the dollars flowed in, but he had another reason for happiness as well. He had met Lillian Appel Herman, and on November 21, 1948, they were married, filling the empty gap in his home life.

Lionel's motive power shifted to dual motors in its diesels and GG1 electric so that longer freight and passenger trains were strung out behind powerful worm drive-motored steamlined locomotives. New operating cars and accessories all required more electricity. A power source with much greater capacity was needed, and the result became another Lionel icon. The 250-watt ZW transformer was announced and quickly became the ultimate of toy train power packs. Four of the brutes held down the control center at the new Lionel showroom layout.

With dual-control throttles and accessory outputs, the beast was capable of operating four trains simultaneously. Its "football-in-a-box" design with numerous lights gave it massive feel that won the hearts of young railroaders and reflected the brutish streamlining finding its way into American life.

Big power for Lionel's elite trains pulled the company one way as the sales staff looked over their

The first Lionel "Scout" set was produced in 1948. This No. 1110 Scout train from 1949 rounds a curve with its four-car freight consist. Created as an O-27 entry-level set, it offered a small locomotive with a very unreliable plastic-sided motor, a tin box tender, and plastic cars with plastic couplers at $18.95, half the price of most sets. It was produced only through 1952. *Chris Rohlfing collection*

A hauntingly prescient 1951 ad looks like a co-op venture with General Mills which would later buy Lionel to form a conglomerate in the 1970s and 1980s. Entrants in the contest could win ". . . a cross-country luxurious Pullman trip for you and your family, plus hundreds of Lionel trains." All they had to do was complete in 25 words or less: "I would like to ride in a Pullman car because. . ." The entry was sent along with a Cheerios boxtop. *Train Collectors Association Toy Train Museum, Strasburg, Pennsylvania*

The Lionel Airex spinning reel and its original box shown here with lures that were included in a set . The Airex was probably the most successful non-train product offered by Lionel. It was discovered by Joshua and his son Lawrence Cowen while fishing on the St. Lawrence River. They bought the company and helped pioneer the spinning reel in America. They were eventually under-priced by Japanese competition, but the Airex was a winner in its time. *Dan Basore collection*

shoulders at Louis Marx, still nibbling away at low-end market share. To counter, sets even cheaper than the low-end O-27 were brought out during the late 1940s and through the 1950s under the "Scout" label. Plastic freight cars and a cheap plastic-cased motor in little 2-4-2 and 0-4-0 steamers were were fed by a 25-watt transformer. Marx's people looked at the Spartan offerings and countered with sets that offered more cars, track, and accessories for $8 less. Lionel could not win the low-end game, but it never stopped trying.

Lionel train and accessory designers stacked the 1948 deck with new products such as the Model 397 operating diesel-type coal loader that noisily clattered coal from a bright red bin up a rubber conveyor to a waiting car. Nevertheless, the Cowens continued to look for that magic key that would unlock year-round sales. They were sure they had found it on a fishing trip.

Father and son were great fishing fans, and on a trip to try the waters of the St. Lawrence River, they used their bait casting equipment while watching the technique of a world-class freshwater fisherman Bache Brown. More to the point, they took note of the Airex spinning reel he touted for that company and how it helped him cast light lures longer distances without the risk of a backlash on the reel.

A bait-casting reel sends its line down the rod guides like a little winch while the fisherman uses his thumb pressing on the line spool to control its speed. If the lure hits the water before the spool is stopped by the friction of the trained thumb, the spool keeps sending out line that has no place to go and jams into a rats-nest tangle called a "backlash." The Airex spinning reel turned the spool at right angles to the cast and the line looped off over the end with little friction or the possibility of a backlash when the lure hit the water. Anyone

could cast with this reel, and it was a real year-round sales winner. The Cowens hurried back to New York to buy Airex stock as fast as possible.

Lionel owned two-thirds of all Airex stock by January 1948 and took advantage of its hardware store dealers to peddle the line. As spinning technique gathered momentum among fishermen, the Airex took off and sold well. To increase exposure, Lionel added an Airex ad to the back page of its 1953 train catalog. According to some, this blatant infusion of an "adult" toy into the little tykes' private dream machine train catalog threatened to send any number of Little Billys into therapy. The author was 12 when this catalog came out and does not remember any seizures or palpitations, and in fact the author's father bought two Airex reels and used them for years until they wore out.

In 1953, the Airex Division of Lionel netted a before-tax profit of $500,000. By 1956, Airex was the largest U.S. manufacturer of spinning tackle, providing complete sets that included reels, rods, lures, and line. Whatever the ads cost Lionel in loss of sales to traumatized tads, it was the Japanese who spiked the dream in the late 1950s and early 1960s with cheaper fishing gear that worked just as well. As a result, Lionel would exit the fishing-reel business, but it was this singular sideline that proved profitable in the company's long-time search for the year-round product holy grail.

While the Cowens were hunting down stock shares in Airex, their promotion department under Joe Hanson was not idle. Always heavy in the print media, Lionel's young and enthusiastic promotion people were eager to branch out. A new medium called television was exploding across the country, and programming was still scarce for people who owned the small screen black-and-white sets. In his book, *The World's Greatest Toy Train Maker* (Kalmbach Publishing Co.), Roger Carp describes how Hanson persuaded the American Broadcasting Company to add a series of kids' shows called "Tales of the Red Caboose" to its schedule. Working day and night, the Lionel team built

scenic dioramas featuring Lionel trains, wrote scripts, and filmed 13 episodes. Old retired engineer, "Dan MaGee," stopped by the house where young "Larry Lane" lived to help the kid build his Lionel layout. Old Dan regaled young Larry with tales of railroading while the stories magically came to life with Lionel trains taking the parts of the real railroads. Unfortunately, it was the practice of television stations in those days to scrap film once the program was shown unless the sponsor would pay for a kinescope—literally a film taken of the imagery while it appeared on the television screen. Nothing remains of "Tales of the Red Caboose," which may be a blessing unless viewed as an historic footnote. As remembered by one of the team members, the scenes were ". . . primitive by today's standards." However, the show did bring together the team that built the dioramas—now called Diorama Studios—and turned them loose on a new Lionel showroom layout that became a huge success in time for the Toy Fair in March 1949.

Magne-traction sneaked into the line in 1949, hidden in the underside of a switch engine. Lionel had offered a yard goat, the prewar No. 1662, an 0-6-0 diecast beauty that was pushed out the door again in 1946 as the 1665 with its same shiny load of Bakelite coal and new knuckle couplers. It was still shuffling cars

ABOVE: This 624 version of the Lionel NW2 switcher brought out in 1952 is an excellent reproduction of the prototype, though Lionel insisted on calling it an "SW2" which it was not—there was not even a prototype SW2. The original 1949 622 model was the test bed for Magne-traction—magnets placed over the axles—or magnetizing the axles themselves for greater traction. This model has the magnetic coil couplers and rather fragile decals which are rarely found intact today. *Stan Roy collection*

INSET: A prototype NW2 for the Elgin, Joliet & Eastern stands outside Electro-Motive's Cleveland (Ohio) plant. Prototype NW2s were produced for a number of railroads between 1939 and 1949, except during the war years. *Electro-Motive*

Railroad engineers still held some sway as the 1950s opened, leading to ads like this one that says, "Sonny, they're the greatest thing on wheels"—"Lionel Trains with Magne-traction." This ad appeared in the Sunday comics section of the November 26, 1950, edition of the *New York Journal.* Interestingly, Lionel copyrighters drew upon actual railroad landmarks—Sherman Hill in Wyoming, Pennsylvania's Horseshoe Curve, and Santa Fe's Raton Pass in New Mexico—to expound on the virtues of Magne-traction. (The *20th Century Limited* "flagstop" item was bogus in that the *Century* didn't make flagstops.) *Train Collectors Association Toy Train Museum, Strasburg, Pennsylvania*

when Lionel underwent dieselization. Lionel produced the model 622 diesel switcher based—rather accurately—on a prototype Electro-Motive 1000-hp. NW2 switcher. With knuckle couplers fore and aft, this little locomotive also carried two Lionel firsts. A mechanical bell chimed every time the engine turned a wheel. Charming at first, the incessant pinging eventually drove many frazzled dads to their tool box for a screwdriver, pliers, and ball-peen hammer—whatever it took to shut the thing up. The other first was the Magne-traction, an attempt at adding magnetic force to make the locomotive grip the track, increasing pulling power, grade-climbing ability, and top speed into impossibly sharp tinplate curves. For the 622, they magnetized its axles. These hard iron axles lost their force so quickly, the effect was barely noticeable—reason enough for the low profile test run in 1949.

Another mini-winner for 1949 was the No. 3656 Operating Cattle Car and corral. Little bovines vibrated their way out of the double doors of the non-scale car through a mini-maze of corral gates—providing the young engineer had properly spotted the car opposite the ramps. Though this push-button car was popular, the five cows that could fit inside frequently fell over, fouling the mechanism. In 1956, the concept was improved with the 3356 Operating Horse Car by raising the height of the interior channel guides.

Lionel improved Magne-traction by using metal powder technology—pressing metal powder into a wheel die, then heating it in a sintering furnace—to achieve a precision molded "softer" iron wheel that would retain the magnetic energy for a longer period of time. The precision casting also eliminated the grinding and finishing process to reduce costs.

Lionel trumpeted the innovation in 1950, attracting the witty attention of *Tradewinds* columnist, Bennett Cerf, in the December 1950 *Saturday Review*. In his column featuring Lionel's success, he commented that Magne-traction permitted ". . . trains to whiz around curves at tremendously increased speed without derailing. Putting upset trains together again and back on the tracks has been the bane of many a father's life—also causing him to waste many precious hours he might otherwise have devoted to Plato, Spinoza, and Gaylord Hauser."

Dating from those first chilly days in the fall of 1900 when Joshua Cowen and Harry Grant bent over their work tables attaching fan motors to cheese boxes, 1950 was Lionel's golden anniversary year. In 50 years, Joshua's vision had grown from a battery-powered window display to the largest, most successful toy train manufacturer in the U. S. Lionel's designers and marketers set the pace.

American Flyer, with A. C. Gilbert at the helm, attracted a dedicated core of customers for two-rail, S-gauge trains that did look better than Lionel's chunkier offerings. There was no end of clever accessory designs coming from Flyer's New Haven plant, and its catalogs were every bit as flashy and inviting as Lionel's marketing broadsides. American Flyer showed a cheeky irreverence for choice of prototypes. Lionel modeled the Pennsylvania Railroad's K-4 Pacific (incorrectly) while Flyer modeled the rarely seen sister K-5 (correctly). Lionel used actual road names on its diesel locomotives while American Flyer for a time gave its locomotives fictional generic names such as *Silver Flash* and the *Rocket* while using prototype paint schemes. Lionel built a near prototypically correct 4-8-4 Northern-type in the form of Norfolk & Western's famous J-class locomotive while Flyer built a Union Pacific 4-8-4 Northern-type and quixotically called it the "Challenger"—a name belonging to an articulated 4-6-6-4 locomotive used by the UP.

Mostly, American Flyer was steadily losing the race because it did not have Lionel's deep pockets, manufacturing, and distribution muscle, or that name that had become as much of an American icon as Ford or Coca-Cola. Many products offered in those flashy Flyer catalogs were slow to reach the market. American Flyer's admitted "underdog" image was further fueled by its "link" couplers competing against Lionel's realistic knuckle couplers. Gilbert went to extremes of self-loathing and had the offending links airbrushed from many catalog illustrations. Early in the 1950s, Flyer finally introduced a highly successful knuckle coupler that, because it worked in reverse (by gravity, versus a magnetic charge) of Lionel's, skirted Lionel's patent.

TOP: Lionel's No. 746 Norfolk & Western J-class 4-8-4 locomotive ranks among the best-looking engines Lionel ever produced. The model was first released in 1957—about the time the real N&W J-class Northerns were being phased out. N&W's Js represented the ultimate in fast, efficient steam engine design, but the diesel would still overrule them. *Chris Rohlfing collection*

INSET: Affiliate railroads Norfolk & Western and Southern Railway (eventually both merged to become today's Norfolk Southern) resurrected J-class No. 611—which had been residing at the Roanoke Transportation Museum since its retirement late in the 1950s—early in the 1980s for excursion service. The sleek, streamlined 4-8-4 is shown on an excursion run on the Chicago & North Western Railway at Nelson, Illinois, in 1983. *Mike Schafer*

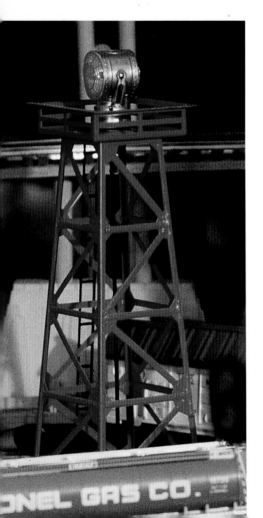

Halfway through the twentieth century the U.S. was at war again, this time as part of a United Nations "police action" in Korea. Only five years after ending World War II, Americans once more approached the holidays with young GIs and Marines lying in snow-covered mud, this time defending South Korea against the North Korean invasion. At home, World War II vets crowded the colleges and technical schools on the GI Bill while suburbs blossomed outside every major city. Air travel was popular as the growing airline industry built up fleets of four-engine Constellations, DC-6, and DC-7 passenger planes. The long- and short-haul trucking industry grew as the U.S. resumed the paving of America. Our railroads, who had helped win the 1941–45 war, looked around for their reward and with a chill realized there would be none.

There were two Americas heading toward the Christmas season of 1950. Across the country, prosperous parents peering in the department store window asked, "Which Lionel Do You Want, Son?" Meanwhile, on December 9, 1950, at Kot'o-ri, North Korea, when a young Marine of the First Marine Division was asked what he wanted for Christmas, he "... reached for the words through frozen lips, then answered, 'Give me tomorrow.'"*

The 1948–49 Railroad Fair in Chicago had been a gala event, showing off America's Railroading heritage and future. Shiny streamliners on show tracks gleamed under the summer sun as fair-goers trooped through beautifully appointed diner, club, and sleeping cars. Few realized that passenger service was bleeding the railroads' profits with every train that rolled half-full from the station. They marveled at the latest big-shouldered steamers, unaware that the last steam engines were then being constructed in the shops of the Norfolk & Western. They gawked at the GM *Train of Tomorrow,* a diesel-powered domed passenger train that had been built as a "test bed for future ideas." Railroad men were licking dry lips and hoping at this halfway mark in the century that some salvation would be found.

On the other hand, toy-train railroad men, like the highly motivated team at Lionel, launched their Golden Anniversary line with new diesels, a semi-new Hudson, a raft of accessories, and a streamliner for the bottom-feeders. They had achieved over $15 million in sales in 1949 and were predicting $21 million for 1950. Life was sweet and the sky was the limit.

"Play value" had always been Cowen's overriding motivation when approving a design, and as the 1950s

(*David Douglas Duncan, *Yankee Nomad,* Holt, Rinehart & Winston, 1966)

began to roll, tinplate "action" was happening all over carpet and plywood layouts. While dump cars dumped and log cars tumbled their loads into bins, oil derricks pumped colored bubbles up a clear tube—looking like a Christmas tree ornament—as the pump bobbed up and down. Aircraft beacon heads rotated, and scrap metal dropped with a clatter into gondolas each time a button tripped the crane's magnet. Every Lionel layout was growing with these amazing remote-control toys. Little men ran up and down switchtower steps as others tossed out parcels from rolling boxcars. Every touch of the button was rewarded with a loud *"zap!"* of an electromagnet performing a task, or a louder and more insistent *"zaaaazzz!"* as a vibrator shivered cows along a ramp, or the moan of a motor moving barrels up a conveyor. The Lionel toy train layout in full operation produced a din of whistle-tooting trains rushing on metal wheels over tinplate track, the *bazok!* of automatic switches shifting their frogs, and the cacophony of operating accessories. Over all hung the smell of ozone and warmth of the lights and heated motors. With the room lights turned off—and those of all the trains and accessories brightly aglow in white, red, and green—the experience was hypnotic, transporting a young engineer into a cozy universe where he had control of a world all his own.

On the three-rail high iron, super-detailed molded plastic and die-cast metal had taken over from stamped steel. Lionel introduced its new 773 model Hudson at the head end of three passenger cars called the "Anniversary Set" and costing $85. These *Irvington, Madison,* and *Manhattan* cars were older style "heavyweight" cars, and the set was offered only in 1950. After that, shiny replicas of the new streamlined extruded-aluminum cars were hung on the drawbars of Lionel's elite locomotives.

The 773 Hudson was a new breed of cat, joining the ranks of Hudsons that followed in the shadow of the magnificent 1937 Model 700E. It used the boiler off the less detailed 763E and added the boiler front of the 726 Berkshire. Its smoke unit clanked and was often ripped out by the owner when it became annoying. The six drivers offered Magne-traction, but the spokes were simulated. Pilot wheels were shrunk to navigate beneath the swinging cowcatcher pilot—also modified—to rush around the tight O-gauge curves instead of the sweeping O-72 turns of her pre-war predecessor. A "smaller Hudson" was also offered in 1950—the No. 2046—using the same steam chest and pilot as the 726 Berkshire. A new four-wheel truck was crammed in under the pilot so the wheel configuration would be correct.

Whatever their merits as models—and they are prized today by collectors—they failed to sell in 1950. The 773 was dropped after its 1950 debut, and the 2046 lasted until 1951. Kids wanted colorful streamliners, not old fogy steam engines whose prototypes were beginning to queue up at scrap yards around the country. And yet, steam locomotives would always be a part of the Lionel line of trains. They were built in a dozen variations—subtle variations of valve gear type, steam dome shape, piping, and air compressor placement—all conforming to some kissing cousin prototype that was probably being melted down to make girders for new highway overpasses. Even as steam faded away from American railroads, some Lionel classics were yet to come.

Really starved for some streamliner action were the bottom-feeders who watched their stubby steam locomotives whiz around the tight curves of O-27 track. They could only wistfully watch a Santa Fe *Super Chief* glide past on the O-gauge high iron in department store windows. In 1950, Lionel's bright orange box opened to reveal a Union Pacific Alco FA-type diesel locomotive—two of them, locked back-to-back in the "A-A" configuration just like the snobbish EMD F3s in fancy-schmancy O-gauge. Your author was one of those fortunate recipients and couldn't wait until we could get her on the track.

The prototype Alco FA-type diesel locomotive was always an also-ran to Electro-Motive's F-series diesel-electrics. Alcos leaked so much oil, sending plumes of smoke skyward, that railroad men referred to them as "honorary Steam Engines."

Lionel's flat-nose Alco FA set, No. 2023, initially was released in Union Pacific livery, painted bright Armour yellow with Harbor Mist gray roofs and red lettering. They had a good motor, a realistic horn, and dual headlights. So what if they were a bit smaller than the F3 (in real life, Alco FAs and EMD F-units were of nearly equal size) and so what if the trucks

were supposed to be American Association of Railroads Type-B trucks but were AAR Type-A borrowed from the Lionel 6220 EMD Switcher. These O-27 diesels filled a vast void and sold well. New road names were added over the years until Lionel's FA became a pale shadow of itself in the end: no horn, no Magne-traction—only a stamped plastic shell glued together over a tinny motor fighting for shelf space in a discount store. But the 1950 Alco FA really cooked and gave way-overdue O-27 operators diesel streamliner action at last.

The Korean War ebbed and flowed with a cycle of defeats, victories, and stalemates, drawing in more young men and women and diverting critical manufacturing resources to the military. Alnico magnets became impossible to get, so Magne-traction was left off of the 1951 locomotives. But, as with both world wars, Lionel easily shifted to armed-forces contracts. These defense dollars earned from developing such diverse gear as bomb fuses and improved radio headsets helped add to research and development budgets. Unlike the restrictions demanded by the world wars, toy train manufacturing was not halted, and Lionel's sales reached their peak of $32.9 million in 1953.

Variations on the Hudson theme: The 1937–38 763E sits on the trestle; in front of it is the Hudson revival model of 1950, the 773. Made up from parts of the successful Berkshire locomotive, it is prized by collectors today, but was yanked in 1951—then resurrected in 1964 using the old dies and trimming it with even more detail. Up front is a "small" Hudson, the 2046, which presaged a veritable fleet of Hudsons that appeared from 1953 through 1956 using both Santa Fe and NYC boiler types. *Toy Collectors Association Toy Train Museum, Strasburg, Pennsylvania*

Richard Smith, designer of the operating milk car, had come through with a pair of accessories that, when combined, allowed special gondolas to be loaded with culvert pipes or relieved of their burden. A lumber yard accepted logs from an operating car, then magically turned the little dowels into "planks" through some behind-the-scenes sleight-of-hand. Train stations spoke, calling out arriving "specials," and forklift loaders endlessly pivoted in their slots, hoisting lumber loads into waiting cars. Play value merged with education as kids discovered how different industries related to each other. In the toy train world, locomotives and rolling stock were essential to America's industries.

Beyond the living-room-carpet railroads, President Dwight D. Eisenhower embarked on a taxpayer-funded "national defense" plan of interstate highway arteries that enabled the long-haul trucking industry to provide door-to-door deliveries across the continent at speeds no railroad could match. Faster and more efficient transcontinental air travel as well as those same Interstate highways gave stiff competition to the railroads' passenger service. However, regulations set by the Interstate Commerce Commission forced the railroads to maintain many money-losing schedules.

America's railroads were losing their glamour and their relevance to the blooming economy. Towns that once welcomed the railroads now abhorred the smoke-belching steamers raining ash on their new pristine housing developments. In 1956, the Chicago & North Western Railway dieselized its entire commuter fleet between Friday, May 8, when riders came home from Chicago behind a steam engine, and May 11, when riders went back to work in Chicago behind a diesel. One hundred and seventeen steam locomotives were hauled off to the scrap yards.

None of this was lost on Lionel. The company had one main product—toy trains. As the railroads' image began foundering, so did Lionel's. Its Airex fishing equipment line was doing well and was featured on the 1953 catalog back cover with the traumatic results discussed earlier. But more diversification was

Lionel chose to model American Locomotive Company's freight carbody-type diesel—the FA—for the 0-27 crowd. The FA and its FB booster, a four-unit set of which is shown on the Lehigh & New England Railroad circa 1960—was Alco's answer to Electro-Motive's phenomenally popular F-series diesel. *John Krause, Andover Junction Publications collection*

The savior diesel locomotive for the O-27 bottom-feeders who had lived only with steam for years was this Lionel No. 2023 Union Pacific FA diesel set. Each locomotive was smaller than the snooty O-gauge F3s and ran on trucks appropriated from a switch engine, but O-27 railroaders didn't care. They had their diesel at last! *Train Collectors Association Toy Train Museum, Strasburg, Pennsylvania*

A popular operating industrial "complex" made from two separate models designed to be combined, the 342 culvert loader was produced from 1956 to 1958 while the companion unloader was offered from 1957 until 1959. Watching the model work—when it works properly—helps convey the intricate design engineering that went into these toys. *Chris Rohlfing collection*

needed. Stepping outside the toy train business had been profitable for Lionel during three wars—and technology learned from dealing with military requirements had spurred new innovations in the train lines, most notably, the application of modern electronics, precision die-casting, optics, and assembly efficiencies. The company would get its chance once again, following a trip the elder Cowens made to Hawaii.

With Lawrence now at the helm, Joshua and his wife Lillian took up the globe-trotting. On a trip to Hawaii in 1949, Joshua took a stereo camera with him. Stereo cameras were a common sight at tourist venues in the mid-1950s, but while stereo photography had been around since the stereopticon cameras of the nineteenth century, the "3-D" movie fad of the 1950s had re-introduced the process in living color. Filmmakers in Hollywood were doing everything they could to counter the popularity of television with its tiny black-and-white screen. Films such as "Bwana Devil" had lions and spears flying at the camera while the audience, wearing stiff cardboard glasses, all screamed at the realism. Stereo Realist and Kodak were among a number of companies who offered photographers special twin-lens stereo cameras that produced color slides mounted side-by-side in cardboard frames. These frames fit into a special hand-held binocular viewer that merged the two images into one with apparent three-dimensional depth. A huge hit at this time was the Viewmaster, a toy viewer that used pre-packaged images on a disc that rotated into place telling children's stories and offering scenic views. Many casual photographers who could afford the relatively expensive cameras ventured forth to make their own "3-D" scenic views.

When Joshua returned from his vacation, he was impressed by the results, but overwhelmed by the complexity of the light meter and exposure settings. He kept the camera on one setting and shot on sunny days. With the 3-D camera industry grinding out these high-end cameras, the designers at Lionel thought they could—as Louis Marx was doing with toys—grab the low-end business. To this end, in 1954, Lionel produced the Linex camera.

The Linex was a sunny-day camera with a fixed lens aperture and a fixed shutter speed. The film was supplied in special cassettes holding enough film for eight shots that were returned to Ansco for processing—not unlike the original Kodak box camera or the one-time cameras popular today. The transparencies were returned as stereo pairs to be fit into two cardboard viewing mounts that were in turn viewed with a special Linex battery-powered viewer. In effect, Lionel

The Linex camera was Lionel's attempt to push its way into the photography market following the 3-D stereo fad of the mid-1950s led by Eastman Kodak and Stereo Realist. Lionel's Linex had a fixed shutter speed and a special film magazine that had to be sent to Ansco to produce eight stereo pairs that had to be fitted into cardboard holders and viewed in a special battery-powered viewer. Shown here is the plaid case, package of cardboard viewers, the battery-powered viewer, the Linex camera, and its flashgun. *Bruce Malmin collection*

substituted complex picture-taking for complex viewing. The camera itself resembled a scientific instrument, and its eight-shot capacity required a considerable load of film cassettes to be carried by the photographer. Although priced at $44.50 complete with snappy plaid carrying case and viewer—half the price of a Revere or Stereo Realist camera—the concept was doomed. By 1956, after draining considerable design and marketing resources, the venture was considered a bust and 65,000 purchasers were abandoned while the remaining 20,000 unsold cameras were fobbed off to discounters.

As diversity eluded Lionel, it doggedly pursued what it did best: making excellent electric trains. While the Linex was struggling for market acceptance in 1954, the No. 2321 Fairbanks-Morse Train Master diesel locomotive had no trouble at all meeting sales expectations.

Like the Pennsylvania S2 turbine steamer, the prototype F-M Train Master was produced in limited numbers and failed to find wide acceptance except where a heavy-weight hauler with fast acceleration was needed. Unlike the S2 turbine, the FM was a well thought-out design, but some of its concepts were radical. It emerged from the Fairbanks-Morse plant in Beloit, Wisconsin, in 1953, with 2400-hp. in a single engine, the type that powered Navy submarines. Since many individual diesels at that time employed two 1,200-hp engines, maintenance costs on a single prime mover would be reduced by half. Its unusual opposed-piston power plant, however, caused service crews numerous headaches until they mastered its

eccentricities. Being highly suspicious of radical concepts, the railroad companies adopted a wait-and-see attitude. In three years, only 127 FMs were sold in the U.S. and Canada. Electro-Motive and Alco had time to build similar—but with more-conventional technology—high-horsepower locomotives, and production of the FM Train Master halted in 1956.

Not so with the Lionel FM. Its first model in Delaware, Lackawanna & Western livery was a 17 inch-long heavyweight in gray plastic with maroon stripes on a stamped metal frame powered by twin motors. With its stamped frame hunkering down on the track, the Train Master was less expensive to build, and it carried two interesting innovations. First, the wheels in each truck nearest the center of the locomotive were blind—i.e., without flanges—so the trucks could swing around those tight O-gauge turns. Next, the coupler attached to each six-wheel truck had a mechanical knuckle system that was uncoupled by a magnet in a special section of track. This new coupler removed the clumsy "sliding shoes" and magnetic coil making it considerably cheaper to produce. However, it occasionally came open under stress and, considering the FM's pulling power, long trains sometimes had trouble staying together. The Train Master added road names to successive generations until 1966. Its brute size and muscle, however, were undermined by cost-cutting in its production—anticipating the shape of things to come.

Rolling stock received a facelift as the injection-molding process allowed highly detailed cars to be produced for less and invited considerable variety of decoration within the same series. The 6464 boxcar was introduced in 1953 in single colors and then took off in 1954 employing two- and three-color paint schemes. Though the schemes are essentially correct, they had been "adapted" by Lionel artists to fit the scale of the car. Getting boxcar decorations as close to prototype as possible was important. A particular incident, however, revealed some "censorship" in the process as told in Roger Carp's book, *The World's Greatest Toy Train Maker.*

Louis Melchionne, a Lionel artist, was directed by Joseph Bonanno to create a car side for Ballantine Beer. Melchionne labored hard to get the three intertwined circles of Ballantine's logo correct. When finished, the car was shown to Cowen who promptly went through the roof. "Lionel will never advertise products that aren't good for children!" the boss boomed. The beer car was promptly yanked.

Some 29 number designations beginning with 6464-1 were introduced as well as numerous variations

Two Fairbanks-Morse demonstrator Train Master diesels head up a passenger train leaving Milwaukee, Wisconsin, on the Milwaukee Road where they were testing circa 1953. At 2400-hp. churning from a single prime mover that had been originally designed for marine application, these burly locomotives were ahead of their time—railroads then were used to regular road diesels, which usually cranked out around 1800-hp. at best. Train Masters could accelerate rapidly, which—despite being unstreamlined—made them ideal for passenger service or high-speed freight runs. *Andover Junction Publications collection*

In 1980, Lionel released Chicago & North Western Train Master diesel to a cool reception. The F-M Train Master was a huge model of a large and powerful prototype. Though the Lionel model has six-wheel trucks, the inside wheelset of each truck never touches the rails allowing the big locomotive to negotiate tight O-gauge curves. It was a dual-motored heavy hauler—second only to the GG1—that could pop couplers loose before its wheels would spin if too many cars were attached.

Three 6464-type boxcars click await pickup by the local freight. The 6464-series cars were introduced in 1953 and continued on with a proliferation of road names, brand names, and, into the 1970s, in short runs as special collectible cars. They came in four body types, two door types and, depending on the years they were built, a variety of trucks and couplers. A collection of these cars breeds like wire coat hangers and can fill a wall of shelves. *Stan Roy collection*

Throughout the mid-1950s, Lionel pressed on, turning out high quality pieces of engineering for its O-gauge train line. Gleaming passenger cars made of extruded aluminum stretched out behind F3 and Alco diesels as well as the revived GG1 electric that shouldered the *Congressional* passenger set. The "General Purpose" GP7 road-switcher from EMD found a place in Lionel's line in 1955. This super flexible "Geep" (pronounced "jeep") found a home on 74 different railroads over its lifetime and debuted with three liveries—Burlington, Pennsylvania, and Milwaukee Road—at the head end of Lionel's rolling stock. Another ubiquitous diesel working the yards of America's railroads was the 400-hp "44-tonner." This bidirectional center-cab locomotive came about through a union dispute that dictated any engine weighing over 90,000 pounds required a fireman to "assist" the engineer (never mind that there was no coal to shovel). Tipping the scales at 88,000 pounds, the 44-tonner could be operated by one man. Prototype-wise, the Lionel O-27 44-tonner flunked the test. It was as long as the much heavier NW2 switcher and used the same road trucks as the GP7—not switcher-type trucks. Its initial run lasted from 1956 to 1958.

However, there were changes in the marketplace beyond Lionel's control. The company was aware of these shifts in the market's basic operating structure

throughout the long life of the series into 1966. With the advent of the magnetic track section, the 3400-series boxcars were introduced. These were operating cars with a plunger in the center that only cost $.50 more than the non-operating cars. Run the boxcar across the magnetic track section, press a remote-control button, and—zap!—the door pops open and a little rubber man peers out. The "finger of God" was used to close the door and re-cock the mechanism.

but either could not or would not adjust or adapt. It was as if a state-or-the-art locomotive came hurtling down the track with a myopic engineer at the throttle who couldn't see the washed out bridge.

In 1947, Joshua Cowen prognosticated that the market between 1948 and 1958 should be excellent for electric trains because the "numerous children born during and after the war will be wanting trains." He was right on the mark and had reason to be enthusiastic. By 1953, Lionel had experienced record profits. Two thirds of America's toy trains and 62 per cent of those played with in foreign countries came out of the Lionel factory. Over 25,000 miles of three-rail track had been laid on living room carpets and in basements and rec rooms across six continents. Compared to America's real railroads whose operating locomotives numbered almost 43,000 hauling some 1.8 million freight and passenger cars, Lionel sold 622,209 locomotives and 2,460,764 pieces of rolling stock.

Celebrity power pushed Lionel sales, including the likes of actor Robert Montgomery, writer Ben Hecht, baseball players Roy Campenella and Lionel spokesman Joe DiMaggio. In India, a rajah used a Lionel train to transport food around the table to his dinner guests. At the Cleveland Radiation Clinic, a gondola towed by a Lionel locomotive moved radioactive materials in and out of lead-shielded vaults. Advertisers, including heavy hitters such as DuPont, General Tire, and Wrigley's gum stood in line to have their product ads miniaturized onto little billboards set up along Lionel tracks. One locomotive manufacturer offered Lionel $20,000 to make a model of its new locomotive. Joshua Cowen rejected the offer because he didn't like the locomotive's paint job.

Back in 1947, Lionel claimed to have saved the mom-and-pop hardware store who, outside of "a few pearl-handled pocket knives," had nothing to offer around Christmas. But by the late 1950s, the mom-and-pop retail stores had other problems—first came the shopping mall, then came the discount store.

One of the first malls, Northgate Mall, opened in 1950 outside of Seattle, Washington. Malls were the product of the suburban expansion that accommodated the baby-boom generation. These new consumers were armed with GI Bill of Rights education and Veterans Housing Administration low down-payment dollars and proceeded to fill new housing developments. Farm fields vanished under parking-lot paving outside traditional rural main streets. In 1956, the first enclosed mall was constructed outside Minneapolis in the little town of Edina. Lionel dealers and hardware store owners stood outside their shops watching cars pass through town to the new meccas where shoppers could browse the year round in shirt sleeves, buying from chain shops who could afford the high rents.

Open malls, enclosed malls, and "strip" malls sprouted everywhere, often anchored by a major department store such as Sears or Montgomery Ward. They were islands of shopping offering convenient

parking in huge unmetered lots. Americans became accustomed to driving to these mega-complexes for a full line of goods and services. By the time John Naisbitt wrote his best seller book, *Megatrends*, in 1982, he recognized that ". . . shopping malls are the third most frequented space in our lives, following home and the work place."

After this pattern was established in the late 1950s, the discount store was born. Merchandisers bought up former cornfields of their own, paved big parking lots, and moved in with huge stocks, few knowledgeable floor employees, and high turnovers that allowed them to offer lower prices to self-shoppers. This was a new generation of consumers who had never experienced the special services offered by the old-line department stores—which built the cost of those services into their margins. Yet, the shopper could still buy reliable brand names stacked on shelves and pay for them at a grocery supermarket-type checkout counter. This aggressive price-cutting alarmed every brand-name manufacturer.

Since California enacted the first "fair trade" law in 1931—a resale price maintenance restraint that set a minimum retail price that could be charged for a

The 3400-series of boxcars came about when Lionel changed its couplers from self-contained electromagnetic to a trackside electromagnetic arrangement that required a special track section. A car was spotted over the track section while a remote-control button activated the electromagnet in the track section which pulled the coupler pin down to uncouple. This design opened the door for new operating cars. In the early 1950s, Lionel mated a 6464 boxcar body with a mechanical system that, when run over the track section and a button was pushed, pulled down a plunger which shot open the boxcar door revealing a little man. In the red, white, and blue mail car, the little man came with a mail bag that he flung out when he appeared. *Chris Rohlfing collection*

General Electric's 44-ton center-cab switcher aimed at reducing the need for engine-crew members. Locomotives weighing 90,000 pounds or more required a fireman in addition to the engineer. The 44-tonner saved railroads considerably on crew costs. Most 44-tonners were sold to industrial and shortline railroads, such as Vermont's Springfield Terminal Railway, where a red, black, and white 44-tonner is returning to the engine house after a morning of switching in 1974. *Mike Schafer*

product—most states had enacted similar laws. In 1941, these anti-price-cutting laws were further strengthened by the Miller-Tydings Act exempting fair-trade laws from federal antitrust actions. But the fair-trade law usually had a non-signer clause that stated even though a store did not ratify the agreement, the minimum price restraint was still binding. As discount stores became more popular, however, the non-signer clause was voided by more and more states until, from a peak of 45 states in 1941, the number of states with a non-signer clause still intact had dropped to 16 in 1967. This downward drift in pegging prices for goods directly affected Lionel.

Lionel's legal department was overburdened with drawing up lawsuits to keep its dealers in line, but gradual disappearance of the non-signers clause took the teeth out of the Fair Trade law allowing more and more aggressive retailers to flourish by building traffic through price-cutting. Even toy stores—the bedrock of Lionel's marketing—were being challenged by mass merchandisers such as the Children's Supermarket that opened its third store in 1958 and whose motto "pile 'em high and sell 'em low" was the typical battle cry of the low-margin, high turnover discounters. From that beginning came the nationwide "Toys-R-Us" chain of stores.

While Lionel and other toy train manufacturers had often built special sets for department-store promotions, now the discount chains with huge buying power were dictating the look of packaging and demanding prices that guaranteed fast turnover. And toy trains in general were not turning over that fast anymore.

On October 4, 1957, the Soviet Union—that backward collection of oppressed communist states where a boy grew up to love his tractor—put a 184-pound sphere into orbit 584 miles above the earth. Though all it did was beep and live less than a year, *Sputnik* galvanized the scientific and rocket exploration and military segments of America's culture into severe catch-up mode. While the media had begun flirting with space-oriented publications and programming back in the early 1950s after the "Atomic Age" had arrived with the leveling of Hiroshima and Nagasaki to end World War II, *Sputnik* accelerated that trend. Driven by television, whose quaint "Captain Video" and "Tom Corbett, Space Cadet" shows of those early days were now becoming reality, the toy industry went into space-craze overdrive.

Since 75 per cent of all American toy companies— including Lionel—had their headquarters within 500 feet of where Broadway crossed Fifth Avenue, the buzz must have sounded like a hive of bees. At New York's Gimbels department store, the staff was garbed in spacesuits while *Sputnik*'s beeps chirped over the store speaker system and parents lined up to buy Ideal's new Satellite Launcher. By the turn of the year, Kenner's Titan II and Bomarc missiles looked out menacingly from merchants' shelves. Monogram advertised kits of U.S. missile ordinance in *Popular Mechanics* magazine as "timely as Sputnik."

Lionel battled for enforcement of the fair-trade laws as its margins were besieged. Traditional product distribution through jobbers and distributors added their taste to the price. Retailers who bought from the jobbers were confronted with price-slashing discount stores and, in turn, cut their prices to remain competitive. From 1953 to 1955, Lionel's sales had dropped by 38 per cent, and by 1959 sales had been chopped by half. Three strikes since the World War II were capped by a fourth strike in 1954, brought on by a proposed

wage reduction, further diminishing the "family" environment that had been the heart of the company since Lionel's founding. Adding to the market change, America's disposable income for toys and luxuries was savaged by a recession that had the effect of reducing employment. Companies undergoing severe downsizing looked to government contracts to take up the slack and caused Lionel to desperately underbid for what had become a stable part of its income.

Scrambling to regain some needed cash and marketing share, Lionel set its designers to working on trendy space and military rolling stock. At the 1957 Toy Fair buyers viewed a tragic miscalculation in the product line-up of "The World's Greatest Toy train Maker."

Trains had always been "guy things." Girls got dolls; boys got trains. In 1957, Lionel introduced a train designed for girls that was pulled by a pink 2-6-2 Prairie-type locomotive, a pink gondola, robin's egg blue boxcar, buttercup yellow boxcar, a lilac-colored hopper, and an illuminated caboose dipped in sky-blue paint. Girls for whom the set was intended felt put down as if they were incapable of appreciating a "regular" electric train. Even fathers who were button-holed by Lionel dealers and salesmen refused to take the "Lady Lionel" home to their daughters.

The Girls' Train was a monumental gaffe, and although it is prized by collectors today for its scarcity, retailers who were stuck with the klinker were not amused. Salesmen took sets home to their daughters

A Lionel 400-hp "44-tonner" moves some freight at the famous Choo Choo Barn. Lionel introduced a model of the prototype (facing page) in 1956; only one axle had Magne-traction. The model shown wears Rock Island colors and was made much later, complete with hand railings. *The Choo Choo Barn, Strasburg, Pennsylvania*

The "Lady Lionel" or "Girls' Train" of 1957 was a marketing stinker from its pink locomotive to its pastel-colored cars. While the toy train market was definitely a "guy thing," girls who did want trains refused to be patronized and the sets gathered cobwebs on dealers' shelves. Eventually, the unsold sets were returned and the locomotives were sprayed black for re-sale. Original Lady Lionel sets are very prized today. The model shown is a re-issue from the 1990s especially for collectors. *Stan Roy collection*

Lionel made a major effort to storm the HO-gauge scale hobbyist market. After a flirtation with Italy's Rivarossi, Lionel subcontracted to Athearn but never truly captured the hobbyists' hearts. This Soo Line HO locomotive with it original box shows the plastic parts and cheap look that, along with trying to peddle kiddy cars (such as an operating giraffe car) to adults, eventually killed the line. *John Hertree collection*

who were also not amused. Though it was a popular re-issue in the 1990s to collectors, the Girls' Train turned into an indicator for the marketing drift that had settled on Lionel.

If only Lionel had managed to balance the Girls' Train with a brilliant, long-term success, it might have weathered the disaster. Instead, Lionel chose 1957 to abandon its core business and introduce a line of HO-gauge trains. Once again, Italy figured into Lionel's plans, and Alan Ginsburg, vice president of sales, traveled to the respected HO manufacturer Rivarossi to consummate a deal whereby that company would produce Lionel's HO line. Rivarossi was already selling its own high-quality HO trains in the U.S. and figured that Lionel's prestige name would enhance its own market position.

Lionel's market research had shown that there was growing interest in the smaller gauge by adult hobby-

ists. Joshua Cowen, by then 80 years old and chairman of the board, along with other Lionel veterans felt the HO line would draw resources from their signature O-gauge trains. Lawrence, as president, disagreed, believing that Lionel's name and a good track record for excellent quality would capture part of the miniature gauge market and bring in new customers buying that coveted year-round product. Too late for the Toy Fair, Lionel issued a separate HO catalog—a four-page folder that came along with the 1957 catalog. Lionel's emergence in this gauge—half the size of O—had the curious effect of "validating" HO; that is, giving it the imprimatur of a major toy train manufacturer.

The Rivarossi models from Italy were excellent, highly detailed, and well-running; Lionel's packaging and promotion were right on target. Hobby magazines and merchants all hailed this HO line as a potentially profitable year-round seller. As the year 1957 turned over, Lionel happily acknowledged a profit, but it was the last profit they would make from toy trains.

The honeymoon with Rivarossi was short. Lionel's cost problems were reflected in its subsequent financial deal that offered to pay off the letter of credit they had opened with Rivarossi without posting any guarantee bond or security for the shipped merchandise. Rivarossi backed out in 1958 and left Lionel to find a domestic supplier. Athearn, an equally respected American HO manufacturer, was tapped and accepted a down-payment and remittance deal.

Athearn made cheaper models than Rivarossi. According to Vincent Rosa and George J. Horan in Greenberg's *Guide to Lionel HO Trains*, they state that a Rivarossi boxcar was priced at $3.75 in 1957 while the same car from Athearn sold at $2.50. Another departure was the "power truck" motor used by Athearn and many other contemporary modelmakers. Although the Rivarossi motor used a gear drive and precision-made steel bearings, Athearn's power truck transferred its torque to the wheels via a "rubber band" from the motor shaft to a gear box. Since the joy of HO-gauge railroading is coming as close to prototype as possible, this rubber band motor made inching along at prototype speeds virtually impossible. And while details such as brake wheels and ladders had been hand-affixed to Rivarossi rolling stock, they were molded into the Athearn body casting to save costs. Strike two.

Finally, Lionel was caught in a philosophical quandary. For decades, it had touted three-rail track as far superior to two-rail track. In its catalogs Lionel flogged American Flyer (though not by name) mercilessly for the complex wiring needed by AF to accomplish layouts that were built with ease using Lionel track. It was like George Orwell's *Animal Farm* where the rebelling pigs' chant "Four feet good, Two feet bad" when they were at war with the farmer, but the cry became "Four feet good, two feet better" once the pigs learned to walk upright. Even then, Lionel came out with a strange three-rail HO gauge track that was anathema to its primary hobbyist market.

Lionel subcontracted flatcar loads to increase variety without raising tooling costs. It outsourced accessory buildings to the Bachmann Brothers in Philadelphia who shipped Plasticville structures to Lionel for distribution in the familiar Lionel orange-and-blue boxes. A rocket could be blasted ceiling-ward from the No. 175 plastic launcher while "atomic waste" containers rode the rails on a flatcar. Whizzing around the track on a single power truck was a DeSoto Model 68 inspection car, bright red and complete with fins. Could there have been a better harbinger of Lionel's coming fate?

Unfortunately, the year 1957 died with a whimper rather than a bang.

Perhaps as a desperate appeal to the growing fascination that American kids had with the automobile, Lionel released this "inspection car" late in the 1950s. It seemed to be a precursor of the slot-car racing craze that would burst upon the 1960s like a supernova.

NEW "SUPER" O TRACK

Lionel's 1957 catalog featured the beautiful 746 model of Norfolk & Western's J-class streamlined 4-8-4s and the great toy train marketing clunker of all time (fortunately not featured on the cover), the "Lady Lionel." Also new in 1957 was the revolutionary Super O track which featured "T"-style running rails like the prototype and a de-emphasized center third power rail made of thin brass. The new track was attached to tough, molded plastic ties that were a realistic brown color. The track was beset with two principal problems: First, the center rail required special bridging rail joiners to maintain electrical continuity (the rail was too thin for the usual pin arrangement)—since they were completely separate, these special brass joiners were also easy to lose. Second, the almost knife-thin center rail quickly wore grooves in pickup shoes. Regardless, it was arguable the most-realistic track offered by a toy train manufacturer. *Jim Flynn collection*

By 1959, Lionel was thrashing about, mixing antique concepts like the *General*, a colorful diamond-stack throwback to Civil War railroading, with missile-firing cars, ballistic rockets, and bunkers in keeping with Cold War headlines. Featuring "duck-and-cover" nuclear war fears with nostalgia for a simpler time seemed appropriate to Lionel's fevered marketers. *Jim Flynn collection*

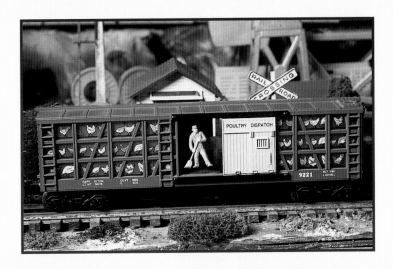

chapter 4

The Fox in the Poultry Car

An Empire Derails: 1957-1969

"Let me have men about me that are fat

Sleek-headed men and such as sleep o' nights.

Yon Cassius has a lean and hungry look,

He thinks too much,

Such men are dangerous."

—William Shakespeare
Julius Caesar, Act 1, Scene 2

If there is a metaphor for Lionel's flat-out rush to destruction from 1959 until the mid-1960s, it can be found on the cover of the 1959 catalog. One of Lionel's classic locomotives—the Berkshire steamer—clanks along atop an embankment while behind it a Navy missile blasts off from a launch pad. Below the Berkshire, a new locomotive, the *General,* an old diamond-stack steamer dating back to the Civil War, puffs along at the head-end of antique wooden, open-vestibule coaches. Below the *General* is a self-propelled Army rocket launcher. Below the launcher is a radar-equipped missile launch bunker and from both the Army launcher and the bunker, missile tracks form an arc over the elderly steam engines. Make something of that if you will.

This artistic hodge-podge reflects the panic in the halls of the Lionel H.Q. on New York's 26th Street as the company's management watched toy train profits move from an "acceptable downturn due to market readjustment" to the arterial pulse of red ink. As the Cold War and space race with the Soviet Union heated up, toy manufacturers like Lionel dashed off into two separate, but parallel directions: old values and new challenges.

First, came the look back at the wars we had won. Fess Parker's *Davy Crocket* TV series—history as interpreted by Walt Disney—showed how we had won the West with a long rifle, grit, and snappy frontier-style one-liners. Every kid wanted a coonskin cap like Davy's. *The Great Locomotive Chase*—also a Disney movie and also starring Fess Parker—showed how a gritty band of Union spies captured a Confederate diamond-stack locomotive during the Civil War to tear up enemy bridges. So what if they were caught. So what if they were hanged. We all knew who won that war. Television screens were sodden with Westerns whose grimly efficient heroes stood for American values in the face of evil.

The other path led to science in the form of technology. Jet-powered flight, space exploration, robots, and radar control were applied to defend American values in the face of evil. On Lionel tracks, rockets launched, helicopters flew, missiles screamed from

This 9221 "Poultry Dispatch" car is a 1983 re-issue of the 3434 operating boxcar built from 1959 through 1960. Drive over an electromagnetic track section, push a button, and the door pops open; a little man appears with a broom and begins to sweep out chicken droppings. When originally offered, the car was prophetic concerning Lionel's immediate future.
Stan Roy collection

their launchers, and boxcars exploded. Long-range artillery poked from the roofs of O-gauge rolling stock while flatcars formed the perfect platforms for a variety of killing machines. While this high-tech blood bath rained destruction on unseen enemies, Lionel designers still tried to keep an even keel by putting fish and chickens on the rails.

The No. 3435 Aquarium Car remains one of Lionel's most creative designs. Two windows on the side of the boxcar are made of wavy clear plastic. Inside, a strip of 35mm clear film with fish painted on it moves past the windows when the activation button is pressed as the car passes over the magnetic track section. The illusion of fish swimming underwater is amusing and very well executed. A modification of the original animated boxcar where a little rubber man peered out when the door slid open was carried over into the No. 3434 Poultry Car. This chicken car had a door fly open and a little man sweep out chicken droppings, which is another metaphor all its own.

That 1959 catalog also saw the integration of HO trains into Lionel's mainline offering—thought by some to be a major mistake since HO was appealing to

a different market apart from the bigger toy trains. However, even as dollars drained out, Lionel attempted to strengthen its HO line-up by buying freight-car tooling from John English's Hobbyline company. These cars were very well made and offered the same sprung trucks as Lionel's HO competition. Though the rolling stock improved, locomotives continued with sluggish-at-slow-speeds rubber-band power transfer instead of the new worm-drive motors.

Orders from the Toy Fair were not promising. The annual stockholders' meeting in the spring of 1959 was foreshadowed by a cut in dividends and a drop in profits. It was a grim little band that faced the board. Family members who owned blocks of shares turned up to oversee the overseers of their considerable holdings. Isabel Cowen Brandaleone, Joshua's daughter, was there in person instead of just mailing in her proxy as usual. Although Lawrence held 42,266 shares, his sister was the major Lionel stockholder, voting 67,225 shares when those held in trust for her grown children were counted. She had always been the stronger of the pair and her presence raised a red flag concerning her brother's stewardship of the company.

Here is a lineup of Lionel military cars that failed to prop up their sinking company from 1959 through the early 1960s. As Joshua Cowen had urged back in 1909, play value is important to keep a kid interested. Many of these cars encouraged demolition and destruction, distorting the job of the railroads. Shown are the 3619 helicopter reconnaissance boxcar, 6805 radioactive waste flatcar, 6650 missile-launching car, 6470 explosives boxcar, 3419 helicopter flatcar, 3664 Minuteman boxcar, and a radar flatcar to locate your target. *Train Collectors Association Toy Train Museum, Strasburg, Pennsylvania*

Lionel's income had plummeted $583,000 by September, and at a board meeting on the 17th of that month, Lawrence looked up and was surprised to see Joshua arrive and take a seat as a guest. After nine months away from the action, the elder Cowen watched and listened, taking in what was said. When the meeting was over an hour and a half later, Lawrence Cowen caught a plane for the Orient. He and his wife, Vicki, were shopping for sporting goods equipment to sell under the World Wide Sporting Goods trademark that Lionel had acquired through its dormant and hemorrhaging Airex Division. Joshua Cowen went home and sold all his Lionel stock to Roy Cohn.

In 1959, Roy Marcus Cohn was at the peak of his game. He had gained his fame as chief council from 1953 to 1954 for Senator Joseph McCarthy who ran the U. S. Senate permanent investigations committee, hunting down communists both real and imagined. Televised hearings had shown Cohn whispering legal points in McCarthy's ear as "Tail Gunner Joe" bore down on a witness with brutal intensity. Roy was only 26 when he was launched into the public arena and carried that first blush of fame with him to New York City where he became a power broker with politicians and flirted with members of the underworld. He also managed a very busy legal schedule as a partner in the firm of Saxe, Bacon & Bolan. To his clients, he was a loyal advocate. To his opponents, he was an unethical shark. Most of all, he loved the action.

He was Joshua Cowen's great-nephew through Rachel Cohen Marcus, Cowen's sister. It is assumed that this tenuous family link and Cohn's growing reputation as a deal-maker brought Cowen's daughter, Isabel, and her two children, Cynthia Saypol and Anthony Otis, to him in 1958 to "talk" about Lionel's skidding fortunes. Since their combined shares in Lionel made them extremely vulnerable to any drop in Lionel's value, they wanted to explore their options. As the 1959 September board meeting approached, their concerns had probably been communicated to the elder Cowen. His holdings were also in jeopardy, so his attendance at that meeting must have been his last attempt to see a ray of light, a spark of hope that Lionel's fortunes could be reversed. He saw none. Five days later, he called in Cohn and offered his 55,000 shares to Cohn's group for $15 a share, five dollars higher than the current price. With Cowen's and Isabel's shares in hand, Cohn rounded up another 21,000 loose shares and achieved control.

Time magazine gave an insight to Cohn's fast-handed methods of acquisition in an April 23, 1960, article entitled "Fast Switching at Lionel."

". . . Cohn last October borrowed $339,000 from the Mastan Corp. in Manhattan at a monthly interest rate of $1^{1}/_{2}$ per cent and $532,000 from a Hong Kong moneylender, Commercial Investment Co., Ltd. With the help of this money, the Cohn Group bought controlling interest in Lionel. A month later, Cohn borrowed $400,000 from Atlantidi, S.A., a Panamanian moneylender to pay off the Mastan Corp loan. Last month, Cohn borrowed another $147,000 from Austin Associates, used it to pay off the remainder of the Hong Kong loan. Despite this razzle-dazzle, the Cohn Group still owes $912,000 on Lionel stock it purchased."

Lawrence was buying Pacific Rim baseballs and catcher's mitts when he got the word. Shaken, he returned to New York and, apparently crushed by his father's perceived betrayal, gave up his shares to Cohn without a fight. He asked the men who had helped create Lionel, but had proved powerless to stop its decline, to resign from the board. In October, Roy Cohn was elected president and Lawrence Cowen was bumped upstairs with the title of chairman. He resigned that post two months later and his sister Isabel was elected to the board. Her son-in-law, Ronald Saypol, became vice president in charge of administration. The palace coup was concluded, but the worst was yet to come.

Train-wise, Lionel's O-gauge and HO-gauge products that had been hurt by kids' new interests in cars, airplanes, and rocket ships, now began a precipitous decline under the new management.

In 1956, Lionel (and American Flyer) had introduced a plastic model of the prototype General Electric EP5 "rectifier" electric—a double-ended passenger locomotive. Rectifier locomotives convert AC current from the overhead wire into DC current for the traction motors that turn the wheels. The prototype rectifiers packed a lot of power into a more compact locomotive than the huge GG1.

Lionel's model of this unique locomotive employed a plastic shell over the same trucks used on the F3 diesel, pantographs from the GG1 (though without the insulators because of the plastic body shell), a single motor, and a horn casting that was

Roy Marcus Cohn, Joshua Cowen's great nephew and Senator Joseph McCarthy's legal whisperer during the McCarthy communist witch-hunt hearings of 1953–54, assumed the mantle of CEO of Lionel in 1960. He was a well-connected and rapacious lawyer as well as a financial gadfly. With Cohn at the helm, Lionel almost sank out of sight under a burden of conglomerate acquisitions and bad product judgement. Cohn skipped out just ahead of the sheriff with a lien on the former CEO's limousine. *Train Collectors Association Toy Train Museum, Strasburg, Pennsylvania*

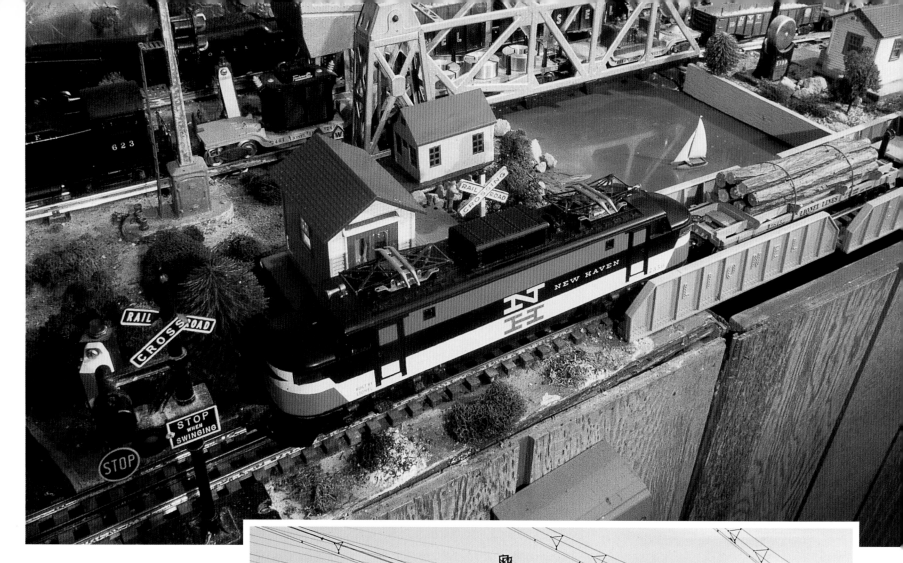

General Electric's EP5 rectifier electric locomotive was considered state-of-the-art technology when introduced in 1955, and both Lionel and American Flyer wasted little time in introducing their own model versions the following year. Lionel's model captured the overall look of the prototype EP5, although it rode on two-axle Electro-Motive trucks versus three-axle trucks on real EP5s. This EP5-powered freight passes two accessories from the 1930s and 1940s: the 1935 gateman's shanty and the 1940 bascule bridge in the background. At lower left in the photo is Lionel's "wig-wag" crossing signal from the late 1950s.

The New Haven Railroad bought ten EP5s for passenger service on its electrified main line between New York and New Haven. New Haven was the only railroad to purchase these locomotives new, but Lionel offered its model version in several liveries. Prototype EP5 No. 374 is shown in 1966. *Jim Boyd*

also swiped from the F3. The model appeared in the vivid, modern-day orange, white, and black "McGinnis" scheme of the New York, New Haven & Hartford Railroad, then under the direction of president Patrick B. McGinnis. Other road names applied to the EP5 were the Pennsylvania, Milwaukee Road, and Great Northern even though those railroads never owned an EP5. The locomotive was featured in catalogs from 1956 through 1960 when it was purged along with many of Lionel's best locomotives, rolling stock, and accessories.

Where possible, unpainted colored plastic was used for carbodies and also replaced stamped metal truck frames. With all the cost-cutting, two interesting sets were offered in 1959: the Alaska set and a set featuring a collection of antique wood coaches and flatcars hauled by a wood-burning steamer dating from the Civil War. The Alaska set is less interesting as trains go: an NW2 diesel switcher without operating couplers and two yellow cylinders atop the hood that represented "dynamic brakes" (never an appliance on real NW2s) plus some freight cars. The Alaska set

commemorated Alaska's 1959 admission as the 49th state along with a selling pitch claiming Alaska as "an outpost of freedom…" being closer to the Soviet Union than the "Lower 48." More Cold War sword rattling.

The 4-4-0 American-type *General* was offered with "Super O" gauge, the new, more realistic track that had been introduced two years earlier. Though American Flyer was no longer the real threat to Lionel's market, management's concern about the "realistic" quality of its two-rail track prompted the "concealed" third rail and more prototypical ties. The antique steamer was also offered as a special set for Sears and in O-27 gauge. During its four-year life, the sets that trailed behind the wood-burner offered a bewildering variety of cars ranging from the fanciful 6445 Fort Knox Gold Bullion transport car to the 3376 stockcar that had a giraffe poke its head up through a roof trap door—and duck down for overhead obstructions at the touch of a button. The set catered to the kids who flocked to the rush of Westerns shown on television during this period, and when these shows waned, so did the popularity of the *General*.

Comparing two eras of locomotives from Lionel is almost like kicking a puppy. The No. 763 from 1938 rests on the trestle above a sad plastic No. 246 2-4-2 from the even sadder 1959 period. The 763 itself represents the tinplate half-price ($37.50) version of the famous $75 700E. To get the 246 as part of a set of cars and track, all you needed were two Quaker Oats box tops and $11.95. *Train Collectors Association Toy Train Museum, Strasburg, Pennsylvania*

In 1977, the *General* returned to the O-gauge rails complete with passenger cars and a horse car. This 4-4-0 diamond-stack locomotive had been introduced in 1959 and appears on that year's catalog cover along with missile-launching cars as Lionel scrambled to save itself in the changing marketplace. As with other Lionel favorites, it was resurrected a number of times into the 1990s painted in different schemes and in 1980 with a chromed boiler. *John Hetreed collection*

The 4-4-0 wheel arrangement was the most popular of the mid-to-late nineteenth century and is closely associated with Civil War-era railroading. Among the best-known locomotives of that period was Western & Atlantic's *General*, made famous by the Disney movie *The Great Locomotive Chase*. It is shown, restored, on an exhibition run to Wisconsin in 1963. Both Lionel and Flyer offered models of the *General* beginning in 1959. Flyer's model was based on photos of Lionel's pilot *General* model taken by a "spy" from A. C. Gilbert! *Robert Bullerman*

As the year 1960 began under Cohn's stewardship, he blew on the coals of the limping HO-gauge line, seeking to lure kids to the miniature gauge by offering "Brand New Action Packed Operating Cars." In effect, Lionel shrunk the O-gauge operating cars down to HO size—no mean feat for its engineers. Today, these exploding, launching, dumping, and giraffe-head-bobbing cars are collectible as examples of inventive engineering. In 1960, though, Lionel's HO-gauge line landed with a wet thud. Adult hobbyists—the main supporters of the Rivarossi, Hobbyline, and Athearn models—recoiled at the tinplate-concept "action" rolling stock and, in a state of high dudgeon, went so far as to abandon all Lionel HO products. The kids

didn't want the big trains any more; why would they queue up to own a smaller version? Lionel even produced a double-decker circle of track with an HO freight train running below and O-gauge set running above. Both trains were headed up by Santa Fe F3 diesels in an effort to sweeten the pot. The ad shows Dad, son, and Spot the dog all enthralled at the sight of this over-and-under wonder circling and circling and circling . . . Lionel's HO-gauge product line lasted until 1966 when it was mercifully dropped.

Roy Cohn and his soldiers had bigger fish to fry than the fading train division. They went chasing electronics firms. They sucked up three companies in that year: Anton Electronics, Intercontinental Manufacturing, and Telerad Manufacturing Corporation—all for shares of Lionel stock. By the end of the year, stockholders could rejoice. The old management had left Lionel with a loss of $1.2 million on sales of 15.7 million while Cohn's buying spree netted $31.3 million with an in-the-black profit of $681,000 on paper. His flurry of acquisitions would eventually ensnare seven companies into the Lionel fold, expanding his usual cat's cradle of financial string-pulling.

Major General (ret.) John B. Medaris, age 58, delivered this profit statement to stockholders with a guileless straight face. He had been recruited by Cohn to become president of Lionel in order to scoop up big military contracts. Medaris had just retired from commanding the U. S. Army's Redstone Missile Project at Huntsville, Alabama and professed ". . . a longtime fondness for electric trains." At one point, Medaris was quizzed about how it felt to work for Cohn, who persecuted and prosecuted Army officials in the Army-McCarthy hearings six years earlier. He replied, "Let us forgive the mistakes of youth." His military connections together with the public's long-held belief that ex-generals make supremely excellent executives drove Lionel's stock up to $31 a share. The board bought Medaris an airplane. Rumors were bandied about that Wernher Von Braun was waiting in the wings to join the Lionel team.

Well, Wernher never showed up, and the fact that Medaris had quit the Army in a huff over its plodding missile program undermined his contract-scooping ability. His handsome visage graced numerous public-relations photos pointing out the wonders of Lionel trains to goggle-eyed youngsters while, on the side, he worked on a book that sharply criticized the U.S. Army. His liabilities began to overwhelm his capabilities. In 1961, after one full year as president, the accomplishments for which he was front man amounted to an all-time high loss for Lionel of $1.8 million. Following a particularly poor on-stage performance at a minority stockholders' meeting where his perks and salary were savaged by the folks in the seats, he was shunted off to become vice chairman and, to paraphrase General MacArthur, ". . . just faded away."

Science kits led the 1961 catalog, elbowing aside the poor trains. And there were many poor trains alongside the only quality

holdovers from the 1950s' days of glory: the Berkshire steamer, the Santa Fe F3 diesel, and the often resurrected GG1 electric.

At the recently built plant at Hillside, New Jersey, a steady stream of old-line Lionel employees filed out the parking lot door carrying cardboard boxes filled with memories. Downsizing among the actual workers offset the cost of a management top-heavy with bewildered officers of acquired companies wandering the halls trying to figure out what to do. Toy trains were simply a puzzle piece in the elaborate mosaic Cohn was fashioning—and not even a good loss

Glittering on a siding is the No. 6445 Fort Knox Gold Bullion Car. This gem was produced from 1961 to 1963 and must have been a favorite of Roy Cohn, Lionel's entrepreneur-president. The aquarium car body was modified to hold the gold. It came in a variety of colors and was one of Lionel's more whimsical designs. Think about it—transporting gold bars under glass for all the public to see. . . *Chris Rohlfing collection*

A giraffe ducking its head out of the roof of a stockcar when it hit a "tell-tale" (a trackside device that warned switchmen walking on top of moving cars that an overhead obstruction loomed ahead) was a real grabber idea from the whiz kids who were running Lionel in the 1960s. While Roy Cohn was playing puppetmaster, the whimsical gem was shopped out as a 3376 or 3386 car. This particular 7904 model is a re-issue from 1983. *Stan Roy collection*

In 1960, Lionel launched an array of HO-gauge "action" cars that fit in with the military/Cold War theme. These two cars represented a destructive pair—in more ways than one—that typified the line. The 0847 "Explosives" car has a mouse-trap spring device inside that, when hit by the "Minuteman" rocket from the Lionel 0365 boxcar, "exploded." (The example shown is minus its rocket). This line of kiddy-market cars went over like the proverbial lead balloon with HO hobbyists and only served to sink Lionel's scrambling efforts in that market. *Patrick Martin collection*

leader at that. Cohn, the master puppeteer, was not even a fulltime leader. He was involved in a championship fight promotion between Floyd Patterson and Ingemar Johansson, travel agencies, a bus company, and his very brisk law practice. Cohn's executive administrative assistant—keeping an eye on Lionel while Roy was busy serving and ducking subpoenas—was Paul Hughes.

Murray Kempton, a columnist for the *New Republic*, wrote of Cohn's right-hand man . . .

> "Hughes' past experience with administration was an unbroken record of misjudgment: he had been an assistant to Alexander Guterma, the swindler; he had been indicted and pled guilty in the market-rigging of United Dye; he has been president of a company said to be controlled by Las Vegas gamblers."

Cohn stated the charges were unfair since Paul came from a large New England family and had been an altar boy at Villanova.

A sorry stew of tape recorders, science labs, chemistry sets, phonographs, model cars, and a few electric trains greeted the receiver of the 1962 catalog. As with the 1959 catalog cover, this collection reflected Lionel as a whole. By 1963, even Cohn had reached the limit of his attention span for the corporate goulash that had become Lionel. Since he had many balls in the air at once and Lionel was just one of his balls, he took the smart-money way out. Cohn cut his losses by selling his stock at a loss to another rapacious group of corporate fixer-uppers and bailed. At his last Lionel stockholders meeting as chairman of the board, he skipped out the back door to avoid a deputy sheriff trying to serve a non-payment judgment. This curtain-closer would be his remembered legacy. As Murray Kempton commented at the end, "The Lionel Corporation was Roy's single venture in productive enterprise."

The following years of the 1960s is a blur of cutting and hacking by various merchant messiahs who further reduced the company to just its name value. The 665 Hudson, smaller cousin of the 773 that was a shadow of the 700E scale Hudson of 1937, was dragged out for a last hurrah in 1966. It was saddled with a Pennsylvania Railroad tender that must have sent long-dead NYC officials into high RPMs in their graves. Ronald Saypol, grandson-in-law to Joshua Cowen and former officer in Cohn's regime, became president in 1968. That year, Lionel offered one train set made by a subsidiary company. The accessories were farmed out. The 2-6-4 model 2029 steamer with rubber "gripper" wheels instead of Magne-traction was made in Japan. Next year, so was its motor. Lionel's name had been affixed to a number of toy and leisure stores that eventually sought protection under Chapter 11 bankruptcy.

Sadly, Joshua Lionel Cowen lived to see his life's work skidding toward oblivion. At age 88, living with his wife, Lillian, in Palm Beach, Florida, his health steadily declined. On September 8, 1965, he suffered a stroke and died. Sixty-five years after tacking a fan motor onto a cheese box, powering it with batteries, and sending it around a circle of steel strip track, he could look back and reflect that he had truly found his product that would sell and make his fortune. He was buried in his hometown of Brooklyn, appropriately near a railroad track where trains pass daily.

In 1967, six years after the death of A. C. Gilbert, American Flyer was rudderless and foundering. The company sailed into Lionel's camp for a mere $150,000. That rivalry was concluded once and for all. Three years later, Lawrence Cowen, the boy who had once become the symbol of Lionel by spreading his arms over a circle of Lionel track for a photographer, died of a heart attack at age 63.

Lionel's name power continued to make lease money for Saypol, but it was used in the same way a primitive tribe would have preserved the head of their dead king on a tall pole to inspire awe in their fellow tribesmen.

Lionel's 1961 catalog featured trains and Porter Science sets. The mix was unsuccessful and Lionel only managed to run its Porter acquisition into the ground and spin it off. *Jim Flynn collection*

Joshua Lionel Cowen is smiling in this photo, but it was taken during Lionel's later years when there was little to smile about. On September 8, 1965, Joshua suffered a stroke and died in Palm Beach, Florida. He had seen his company grow from two guys working in a loft to the world's largest toy train manufacturer. He also lived through its steep decline into desperate measures to save the Lionel name. He was 88, and if he could have borrowed a few more years, he might have seen Lionel rise again from the ashes. *Lionel L.L.C.*

In 1973, Lionel brought out the 8359 GM50 GP7 diesel to commemorate the 50th anniversary of General Motors' locomotive-building Electro-Motive Division. This limited edition run sold out so quickly that General Mills executives suddenly realized there was a collectors' market out there. This was the first of the "Collectors" locomotives and rolling stock. The GP7's production was limited to 9,000 units. *Chris Rohlfing collection*

chapter 5

The Fundimensions Era

The "Grain Grinders" Give it Their Best: 1969-1986

By 1969, the U. S. was neck deep in the Vietnam War and moving toward the "Swinging Seventies." This was a time of bell-bottom pants, white shoes with matching belts, big hair, neck medallions, and social consciousness on display. Gas guzzling automobiles dominated the fast lane, jet airliners screamed overhead, citizens-band radio made truckers into cultural icons as with their own southern-twangy "CB-speak." Meanwhile, the railroads went deeper into the dumper both financially and in public esteem. It was not a good time for the toy train market.

Famous American railroads—cultural fixtures a hundred years old—vanished into seas of red ink. In a desperate attempt to save what could be salvaged, some roads merged their resources. The Pennsylvania had already merged with the New York Central in 1968 in an effort to seamlessly blend two rival management systems into the Penn Central Railroad. Together, they achieved the largest bankruptcy in U.S. history up to that time. Pretty-colored diesels with shiny stainless-steel cars couldn't save the passenger services as schedules were cut, whole trains were cut, employees were let go in wholesale lots, and entire communities were stranded as secondary services were discontinued. America's passenger trains had lost their allure, their luster, and their lease, forcing the government to

step in. The result was the Rail Passenger Service Act of 1970 that created the National Railroad Passenger Corporation, marketed as "Amtrak" (for <u>Am</u>erican, <u>tra</u>vel, and trac<u>k</u>). Technically a railroad and not a government agency, Amtrak began years of struggle against the public perception that the railroads were a dead issue, that tracks should be replaced with highways or bicycle and jogging trails.

This attitude did not help toy train sales. Louis Marx prospered because of his overseas plants and wide range of toy products including electric and wind-up trains from the Girard and Erie plants. He had outlasted them all with sales of $67 million in 1971. When he passed away in 1982, like Joshua Lionel Cowen and Alfred C. Gilbert before him, he left a void in his company that could not be filled. Quaker Oats eventually bought the company.

By 1969, the Lionel name was attached to a growing line of Lionel Leisure Stores run by Ron Saypol, the husband of Joshua Cowen's granddaughter. While some toy train inventory trickled off dealers' shelves at knock-down prices, the rest were represented by crates of tools, dies, and unsold products warehoused away and gathering spider nests. However, with the approach of the Swinging Seventies came a business phenomenon that lifted Lionel phoenix-like from the

The ubiquitous little gateman that pops out of his little house arrived in 1935 carrying his lantern. Tossing scale to the winds, the figure is as tall as a tank car, but the accessory proved to be one of Lionel's all-time hits and has rarely been out of the catalogs. *Stan Roy collection*

$1.00
A LIFETIME OF RAILROADING
1903
1970
LIONEL®
TOY DIVISION OF
ALL ABOARD . . . for a lifetime of railroading, for the thrill and excitement of trains, for the sharing of an experience by father and son. Here is everything every boy wants. Here is Lionel. Big cars, big locomotives, detail and realism. Here is Lionel. The great grand name in model railroading . . . in outstanding quality. Lionel . . . great for parents, great for youngsters, great for a lifetime of fun.
BONUS . . . OPEN UP TO A 22" x 34" POSTER
BURLINGTON
WABASH CANNONBALL
No. 1081
New heavy duty Pullmor motor and Pullmor Power that hauls five times as many cars as ever before. Forward, reverse and neutral selective on the loco. Uncouple cars automatically. Set measures 43" long. New Nickel Plate Road Steam Locomotive • Nickel Plate Road Tender • New Burlington Gondola • New Santa Fe All-Purpose Flat Car with Side Stakes • New Nickel Plate Caboose • New 6,600 h.p. Trainmaster® Safety Transformer — UL Listed • 8 Curved Tracks • 2 Straight Tracks • New Mechanical Automatic Uncoupler • Lockon and Wire • Owner's Maintenance and Instruction Manual
FITS 27" x 36" SPACE
BURLINGTON
YARD BOSS
No. 1082
Powerful switch engine with Pullmor Power, forward, reverse and neutral selective on loco, and beaming headlight. Freight cars uncouple automatically. Set measures 42" long. Santa Fe Diesel Switcher with Headlight • New Burlington All-Purpose Gondola • New Great Northern Hopper • New Santa Fe Convertible Work Caboose — Convertible to a Flat Car • New 6,600 h.p. Trainmaster® Safety Transformer — UL Listed • 8 Curved Tracks • 2 Straight Tracks • New Automatic Uncoupler • Lockon and Wire • Owner's Maintenance and Instruction Manual
FITS 27" x 36" SPACE
LIONEL 027 MODEL RAILROADING . . . THE RIGHT SCALE
FOR EASY HANDLING, FOR EASY OPERATION AND FOR ALL-AROUND FUN

The 1970 consumer catalog that opened out into a 22 x 24-inch poster produced by the Lionel Toy Division of General Mills' Model Products Corporation—one of the many Lionel organization titles that were used after 1969. *Jim Flynn collection*

dust bunnies. Known as the "corporate conglomerate," it consisted of a ". . . mass created with fragments from different sources."

Cash-rich corporations fell under a spell of logic based on the premise that more companies housed under one umbrella would yield greater profits. With checkbooks in hand, America's industrial giants swooped down and gathered up scores of smaller companies and brand names that had nothing to do with the giants' core businesses. In the midst of this check-floating frenzy, the cereal corporations chose toys as the obvious extension of their puffed, toasted, and sugar-coated products already aimed at kids.

Quaker Oats bought Fisher-Price. Consolidated Foods snagged Tyco while General Foods picked up Kohner. General Mills purchased Rainbow Crafts, Chad Valley, Regal Toy, Kenner, Parker Brothers, and made Ron Saypol an offer for Lionel electric trains. Saypol leased the famous name to General Mills for a 3.5 per cent royalty on annual sales—a wise decision since in little more than a decade's time, Saypol's leisure-wear stores would be treading red ink in Chapter 11 bankruptcy. Delighted with the transaction, the cereal people added Lionel to their new umbrella division called Fundimensions, headquartered in Mt. Clemens, Michigan, then ran off to the warehouse with hammers and pry-bars to peer into the crates and see what they had bought.

To their undying credit, General Mills' Fundimensions Division gave the toy train market its very best shot. It is beyond the scope of this book to examine the entire explosion of Lionel products resurrected and created between 1970 and 1986, when the romance ended, but even the most casual perusal of this period reveals an almost heart-breaking attempt to restore Lionel electric trains to their former stature.

What they discovered when they opened all those crates and cartons was a large inventory of accessory parts ready for assembly plus a collection of tools, dies, and molds that would allow re-issuing Lionel's line of classic rolling stock and motive power. The two main problems were (1) how to begin selling new products into a market that was still trying to peddle unsold leftovers from Lionel's days of steep decline, and (2) how to stimulate a market that was truly jaded toward toy trains.

The toy industry was recovering from child-safety and morality groups who had come out against war toys. Because of the growing unpopularity of the Vietnam conflict, G. I. Joe had shed his military togs for "adventure" wear. Gross-out toys of gruesome fantasy from Aurora Plastics—"Rated X for Excitement"—were pulled from the shelves. Fantasy figures from comics became "action" figure kid collectibles fired by television commercials sponsoring Saturday morning cartoon series. Sesame Street had become a toy generator elbowing other slower-moving toys from the discount store shelves. While General Mills laid the lash onto Kenner and Parker Brothers to create new toy innovations, Lionel was what it was—a toy train company in an era when most 9- and 10-year-olds had never even seen a steam locomotive and could care less about the grimy, faded diesels of railroads no longer interested in public awareness. There was no more venerable engineer, no Bob Butterworth to inspire youthful dreams. Diesel engineers went to work in a strike-torn, down-sizing industry looking like the day shift at an assembly plant rather than denim-clad knights of the rails oiling up their giant Hudson's drivers for another railroad adventure on the high iron. The Fundimensions marketing spin-meisters decided they would re-launch Lionel in rainbow hues of diesel-hauled train sets.

The 1970 Lionel catalog featured a colorful profusion of low-end diesels including Santa Fe Alcos resplendent in "warbonnet" red, yellow, silver and black and a delightfully garish Illinois Central Gulf GP9 in orange and white. Although steamers were not ignored, only the dies for a pair of 2-4-2 Columbia-type locomotives were dusted off for production—one in plastic and the other in die-cast metal. This oddball wheel arrangement made a brief appearance circa 1895 on the Chicago, Burlington & Quincy, and it is doubtful that Lionel had this prototype in mind when it cobbled something together to ride on its ubiquitous four-wheel chassis and motor. Its re-introduction nibbled away at the vast mound of four-wheel drives that Fundimensions uncrated. Sharing the catalog with the 2-4-2 locomotives was a big Hudson-type in Great Northern livery (never mind that GN never bought Hudsons), but it was never produced.

Helping Fundimensions' concentration on brightly colored train sets were new application processes that allowed more complex logos and color combinations. One of these was the "electrocal" system that came along in the late 1970s and premiered in large scale on the 9400-series boxcars. This electrothermal method of applying highly detailed logos and striping to cars replaced the peel-off decals and heat stamping. Its one flaw left a flat paint area around the decoration when applied to a high-sheen car side. The other application process was called "tampo" and used a changeable color pad and fast drying paints. These new technologies coupled with a variety of colored plastics in pellet and liquid form widely expanded Fundimensions' palette.

This first bevy of diesels arrived somewhat stripped down from their postwar Lionel counterparts. They lacked delicacy of trim, Magne-traction, and horns. The early GP-type diesels were fitted with hollow rollers to draw power from the third rail. These lighter rollers refused to bridge the non-current areas of the switches and caused locomotives to stall. Solid rollers were offered in a swap plan at Fundimensions' expense. The new diesels' most important qualification for heading up Lionel's re-introduction was their low production cost and potential variety of road names using the same castings. From the Alcos reintroduced in 1970 to the F3s brought back in 1973 with B&O livery added, this philosophy held true over the years. Six body variations were cast for the F3, presenting different porthole and louver locations for specific road types. In 1979, however, the last body type—known as Type Six—was used for all the F3s to come.

Fundimensions had launched Lionel into the mummified toy train market in 1970 using up leftover parts and low-cost, low-risk sets. In 1973, however, stirrings were heard in a virtually untouched corner of the toy train market—adult collectors and operators. The Train Collectors Association––TCA—had started up in 1954 and grew to include divisions across

Three boxcars from the 9400 series. These cars saw the first extensive use of electrocal decoration that replaced fragile decals. They also featured cars exclusively from shortline railroads instead of more recognizable Class1 roads. Their most unique feature, however, is their use as collectibles offered separately or in sets. Sometimes a special car needed to complete a set would only be offered as part of another set—which thus had to be purchased as a whole to get that one car. Outraged collectors brought this Fundimensions practice to a halt—for the time being. The heavyweight passenger cars in the background wear the colorful livery of the prototype Chessie System's *Chessie Steam Special* exhibition and excursion train, which in real life during the 1970s was pulled by a restored steam locomotive. *Stan Roy collection*

America. By 1976, ground was being broken for the TCA Toy Train Museum in Strasburg, Pennsylvania. In 1966, the TTOS—Toy Train Operating Society—opened as an organization for members who enjoyed running their collectible trains on elaborate layouts. These groups with their bulletins and newsletters formed a growing inter-connected market that appreciated Lionel's re-emergence. They had disposable income and a nostalgic attachment to the electric trains of their youth. The operators in particular desired re-issues of classic motive power and rolling stock that could be run, saving wear and tear on their collectible trains that were increasing in value dependent on condition. Most important of all, these collectors and operators held the promise of that holy grail of the toy train industry—the long sought-after year-round consumer. Their wallets were open all the time and they eagerly anticipated each new addition to the Lionel line.

Together with the B&O F3 diesel issued in 1973, Lionel brought out a GP7 diesel locomotive that com-

memorated the 50th anniversary (which happened in 1972) of GM's Electro-Motive Division decked out in Chessie System (in the prototype world, a new amalgamation of B&O, Chesapeake & Ohio, and Western Maryland) yellow, blue, and vermillion colors. The locomotive sold out its run of 9,000, proving the value of the collectors' market. That same year, the Lionel die-masters were hitting their stride by adding an insert to the standard GP series die and slicing the high short nose in half to produce a "new" locomotive—the Electro-Motive turbocharged GP20—that also mounted Lionel's first electronic horn.

By 1974, Fundimensions built the U36B, a model of a General Electric prototype. This model "U-Boat" (as all the prototype models in GE's Universal series were nicknamed) headed up Lionel's high-end freight set that year and went on to haul Fundimensions' expensive freights through 1980. The Disney-licensed freight set of 1977–78 featuring Disney characters applied to the sides of "Hi-Cube" boxcars was hauled by a U-Boat adorned with a smiling Mickey Mouse.

Three F3 diesel locomotives wait on work tracks for their next runs. These three inherited the popularity of the original Santa Fe and New York Central models introduced in 1948. Over the years, Lionel added other road names such as the Western Pacific in 1952. The Milwaukee Road and B&O locomotives were produced for only one year after appearing in 1956. *Chris Rohlfing collection*

Another unique car that showed Fundimensions was in tune with modern railroad trends was the TOFC car—Trailer On Flat Car or "piggyback" car. These cars, picked up in the 1970 catalog, used realistic application of trucking company logos to add both color and play value to freight sets that were familiar sights on most major railroads. Unfortunately, there were no accessories or tractor-trailer combinations offered until 1977 to make a true intermodal facility to handle the trailers, limiting play value. In 1973, another blend of road vehicles and train loads was attempted with the open automobile carriers made of colored plastic and allowing both single and double tiers of die-cast metal automobiles. These cars suffered in that they could accommodate only HO autos, giving them an odd appearance, and they tipped over on turns because of their being top-heavy.

Another 1973 experiment that lasted exactly one year was the introduction of the Lionel Tru-Track system. This track looked great, harking back to the prototypically accurate T-shaped rail of 1937 with wood-grain plastic ties and rails that could be mounted on rubberized roadbed strips. Unfortunately, the Fundimensions folks overlooked one trumpet-blaring flaw: the track was aluminum and Magne-traction does not work on aluminum. Operators—that new market outlet being courted—wanted their Magne-traction for those prototypically long trains stringing out behind laboring, double-motored locomotives. In the trade-off between the toy look of tinplate three-rail track and watching their prize motive power spin its wheels until it started to smell bad, Tru-track lost out.

Overlooked so far has been any mention of passenger cars. That watershed year in Fundimensions' stewardship, 1973, also produced the first of its 9500-series passenger cars in a set headed by a black Milwaukee Road 4-4-2 Atlantic-type steamer complete with the

electronic Sound of Steam feature and a whistle. The cars, though nicely detailed, were hardly auspicious. They were old-time illuminated heavyweights decked out with maroon roofs and orange sides complete with an open-platform observation car. In design and color, they were the postwar Madison-series cars, but they were too short and their body-mounted (versus truck-mounted which provides better track-negotiation) couplers were not automatic. Grumpy rivet-counters out in the collectors' market would only allow them a passing "harrumph."

Following this bad start, however, Fundimensions burned the bad mail and got down to cases with a flurry of colorful, reasonably accurate modern cars leading up to a breathtaking set in 1981. It was headed up by a re-issued Norfolk & Western J-class steamer—the 746 Northern-type (4-8-4) that is arguably the most graceful steam locomotive Lionel ever built. Its

Longtime Disney animator and railroad and toy train aficionado Ward Kimball designed this 6464-1971 Disney boxcar for the Train Collectors Association for their National Convention in 1971. Many clubs and associations across the country have commissioned special cars to commemorate special events or anniversaries. Only 1,500 of this particular car were built, making it a rare collectible in today's market. *Train Collectors Association Toy Train Museum, Strasburg, Pennsylvania*

The U36B road-switcher built by General Electric was reproduced by Fundimensions as a semi-scale (a bit shorter than the prototype so that it could negotiate O-27 curves) freight-hauler with a stamped metal frame, a plastic shell, and a single motor. This model was manufacturered in 1976 and came in the Bicentennial paint scheme worn by its Seaboard Coast Line prototype. It accompanied a set of boxcars celebrating the original 13 colonies. *John Hetreed collection*

Contemporary Lionel owners went a long way to offer products that younger buyers could relate to. In response to the boom in "piggyback" (trailer-on-flatcar or TOFC) transport that took hold in the real railroad world beginning in the late 1960s, Lionel issued its own fleet of TOFC cars, complete with truck trailers wearing appropriate prototype markings. *The Choo Choo Barn*

Bonding with the automobile industry in the 1970s, Lionel created these extra-long open automobile carriers, each made of colored plastic and having off-set trucks, loosely attached to allow negotiation of tight curves. They are good reproductions, but had a habit of tipping over. Only the car offered in 1989 actually came with automobiles and they were HO scale, as these on the No. 9145 car of 1977. No other size auto would fit on the ramps. *Stan Roy collection*

passenger consist was a replica of N&W's famous *Powhatan Arrow* post-World War II streamliner on the Cincinnati–Norfolk route. The following year, a model of the Southern Pacific *Daylight* locomotive came down the three-rail pike leading its own matching passenger cars.

But along the way, living up to collectors' expectations proved difficult. Ragged paint jobs, ill-fitting plastic components, and indifferent lighting schemes were criticized. When Lionel managed to produce a slam-bang winner passenger set, its asking price was also stratospheric. The pockets of Lionel collectors were not bottomless.

Fundimensions re-introduced the EP5 electric motors and their boxy E33 freight companions—also

in a bevy of colors. The classic GG1 was long anticipated and finally delivered in 1977. It was the Tuscan red model complete with Magne-traction and dual motors for hauling long trains. This moment lost some of its sublime reverence when the castings proved to be a bit rough and the nylon gears were not durable. To round out the line of GG1s, Fundimensions pushed a model out the door in Penn Central black livery with its infamous "mating worms" logo. The marketplace yawned and stayed away. Though PC had indeed inherited the Pennsy's GG1 fleet, Penn Central itself had disappeared in 1976 with the coming of Conrail.

Up at the General Mills corporate towers, high sales quotas had been assigned to all the toy manufacturers under the Fundimensions umbrella and Lionel was no different. The "grain grinders"—a name given to the top echelon cereal company strategists by the harried *unter muenchen* toiling farther down the food chain—wanted profits from all their acquisitions, but not at any cost.

The production of steam locomotives became a testing point. While the kiddies liked the vibrant colors of the diesels, adult collectors wanted Lionel's classic steamers revived—and then some. The little 2-4-2 faux-Columbia whizzing around the tracks on its Type 1 four-wheel motor was not what they had in mind. Fundimensions took a deep breath and responded with a beautiful collection of high-iron smokers.

This was no small commitment. The market leader diesel dies were simplicity itself compared to the cylindrical boiler, firebox, sand and steam domes, piping, cylinders, headlight, smokebox fittings, stack, cab, and pilot of a steam locomotive. The warehouse crates had yielded a collection of used steamer tools and dies that would have to fill the bill until the market was more firmly established. Convincing the suits in the top-floor conference rooms to drop $100,000-plus on a new set of steam engine dies required more than hopeful optimism.

Tentatively, Fundimensions pushed a little Hudson out the door in 1972. The 8206 was well-motored and accessorized with Sound of Steam, a whistle, headlight, and a new wrinkle—a small rubber traction tire on one driver in lieu of Magne-traction. It was beetle-browed with an Elesco feedwater heater above its smokebox to give it a bulky look, but its drivers were sometimes drilled off-center, giving it an ugly duckling waddle down the straights. It also suffered from the re-use of postwar molds, causing a softening of what were once sharp details. This problem would be a constant concern as Fundimensions developed its steamer line using these old molds. But, it managed to resurrect many of the old dies, modifying them in clever ways—as engineers had done to create the GP20 from a GP7 die mentioned earlier—and chrome-plating die surfaces to extend their life.

One unique locomotive emerged in 1972, the 8209 Pioneer Dockside switcher, an 0-4-0 tank-type locomotive. Although this diminutive steam switcher is considered to be an oddball among Lionel's standard fare, it is actually closer to being prototype than the bogus Columbias and "Porters" surrounding the ubiquitous four-wheel motor. The Dockside tanker—carrying its own coal and water on board—resembles a number of Pacific Northwest logging engines that shared the rails with geared steam locomotives such as the Climax, Shay, and Heisler. Actual tank-type locomotives were somewhat common switching the tight confines of heavily urbanized industrial areas (hence their lack of separate tender). Interestingly, when the 8209 was offered, it came with a tender so as not to confuse buyers who were unaware of tank-type engines. On seeing a tanker for the first time, one irate buyer who felt he was being short-changed asked, "What do you call a locomotive with no tender?" Having answered this question too many times, one demonstrator looked up wearily and said, "A diesel."

The No. 8600 Hudson was issued in 1976 fully tricked out and including smoke and Magne-traction. This locomotive used the Alco body worked over from its original postwar 646 dies. Another Hudson, the 8603, shared the debut in Chesapeake & Ohio livery over a Baldwin-style body with, curiously, a dummy coupler hanging off the back end of the tender. Unfortunately, it shared the same duck waddle as the 8206 and lasted only one year. But the success of the 8600 proved the concept, and Fundimensions engineers gave the old dies a hard squint, considering how they could be creatively modified to produce an elegant fleet of steamers to open the wallets of collectors and operators.

As with the diesels, Fundimensions went for the gaudy wherever possible. The two-tone maroon and gold Chicago & Alton Hudson of 1981 hauled matching passenger cars that in real life in the 1920s had been pulled by a Pacific. An 8003 yellow-and-vermilion-splashed Berkshire 2-8-4 from postwar days sported the Chessie System logo as it swept past the

One of the "small Hudsons," this 8702 *Southern Crescent Limited* locomotive came out in 1977 hauling its own passenger-car set made up of shortened 9500-series Madison cars riding on four-wheel trucks. It was offered in two versions of green: flat and shiny, this being the latter. The locomotive had "Sound of Steam," smoke, and an AC motor powering all six wheels. *John Hetreed collection*

A Lionel EP5-type rectifier locomotive in Great Northern colors rounds a curve hauling freight. This locomotive, whose prototype debuted in 1955 on the New Haven Railroad, was the first electric-type that Lionel re-issued in 1975 (Lionel would also reissue the American Flyer version). The model is relatively accurate compared to its General Electric prototype and can run off the track power or with its steel-spring-reinforced "pans" operate from an overhead wire. However, although the real GN did own electric locomotives, none were EP5s—but Lionel's models looked great in the famous GN green-and-orange livery. *The Choo Choo Barn*

In 1988, this Penn Central GG1 was offered in all its austere glory. Even with its simpler paint job than the former Pennsylvania Railroad Tuscan red with gold striping, Lionel raised the price $50. The PC "mating worms" logo foretold the real-life horror that would swallow both railroads—the Pennsylvania and New York Central—whose merger into PC became the largest corporate bankruptcy in history to that time. Since then, polls among railroad fans have revealed Penn Central to be one of the least liked of America's major railroads, so it's no small wonder that the market did not respond kindly to Lionel's Penn Central model—although some speculate that time may alter this GG1's collectibility. *Chris Rohlfing collection*

8002 Union Pacific "Berk" tarted up in light gray paint with "elephant ear" smoke deflectors on either side of the smokebox. Where remotely possible, every steamer's surface was dabbed with touches of gold, white, silver, or—as with the beautiful Southern Pacific *Daylight* 4-8-4 Northern-type—streaked down the side in prototypical bright orange with a silver smokebox front and dual headlight. A Southern 2-8-2 rolled out in 1983 painted prototype dark green with a red cab and silver smokebox. Its cylinder box was pin-striped in white as was its red-roofed cab and matching tender. Walkways were edged with white or gold, and drivers were left polished steel until corrosion complaints came in, then the drivers were given a whitewall treatment.

Even a facsimile of the Pennsylvania S2 steam turbine was created in 1984. While the prototype was a 6-8-6, the model is a 4-8-4 Northern with a tiny center wheel behind the middle journal box in the front and rear trucks. It rode on small Berkshire-size drivers while a graphite gray smokebox with white striping added non-prototype touches to the gussied-up postwar 682 body casting. Even the fussy and troublesome oiler arm seen only on the 682 was part of the running gear.

Lionel accessories were also sought after. As the inherited spare parts bins containing the bits that made up Lionel's classic accessories emptied, it became obvious that new layout furniture had to be designed and built from scratch. One of the good things about being a conglomerate is picking up the phone, calling one of the attached businesses such as General Mills' Model Products Corporation, and saying, "Start making Lionel stuff next Tuesday." The Model Products division (MPC) had a good industry reputation for building model airplane kits, so when the word came down, Century Series Jet Fighters and Super Sabre molds were shelved and railroad structure kits in rainbow colors began rolling down the lines. Lionel became known as "MPC Lionel."

The first new locomotive made by General Mills' Fundimensions-controlled Lionel was the 8209 Pioneer dockside switcher brought out in 1972. Very inexpensive and sporting a four-wheel tender and balloon stack, this little 0-4-0 locomotive was untrue to any prototype. However, without the tender and "onion" stack, it did replicate the tank-type switchers that apparently inspired its creation. The true dockside switcher worked for the B&O and looked nothing like this. The model was so small that its motor had to be crammed into the boiler *and* the cab. *Chris Rohlfing collection*

The 8600 "small" Hudson shopped out in 1976 was Lionel's second flirtation with mid-size Hudsons since 1964. It was built around the Berkshire boiler casting with a 4-6-4 wheel configuration crammed underneath. This Hudson-type of locomotive has become a fixture with every toy train maker and, for Lionel, resulted in a glut of Hudsons over the next few years—some good, some awful. *Chris Rohlfing collection*

A Berkshire sporting Chessie System livery hauls a lowly freight toward a Lionel sawmill where logs went in and—through a designer's illusion—planks came out. This 2-8-4 Model 8003 locomotive arrived in 1980 as a passenger-hauler with its own set of equally gaudy cars—but it was relatively true to prototype, mimicking Chessie System's real-life *Chessie Steam Special* train, which roamed the system to provide the public with a look at—and a ride behind—a real operating steam train. This re-visiting of Lionel's sturdy "Berk" was a big step for Fundimensions and they loaded it with Sound of Steam, an electronic whistle, smoke, and Magne-traction. *Stan Roy collection*

The little automatic gateman popped out of his shed with his lantern once again. Street lamps, lighting towers, crossing gates, and highway flashers added illumination to new layouts and let collectors retire their original pieces to the investment shelf. Train stations made of colored plastic parts tumbled out of kit boxes and little ready-made freight sheds steam-whistled or diesel-horned when the train went by. New coaling stations that were "Easy to Build!" dumped their loads into multi-hued hopper cars. With all these new accessories and the old classics humming, buzzing, lighting up, and zapping as long trains of rolling stock followed twin-motored locomotives gripping the rails with Magne-traction, power became a real problem.

Gone were the days when straight 110-volt AC caused transformers to become impromptu hot plates as they necked the current down to train-operating needs. Also gone was the manufacture of the classic two-handled ZW transformer that put out up to 275 watts, enough to run four trains at a time. By the time Fundimensions inherited Lionel, the Occupational and Safety Hazard Administration (OSHA) had come into being and clamped down on the amount of juice allowed for toy train running—100 watts was the maximum. Then came the three-prong safety plugs and a shortage of copper wire in 1972—enough to make an engineer cry. The result was low-power transformers offered to traditional—read, "kids"—market and the adult operators doing everything they could to keep their old ZWs going, or—as at least one model railroader did—build a custom power pack that delivered a sizzling eight amps, enough to run 32 trains at once.

Cabooses of all kinds brought up the ends of Lionel freights, everything from porthole, to transfer, to bay-window and wood-sided shown forth in those snappy colors. Other cars that lent themselves to gaudy brilliance were tank cars: single dome, double dome, and triple domes wearing logos from Sinclair to Pennzoil to Life Savers and Tootsie Rolls. Every foodstuff from Cheerios to J&B scotch found their way onto the sides of boxcars. Gone were the days when Joshua Cowen pulled beer ads from the line, because beer was bad for kids. Now Coors, Black Label, and Hamms all had their own reefers. You could also get El Producto cigars or Salem cigarettes. In 1980, the anniversary of Joshua Cowen's birthday, Fundimensions issued a set of 9400-series boxcars, each of them telling part of the Lionel story. At one point a Lionel boxcar had a portrait of Joshua next to his *New York Times* obituary. Fortunately, it was not an operating boxcar where, at the push of a button, the door slammed open and a little miniature Joshua popped out.

In that same 1980 catalog, four pieces of S-gauge rolling stock were offered for the deserted American Flyer fans whose loyalty to two-rail never flagged. A GP7 and an Alco Santa Fe diesel set—made from original Flyer dies that were part of the dowry when General Mills acquired Lionel—would be targeted to these orphans, but they would have to rely on small hobby-manufacturers for their main supply of Flyer-compatible rolling stock or replicas of past glories.

A survey of Fundimensions' catalogs reveals the change from the fantasy artist renderings of creatively stretched locomotives and rolling stock rushing four abreast past grinning boys. Truth-in-advertising mandated by law became the watchword of corporations who had gotten their fingers burned. Some mourned the passing of the fantasy artwork books of the 1950s replaced by photographic catalogs of the 1980s. These mourners reflected the same feelings expressed when television

A bank of Lionel ZW transformers is the backbone of many large layouts. These ZWs were produced by Fundimensions, but shortly thereafter, the Occupational and Safety Hazard Administration (OSHA) cracked down on production of the big, 275-watt controllers, ruling that 100 watts would be the maximum power permitted. Model railroaders who had bought ZWs before the ruling spent their time keeping the beasts going. A cottage industry developed providing parts and service. *Chris Rohlfing*

Lionel has always offered a variety of caboose designs. Here is a colorful collection from the 1980s featuring, from back to front: a Chicago & North Western 9361 bay-window car; the 1974 re-issue of the 2420 work caboose of 1948—only in aqua blue; a yellow-and-blue Chessie System extended-vision cupola caboose coupled to a Southern 17601 standard O-gauge woodside car from 1988. Waiting on the siding is a Pennsylvania NC5 porthole-type "cabin" (which is what PRR called its cabooses) in O-27, and in the foreground is a scale NYC brown woodside from 1987. *Stan Roy collection*

These three boxcars and three reefers represent Lionel's constant flow of collectible sets wherein each car was offered separately over a period of years to the end that a complete set is more valuable than its individual parts. Collectors form a large market for these cars that cost only a change of decor and paint scheme to turn out. The top set is part of a beer collection in the 9800 series offering two regular billboard reefers: the Hamms car and the Old Milwaukee flanking a special "Standard O" Strohs car that is fairly rare. The Standard O reefers had special spring-mounted trucks and were built to scale. They did not sell well because there were very few scale locomotives or other cars to accompany them during the mid-1970s. These beer cars would never have been tolerated by Joshua Cowen because beer was bad for kids—but they demonstrate how the market has changed. Below the beer cars are three 7600-series "colonial state" cars offered between 1974 and 1976 to commemorate the Bicentennial. A complete set comprised 13 cars, and plans were made to add the other 37 states but not carried out. *John Hetreed collection*

The countenance of Joshua Lionel Cowen adorns the side of the commemorative 6421 caboose offered in 1982 to cap off the "Cowen Commemorative Set" issued two years earlier. *Stan Roy collection*

replaced radio and removed images of the imagination from the experience. Straightforward photography showed the Lionel line as tangible products in real colors with airbrush smoke and headlight beams posed against seamless paper backgrounds. The new buyers who patronized the Collector Series wanted to see those to-die-for pieces for which they were shelling out significant sums. And the waning kid market catered to by the Traditional Series was made up of parents who had struggled through a couple of recessions, wage freezes, and gas embargoes who wanted to see what they were getting for downsized disposable income. More often than not, they opted for slot cars and fantasy figures to placate their trend-driven kiddies. As each generation has met new technology, old tech is put on hold but often is brought back, dusted off, and recycled. Today, books on tape have brought back the images of the imagination lost when radio drama went away—albeit at the expense of the reading experience.

To its credit, Fundimensions was churning out products—good ones for the most part—and making

its collector/operator market relatively happy. But Fundimensions was not making its nut according to the General Mills bean-counters and the artificial (read, arguable) quota placed on the toy-train-makers. During this period of supply-side "Reagonomics" and cost-cutting flights to offshore manufacturing facilities, Lionel and its fellow satellites seemed ripe for a change of scenery to boost their bottom line.

In 1983 their marching orders were made known to the press and they packed up their machinery, tools, dies, molds, punches, test tracks, plastic pellets, and zinc ingots and headed for a *maquiladora*—jointly owned factory by Mexico and General Mills—facility just outside of Tijuana, Mexico. Some personnel were sent to Fundimensions' office in San Ysidro outside of San Diego, California. The sprawling Mexican facility housed all of Fundimensions' manufacturing, and Lionel waited its turn as other satellite companies who took precedence set up their operations. When Lionel production resumed, language barriers forced communications breakdowns. The interconnected systems required for toy train manufacture and operation defeated production processes geared to building a single toy. Teddy Ruxpin the Talking Bear was a snap to build compared to the simplest toy train set with locomotive, cars, track, and transformer that all had to work together. One faulty part among hundreds brought train action to a halt.

Production struggled. Quality control sagged. New products were delayed and some were delivered only partly constructed in their boxes. Popular sets never reached the distribution pipeline. Lionel's carefully re-built market began to crumble. By the end of 1983, the horror of the move to Mexico became all too evident as the chart arrows skidded downward from hard-won peaks into dismal valleys. The experiment ended in 1984, and Lionel straggled back to Mt. Clemens like refugees from a bombed-out country. Old hands who were laid off were

begged to come back. After returning to their former facility, Lionel tried to make a splash by re-issuing three quarter-inch-scale Hudsons: the 783 New York Central in black, the 785 in gray, and the 784 trimmed in white with Boston & Albany lettered on the tender. The age of the 773 Hudson's well-worn mold used for these locomotives affected the quality of the castings.

By this time, General Mills wanted nothing more to do with the toy business, period. Hit or miss products, production costs compared to returns, and vagaries of the marketplace all added up to a bruised bottom line that diversity and acquisition were supposed to have

built up. In 1985, General Mills fobbed off its toy businesses one by one and went back to its "core competency," grinding grain. Lionel found itself dumped into Kenner-Parker which didn't have a clue what to do with it.

In Detroit, Michigan, real-estate developer and collector of antique cars and toy trains, Richard Kughn, heard Kenner-Parker wanted to unload its Lionel albatross. His Lionel collection had a big reputation throughout the collector circuit, and many friends ribbed him that he might as well buy the company. In 1986, he did just that and named his new acquisition Lionel Trains Incorporated.

A pair of the "Hudson fleet" locomotives offered to buyers in a variety of detailed and sized variations. The 8606 Boston & Albany engine on the trestle was built in 1986 based on a No. 773 1/4- inch scale body. Fundimensions loaded up all the extras on these engines including smoke escaping from around the cylinders to resemble steam. Below it is a gray New York Central 18002 Hudson introduced in 1987 and shipped in 1988 commemorating the 50th anniversary of the New York Central Hudson prototype. It uses the 773 body shell and its detail is based on the pre-war 763E. *Stan Roy collection*

Dick Kughn, the last sole owner (1986–1995) of the Lionel brand name. He is the millionaire toy train collector who turned around Lionel's fade into obscurity. He moved the brand toward high-quality brass models made overseas as well as rejuvenated rolling stock and accessory offerings. Curiously, he is posed with a Lionel Power House. A competitor, Norman Thomas, who had been producing a replica of this model, had his dies and tools pounded into junk by officers of the court after Lionel sued the company and won. Despite rather ruthless business practices, Kughn should be credited with restoring Lionel to its place of prominence in the toy train market. *Lionel L.L.C.*

The Lionel B-6 switcher, introduced before the war as a scale model die casting, was resurrected in 1989 to use as a test vehicle for the new feature called "Railsounds."™

chapter 6

"Train Guy" at the Throttle

The Kughn Years: 1987-1996

Richard Kughn saved his first Lionel locomotive from a garbage can at age seven. An inveterate model builder at that early age, he stripped the locomotive down, cleaned the brushes and armature in carbon tetrachloride, and watched the little engine scuttle off down the track. Later, on Christmas morning in 1938, the nine-year-old Kughn rushed down the stairs to find a gray *Commodore Vanderbilt* locomotive ready to haul a Shell tank car, a yellow boxcar, and a caboose around an oval of track. As soon as the transformer was plugged in, young Kughn was eyeball-to-eyeball with his Lionel. As he told *Peoples Weekly* in a 1987 interview. "…I was down on the floor—that's what's fun—to lie nose-to-nose with the train."

Kughn turned his hand to diverse activities as he grew, holding down the clarinet chair in a sixth grade band seated next to fellow musician, George Steinbrenner—today the eccentric owner of the New York Yankees—and earning a few bucks as a magician, entertaining the crowd between matinee features in a movie house. His academic life was limited to finishing one year at Ohio University before dropping out. He suffers from diplopia—double vision—which makes reading difficult and to which he attributes his difficulties in school. He started his working life with a shovel in his hand as a construction laborer and rose quickly to foreman and on up to field engineer and estimator. He returned to the town of his birth, Detroit, Michigan, in 1955 and joined the firm of builder Alfred Taubman and became president of that company in 1969. He retired in 1983 as vice chairman of the board to create Kughn Enterprises, a conglomerate of 81 separate businesses that have included a radio station, a luxury restaurant in Detroit, a film company, and tracts of real estate. Besides collecting businesses, he accumulated collectible examples of everything from antique coin banks to antique cars to Lionel trains, and this vast accumulation needed a home. In 1976, Kughn bought a building to convert into "Carail," his own private museum. Its large, open spaces house a portion of his antique auto collection and shelf upon shelf of Lionel and American Flyer electric trains and accessories, representing about half of his actual train collection.

At one point in his agglomeration, he purchased Madison Hardware—considered to be one of the oldest and largest Lionel dealers in the world—and moved its entire stock from Manhattan to Detroit using an imposing string of 18-wheelers to accomplish the job. The best of its Lionel products went

Lionel's No. 18001 Rock Island 4-8-4 was produced in 1987 using the old Berkshire mechanism but beneath a new body casting. Its very massive appearance was typical of its prototype, which was considered among the most efficient operating steam locomotives ever built. However, the model's drivers were somewhat undersize for the typical prototype Northern. Its early castings were rough, but, since it was a unique locomotive for Lionel, collectors and operators snapped it up. The engine ran well and was praised except for its dummy plastic coupler on the tender, which was later upgraded. *Chris Rohlfing collection*

Opposite page: A Southern Pacific 4-8-4 GS4-class *Daylight* locomotive from 1983 rumbles across a bridge above a special-issue GG1—the 8300—launched in 1987. The *Daylight* steamer is a desirable collector's item with a reputation for excellent running. It was powered by the Berkshire motor and featured a complete smoke and electronics package. The GG1 was colored bronze to go with a string of "bullion" cars forming a "money train" complete with a matching caboose based on the Pennsylvania's prototype NC5 caboose. The whimsical color scheme sent prototype worshippers into a foaming tizzy, but the train was a hot item. *Stan Roy collection*

into his collection while he re-opened the store to the public.

As the break-up of Fundimensions became obvious and Kenner-Parker was anxious to drop the money-losing train company, several of General Mills toy executives lead by Arthur Pisner approached Kughn to bankroll a buyout of Lionel. Their pitch was, "You buy it, and we'll run it for you." Kughn bought both the train company and the license to use the Lionel name from the Lionel Corporation, which was sliding toward Chapter 11 bankruptcy. The new company was named Lionel Trains, Incorporated (LTI). Following the purchase, Pisner continued as president and his people became the "new" operating management.

Kughn, as owner and CEO, wanted to reposition Lionel as *the* electric toy train company—the position it held in late pre-war period and golden days of the early 1950s. Pisner and his hand-picked management team had something else in mind. Arthur Pisner had risen through the chaotic and heady world of the toy industry and wanted Lionel to expand beyond toy trains into that world he had left where Mattel and Hasbro were the big names. While Kughn sorted out the mess left behind by the former Lionel stewards who, according to Lionel historian Chris Rohlfing, had jammed the distribution pipeline with unsold products, Pisner and company went ahead with their new toy announcements.

First came a set of action figures augmented with power units along the lines of the popular G.I. Joe™ character. Next came a press release announcing a Saturday morning kids' cartoon show that would sup-

port these figures. The show existed only on paper and was shredded when costs turned out to be considerably more than Lionel's projected yearly advertising budget. Going head-to-head with Mattel's phenomenally successful Hot Wheels™, Pisner's group actually produced a clever toy car series called "Revolvers"—turn them upside down and they transformed into a different vehicle—which died quickly due to toy store buyers' apathy and lack of promotion. After a colorful and clever railroad-themed board game called "Double Crossing" quietly died, the Pisner's business plan was in tatters.

It appears Richard Kughn was caught in an untenable position. He wanted to rebuild Lionel as a toy train company, reissuing Lionel classics while creating new ones, and to do that required considerable investment in tooling and dies. Further, he would have to overhaul the sales and distribution system as well as determine how he could design and build new train models with the limited in-house capabilities at his disposal. New non-train products requiring considerable advertising and tooling resources would sap his own heartfelt agenda. Kughn's astute business instincts, honed while participating in the management of 81 businesses under his Kughn Enterprises banner, told him to stick to what he knew best. Arthur Pisner's plans—which might have succeeded with proper funding and commitment—ended up in cardboard boxes in the parking lot when Pisner was bought out and he and his team were shown the door.

Replacing Pisner was Nick DeGrazia. By this time, however, Kughn was closely overseeing Lionel Trains, Inc., and DeGrazia became more of a roving ambassador, attending club functions and showing the Lionel flag wherever possible. In this capacity, he was also the target for complaints. Kughn beat up on DeGrazia for "permitting" Mike Wolf to bring out a new line of diesels while he—DeGrazia—ducked barbs from customers who were referred to his desk. (Later, however, after Lionel had changed hands to Wellspring Associates, DeGrazia lectured the Turnaround Marketing Association [TMA] in Detroit on how he ". . . saved Lionel" by instituting better quality control, production scheduling, and team tasking. An article appeared in the *Wall Street Journal* the same week as DeGrazia's lecture that claimed Lionel was in big trouble when Wellspring took over. Richard Kughn declined to comment on the discrepancy.)

As Kughn sorted out his problems, the big news in Lionel trains was a Rock Island 4-8-4 set to debut in

1987. This entirely new die-cast design offered all the goodies: Magne-traction, Sound of Steam, and smoke that came not only from the stack, but from around the cylinders. It had teething problems, among them an extremely rough casting that was not up to Lionel's usual standards. However, the 18003 casting offered in 1988 with Lackawanna markings and prototype numbers was greatly improved. According to the authors of *Greenberg's Guide to Lionel Trains, 1970-1991,* Volume 1, the 1988 locomotive's superior casting was made from molds hurriedly created in Taiwan to maintain Lionel's reputation and help stem collector wrath. Unfortunately, that did not end the problems. Operators discovered that the engine's motor armatures quickly burned out. Kughn's demand for high-quality customer service quickly attended to that problem and, once repaired, the locomotive ran very well.

That same year a bronze-colored version of the dual-motored GG1 electric was sent forth with a matching Pennsy-prototype caboose. The set was designed to be hitched up to Lionel's goofy but interesting "bullion" boxcars that had open clear plastic sides showing stacks of gold bars inside. Though they did not speak well for security practices of the U.S. Mint, the whimsical cars were popular.

To his credit, Kughn also chose 1987 to honor his commitment to the little band of American Flyer acolytes waiting expectantly. For these models, he followed Fundimensions' lead and began moving diesel-hauled freight and passenger sets out of the Mt. Clemens' factory. They vanished into a swirl of open wallets and checkbooks—at least until 1988 when a pair of Hudson steamers were announced. The little beauties carried a price tag of $450 to $525 each. The American Flyer fans closed their doors, their wallets, and their checkbooks. Amidst the deafening silence that greeted the locomotives' announcement, Lionel Trains, Inc. dropped the Hudsons and offered up a nice little Wabash freight set hauled by yet another pair of Alco PA passenger diesels. That appeared to be the last gasp of American Flyer steam.

"Large Scale" became a totally new venture for Lionel in 1987. Large Scale was Lionel's version of the huge trains developed in 1968 by Lehmann Gross Bahn (LGB) company of Germany. LGB's design was originally based on European narrow-gauge railroads, giving them a toylike look and compressed size for all their hugeness. They looked like kids' trains, but were ruggedly built with enclosed motors to endure outdoor running in rain or shine and even snow. They became known as "G" gauge—which could stand for

A Mike Wolf reproduction of a Lionel 392 steamer that had been produced by Lionel from 1932 through 1939 rolls past a Model 9E New Haven-style electric with an orange passenger set. Wolf created Standard Gauge reproductions for Richard Kughn while working as design consultant for Lionel beginning in 1989. *Barry Stevenson collection*

A new scale from overseas—LGB (called "G" in America)—ushered in the hobby of "garden railroading" in North America. More than twice the size of O-gauge, these trains are marketed as "Large Scale" by Lionel. In 1991, Lionel Trains, Inc. brought out a powered Burlington Northern GP20 road-switcher in this scale, and in 1992 this massive non-powered dummy unit was offered as a companion piece. *Lionel L.L.C.*

"garden" since their popularity as an outdoor garden railroad sparked a whole new toy train industry that remained popular into the new millennium.

Despite their European prototypes, G-gauge trains—whose track is surprisingly close in width to the beloved Standard Gauge of yore—caught on in the same way that German toy trains captured the American market before World War 1. With the latest injection-molding techniques, considerable detail can be shown in G-gauge cars and locomotives, and when coupled with electronic sounds, smoke, and illumination, they offer designers wonderful opportunities. Kughn saw a chance for Lionel to give an American spin to this market.

Lionel's entry into the garden-railroad market in 1987 followed the European lead by modeling stubby 0-4-0 tank-type steamers hauling narrow-gauge-looking freight cars and open-vestibule passenger cars. In 1989, Lionel even added Railscope—an on-board TV camera system (discussed later)—to one of its 0-4-0 tankers. To bolster this initial line, GP7 and GP20 diesels were were introduced along with a beautifully detailed line-up of 4-4-2 Atlantic-type steamers decorated with a variety of liveries. These engines were fully equipped with fireman and engineer figures plus all the electronic bells and whistles, chuffing sounds, and glowing red firebox.

The entire launch required a huge investment, considering other new product lines rolling out the door. Its drain on production resources resulted in delivery delays. Major chain stores found themselves shorted as the holiday seasons rolled around. Also, Lionel was

selling into a market already served by Bachmann, Aristocraft, and—Lionel's largest mail-order dealer—Charles Ro. The Lionel line of Large Scale trains was barely competitive with the products already available in quantities on dealers' shelves, but one highlight was the set based on Thomas the Tank Engine™—a popular talking kiddie locomotive from a British television program imported into the U.S. By 1996, Lionel's Large Scale sets were being dumped to an outlet store chain for under $50. But after some re-tooling and re-thinking, they would be back.

Meanwhile, back in the realm of O-gauge, a 1/4-inch scale Hudson in gunmetal gray was offered in 1988. Modeled after the pre-war 763 Hudson—with tinplate wheel flanges and reduced detail from the legendary 700E—it offered the high-end smoke package and a headlight, but no Magne-traction because of its spoked drivers with chrome metal rims.

A whoop of joy went up from collectors and operators alike when LTI announced the rebirth of prewar Standard Gauge and O-gauge trains as a "Classic Series." With their stamped metal, enamel paint, nickel and brass trim, they rose from economic banishment as bidden by Kughn, the collector, and his new consultant, Mike Wolf. Mike had already made a reputation building and selling these very models working for Jerry Williams and later with his own company, Mike's Train House.

The Standard Gauge four-wheel drive motor was pushed under a 2-4-2 black-and-brass steamer and a gray and nickel-trimmed 2-4-0. The power plant also settled in comfortably beneath a long-awaited

The Lionel No. 12741 model of the Union Pacific MI Jack Intermodal Trailer Lift was originally offered in 1989. The truck trailers were also introduced in 1989 as Lionel along with the railroads made a "pact with the devil" and profitably embraced the trucking industry with trailer-on-flatcar (TOFC) loads. The red beacon and orange spotlight tower are also Lionel as is the gray and blue Delaware & Hudson Alco road-switcher. A Lionel No. 2352 General Electric EP5 electrifier-type locomotive in a fictitious gold Pennsylvania Railroad scheme pulls a K-Line Barnum & Bailey circus train. *Train Collectors Association Toy Train Museum, Strasburg, Pennsylvania*

resurrection of the famed 4-4-4 *Blue Comet* locomotive followed by a matching set of three passenger cars. A hulking new model of the old 381E—renumbered as the 1381E with a Build-a-Locomotive motor inside—was unveiled in 1989 to haul a set of State passenger cars in matching dark green.

Buffs of pre-war O-gauge snapped up their own *Blue Comet* set—blue trimmed in white and towed by an unspectacular 2-4-2 with a Vanderbilt tender. They also considered an orange 0-4-0 box-cab electric heading a *Hiawatha* freight set. The old racing automobiles were brought back along with the key-wind power boats and even the Model 440N bright red control panel with its meters and knife switches—a classic from 1932.

Back in the mainstream production, small Lionel locomotives were joined by another resuscitation, the 0-6-0 Pennsylvania B6 switcher of 1937. This beautiful little scale locomotive was the test bed for Lionel's new "Railsounds™" electronic system that replaced Sound of Steam. Its introduction in 1989 was part of an explosion of new steamers including a raft of "elongated" Columbia boilers riding atop 4-4-2 Atlantic wheel arrangements in a variety of liveries. Another innovation was the switch from the open armature-type motor—a design that dated back to the modified fan motor used to power Joshua Lionel Cowen's original *Electric Express* gondola—to the fully enclosed "can" motor that has since become state-of-the-art on most of today's fine-running models. When combined with weighted flywheels, the locomotive can sustain slower prototypical speeds.

In the prototype world, a new heavier diesel-electric road locomotive had been created by General Electric, the 4000-hp. C40–8. In 1987 it was snapped up by the Union Pacific and other railroads for heavy-duty freight-hauling. In 1989, the "Dash 8" in UP colors rolled out of the Lionel shops, showing that once again Lionel was in tune with the latest prototype developments. This keen appreciation of real railroad designs was matched by innovation in toy train electronics. The big yellow 12741 operating intermodal crane was introduced. Operating this free-rolling behemoth required a four-lever control panel—each running a different motor—and keen-eyed dexterity to lift and

Railscope was an innovation that came along in 1988, fitted into an O-gauge GP9 locomotive that gave an operator an "engineer's-eye view" of the tracks ahead by fitting a miniature television camera into the locomotive's nose and sending the signal to a "Railscope" TV set (or any black-and-white TV). The system was small enough to fit into an HO locomotive, as shown here. The camera and electronics fit in the front unit of this back-to-back Alco FA locomotive set while the motor occupied the rear. *John Hetreed collection*

This is a reproduction of the Lionel Power House built by T-Reproductions owned by Norman Thomas. When Richard Kughn sought to restore "order" to the toy train market, reproductions of Lionel products had to go. He signed up Mike Wolf to make Standard Gauge reproductions for Lionel, create new models, and utilize Mike's connection to the Korean brass-trains firm of Samhongsa. Kughn sued Norman Thomas who had no money to fight Kughn's attack. When Thomas lost, the tools and dies used to make this reproduction were pounded into garbage with sledge hammers by order of the court. *Stan Roy collection*

Following the close of the steam era in America in the 1950s, many steam locomotives were saved from the scrap yard and preserved. Several were restored to operating condition for exhibition and excursion service, among them Reading T-1 No. 2102, shown here on a railfan trip at Reading, Pennsylvania (where the locomotive was built by Reading shop forces in the late 1940s) in 1985. Sister T-1 No. 2100 was purchased by Lionel president Richard Kughn and would inspire the beautiful O-gauge model shown below. *Jim Boyd*

The Reading 4-8-4 T-1 was the largest steam engine built by Lionel until 1989. At 27 inches long, the locomotive was virtually new in every aspect. Lionel President Richard Kughn had just bought prototype T-1 No. 2100 and asked Mike Wolf to design an O-gauge replica. Mike did the job for his first project as a design consultant for Lionel. The locomotive vaporized off dealers' shelves and Mike Wolf had made his bones as a hot property with the Lionel organization. *Stan Roy collection*

lower the truck trailers on and off flatcars. The canary-colored monster is as inconspicuous as Big Bird and takes up quite a bit of layout real estate, but was a sensational bit of engineering bravado.

Railscope was another one of those great ideas that was introduced in 1988 and refined in concept until today's LionelVision™ has made the idea work in full color with stereo sound. As originally conceived, Railscope was introduced in the body of a GP9 diesel locomotive. It consisted of a miniature TV camera poked out through the front of the locomotive's shell to show an "engineer's view of ridin' the rails." The camera's image was transmitted down the rails to an RF modulator that cabled up to the antenna input terminals of a black-and-white TV set. The camera's field of vision was 22 degrees (very wide angle), its depth of focus was from 4 inches to infinity, and exposure was controlled with an automatic iris. This very sophisticated system came to toyland from television probes designed for medical use to look around inside the human body. By 1988, the technology was fairly mature, but Lionel's application was unique and effective. The miniaturization process even allowed Lionel to offer Railscope stuffed into an Alco FA2 diesel in HO. An FA2 mate carried the motor.

Despite teething problems—Railscope required absolutely clean track at all times and ate batteries by the fistful—the system had novelty value. Improvements in later 1990s technology fulfilled the original idea. At the 1998 giant exhibition of toy trains held annually in York, Pennsylvania, the latest LionelVision™ iteration was shown on a 20-foot-square Sony Jumbotron™ TV screen in full color and Dolby™ stereo sound. Images showing a view down the three-rail tracks as the camera-carrying Dash 8 diesel whipped past stations and oncoming trains mesmerized the crowds.

With products going out the door, Kughn turned his attention to a phenomenon that had sprung up as Lionel's futures had plummeted during its latter Fundimensions period: other people were making Lionel trains and accessories.

Richard Kughn had made a heavy investment in new tooling and refurbishing tools used to create the classic Lionel designs. Not since Joshua Cowen had Lionel been in the hands of a truly driven businessman with a passion for toy trains. And, like Cowen, Kughn would brook no competition as he attempted to "take control" of the toy train hobby market. What appears to be admirable to Kughn's supporters at Lionel can seem heavy-handed and brutal from the point of view of those who are standing at point B when Kughn wanted to move from A to C.

A cottage industry of small manufacturers from garage-builders to small plants with a few employees had grown up as Lionel was slipping under, making everything from spare parts to whole replicas of Lionel trains and accessories. Not that their products were either better or worse than Lionel's and not that their prices were higher or lower than Lionel's, they were just there. From Kughn's perfectly reasonable perspective, they were poachers. The approaches used to eliminate their "intrusion" varied.

Norman Thomas owned T-Reproductions in Tennessee. He built reproductions of discontinued prewar Lionel products. Among these were excellent models of the Power Station and the Hell Gate Bridge, neither of which had been produced in the last 50 years but were in demand by collectors and operators. Lionel sued Thomas. Thomas did not have deep pockets to sustain a defense against Kughn's legal attack, so he capitulated. One morning, agents of the court showed up at his factory and battered his tools into junk with sledgehammers.

Mike's Train House was dealt with in a completely different manner. Mike Wolf was 12 years old when he went to work for Williams Electric Trains in 1973. Jerry

Williams' company made reproductions of prewar Standard Gauge locomotives, cars, and a few accessories. He worked out of his garage and eventually shifted operations to a small factory as sales burgeoned. Mike started out assembling these reproductions, then quickly rose in the company as his skills matured. In 1980, he formed Mike's Train House as a wholesale/retail outlet. By 1983, he bought Williams' Standard Gauge tooling and set up his own production line turning out those prewar Lionel electric and steam locomotives for collectors who wanted to run them while their originals aged quietly on display shelves. Another market was made up of those hobbyists who wanted to run the big Standard Gauge trains, but could not afford classic originals, most of which had been scooped up by collectors.

In 1987, Kughn saw the need to expand Lionel's offerings and not just rely on re-issuing what had gone before. While the in-house design staff was busy keeping the current pipeline filled with re-issues, Kughn needed outside talent to fill in— especially outside talent with connections overseas to produce tools and dies more cheaply. Mike Wolf fit that bill. He literally knew the electric-train-design and manufacturing business from the ground up and had developed a good relationship with Samhongsa, the Korean precision scale train builder whose name roughly translates as "future oriented." (The name was prophetic since today the company claims a 50 per cent share in the precision brass model train market.)

A deal was struck. Lionel would not sue Wolf and hound him out of business if Mike would consult and help build new products for a royalty. As an additional

A Lionel Electro-Motive SD40-2 in Conrail livery crosses a Lionel bridge above a zoo on tracks of the mammoth layout at the Choo-Choo Barn in Strasburg, Pennsylvania. New products rolled out the door of Lionel's Mt. Clemens, Michigan, factory, but problems with delivery and manufacturing quality still plagued customers. *Fred M. Dole photo, courtesy the Choo-Choo Barn*

incentive, Mike was also offered a coveted Lionel dealer-distributorship. To get the ball rolling, Kughn purchased a full-size Reading 4-8-4 T-1 locomotive and asked Mike to design an O-gauge model of this big engine for 1989. Mike did just that, and the No. 18006 steamer rolled out in a year-end "Holiday Collection" flyer. This locomotive surprised and delighted Lionel aficionados both with its size—27 inches long, the largest O-gauge model ever offered by Lionel to that date—and its craftsmanship, which was superb. Sales took off as did Mike Wolf's value to Lionel.

The Mohawk, a 4-8-2, based on the New York Central L-3s class, followed in 1990. This superb engine—offered originally with New York, Ontario & Western lettering but later changed to NYC due to collector clamor—was loaded with all the extras: smoke from the stack and cylinders, headlight, red glowing firebox light, Railsounds™ in the extra-long tender that also had a back-up light and water scoop (scale size). On the front of the engine was another first, a prototypical fold-away coupler in the pilot.

Lionel collectors and operators were ecstatic over this sudden rush of stunning new products, each out-doing the previous in breathtaking scale audacity. The 18010 Pennsylvania scale steam turbine—the formerly squeezed and brutalized S-2 that had sold so well in

postwar days—now emerged as Lionel's most expensive flagship in 1991. Its die-cast body with brass trim took tinplate railroading to a whole new plateau. Full six-wheel pilot and trailing trucks were matched with steel-spoked scale-size drivers and a long tender running on six-wheel trucks that totaled 30 inches worth of motive power. That same year saw a slick set of Lackawanna multiple-unit (MU) commuter cars with pantographs and full underbody details.

Wolf followed up these designs with his Western Maryland Shay in 1992, a busy gear-driven logging locomotive with fully working details. This engine looked great, but had mechanical problems due to its complexity when mass-produced. Though it was snapped up by Lionel fans, it also had one curious and very unprototypical fault. Real logging locomotives were designed to follow twisting, curving tight-radius tracks to and from barely accessible logging camps. The Lionel Shay only ran on 54-inch radius track. In that same year, Wolf's orange-and-silver Rio Grande 18107 Alco PA locomotive and B-unit more than made up for the Shay's operational shortcomings.

But, according to an interview with Mike Wolf in the May 1998 issue of *Classic Toy Trains* magazine, the relationship between Mike and the Lionel in-house staff designers soured and was a factor in ending the

Mike Wolf went on to design the Western Maryland Shay-type steam locomotive locomotive for Lionel in 1992. The model shown here is a 1999 re-issue hauling one of its log cars. Although the prototype—whose small drivers were powered through a gear arrangement rather than drive rods— was built to haul log trains around twisting, undulating woodland tracks, the Lionel model could only negotiate curves that were 54-inch radius or greater. Regardless, it sure looked good thrashing away with all its gears. *Barry Stevenson collection*

consulting relationship. Once ended, Mike and his off-shore collaborator, Samhongsa in Korea, were stuck with considerably more manufacturing capacity than they had customers. Mike and Samhongsa produced a beautiful GE Dash 8 diesel locomotive for Mike's Train House and announced its arrival at the bi-annual meeting of dealers and toy train folk at York. The result of that announcement was the termination of his Lionel dealership agreement. He had violated Lionel's Value Added Reseller (VAR) agreement with dealers.

The VAR was most likely created by the computer industry at a time a few years ago when deep discounting of computer components by non-franchised dealers was disrupting dealers who had signed the manufacturer's "value-added" agreement. Though reminiscent of the "fair trade" laws passed and abandoned by the States back in the 1950s, this agreement skirted anti-trust and market manipulation legalities by "adding value" to the buyer's purchase. It guaranteed the components would be combined in a working "integrated system" backed by the manufacturer.

Lionel's VAR was aimed at curtailing Value Added Dealers (VAD) from dumping slow-selling Lionel goods at swap meets and collectors' get-togethers—even if the meet was only a block away from their store. The VAD had to have a store front, be listed in the local phone directory, and display a working layout during the holiday season. Many Lionel "dealers" had been working out of the back of their vans or renting table space at swap meets and train shows to hawk their Lionel products at below list cost. With very low overhead, they could undersell the VAD who was prohibited from working the same meet. A glaring exception to this VAD agreement is the use of mail-order sales to advertise dealers' lower-cost Lionel products in page upon page of ads in the model train magazines.

Mike Wolf had been shut out of the VAD club, but unlike Thomas, who was forced to cave under Lionel's big legal guns, Wolf hired a prominent Philadelphia law firm who specialized in anti-trust litigation and sued Lionel.

As the lawsuit percolated, the marketplace waited for no one. In 1978, Maury Klein, toy train-struck as a kid growing up in Philadelphia, started the MDK Company selling O- and O-27-gauge track under the K-Line brand. After success in this area, Klein found some rolling-stock molds that had been made by American Model Toys (AMT)—an undercapitalized Lionel competitor that appeared briefly back in the 1950s—which had sold them in 1954 to Bill McLain, president of the

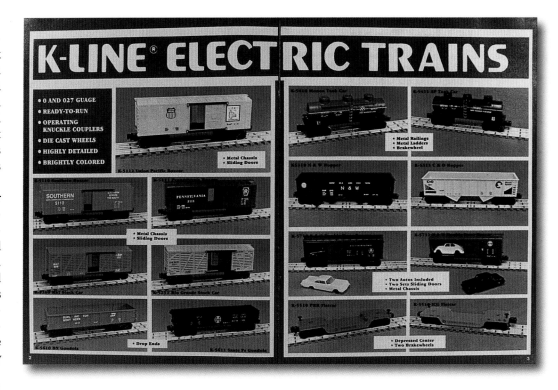

Kusan Corporation. Kusan, in turn, used the molds as a low-end Lionel competitor until the toy train dog-days of the 1960s when Kusan dismantled and sold them to Kris Model Trains in New York. There they remained unused until Jerry Williams bought them and eventually sold the lot to Maury Klein in 1985. From that confused provenance point on, K-Line used the molds to grow its own line of rolling stock and became yet another competitor to Lionel.

With Jerry Williams switching over to O-gauge mainstream models, MTH turning out excellent price-point models, and K-Line coming up fast from the low-end toward its eventual emergence into the front ranks, Lionel's flanks were hard-pressed. Hobbyists were in hog heaven, able to purchase highly detailed Korean-made models of Union Pacific's articulated "Challenger," Southern Pacific Cab-Forward articulateds, the huge Big Boys of the UP, and the graceful Niagara steamer from Jerry Williams. These hobbyists could also compare the low-end starter sets Lionel offered as an attempt to build the market with similar sets from MTH while K-Line offered a raft of rolling stock and accessories.

While free-lance dealers caved under the VAR agreement rules and either took out licenses from Lionel or closed up shop, Kughn and company upped the ante in 1992 with the TrainMaster™ remote-control system. This is where singer Neil Young entered the increasingly convoluted Lionel story.

Maury Klein started selling three-rail tinplate track and then got his rolling stock line started with fourth-hand freight-car molds, the result of which are shown here in his first catalog in 1985. His MDK K-Line™ took off from there to become a major Lionel competitor in the 1990s.

Young was better known as a member of Buffalo Springfield, with whom he recorded three albums; as a member of Crosby, Stills, Nash & Young; and as a rock-and-roll recording artist with more than 32 albums made between 1968 and 1996 under his own name. Less known was the fact that he was also a self-confessed toy train fan. In Northern California he built a ranch that included a 4,000-square-foot barn that has Lionel tracks weaving in and out of live greenery. Young is also a tinkerer and fools around with electronic music. From this tinkering, he developed a remote control for his son who has special needs.

Kughn, always on the hunt for an edge, met with Young and created Lion Tech™—an electronic research and development lab that upgraded and created Crewtalk™ and shaped the TrainMaster Cab-1™ hand-held remote into its final form. With the remote, an engineer can start, stop, control direction, uncouple, activate the Railsounds™ horn (or whistle) that is the exact sound of the prototype and control more than one locomotive on the same track. It's all done with wireless frequencies and computer chips.

When Railsounds™ was first offered, the cost to purchasers went up for this feature and, unlike buying a new transformer, locomotives had to be fitted with the small computer circuit board. This was the culmination of the goals for the postwar "Electronic Set" hauled by the S2 turbine and operated with a pushbutton radio transmitter. In concept, the TrainMaster™

had every reason to be a hit. However, many Lionel dealers did not have the kind of display layout that could use this system effectively. Those hide-bound traditionalists with large layouts who could afford the TrainMaster™ were happy with their two-fisted bank of Z and ZW transformers.

Neil Young's participation in the program was a considerable plus, so he embarked on a cross-country tour to hype the system to dealers. Each dealer was mailed a model truck with undecorated white sides that Neil would autograph for them when they showed up at his presentation. He scored hits with his Train-Master™ promotions but also ran a gauntlet of Lionel buffs complaining and whining. At each complaint, Young shouted back, "Tell it to DeGrazia!" referring to the president of Lionel Trains then operating in Richard Kughn's shadow.

By 1995, after pumping out some 200 new and re-issued products and literally saving the Lionel name from becoming merely a question in a nostalgia test, Richard Kughn had come to the end of his stewardship at Lionel's helm. Almost single-handedly he had raised the bar for toy train manufacturing. He had invested his money and his passion into the hobby. On one hand, his efforts forced other manufacturers to push the envelope in new designs, and on the other he became vilified by many because of his draconian litigation in an attempt to reconstruct Lionel's once-dominant market position. There had been

A beautiful brass interpretation of the Pennsylvania Railroad's "Torpedo" streamlined K-4 Pacific-type locomotive was manufactured by Samhongsa of Korea for Williams Electric Trains in 1987. Small wonder that Lionel's Richard Kughn wanted to work with this superb manufacturer. *Williams Electric Trains*

The TrainMaster™ walkaround throttle and special features controller was revolutionary in world of tinplate and toy train model railroading. A product of Lion Tech, a partnership between Lionel and rock singer Neil Young, the controller was the result of an idea developed by Young for his son who had special needs. The TrainMaster™ provided computer-chip control of more than one train on the same track as well as activating sound and action features. *Chris Rohlfing collection*

production problems—e.g., a crack in the mold that showed up on an entire run of F3s—while the "Classic" train line failed to ignite dealers' and collectors' enthusiasm. These shortcomings were magnified by the highly critical—and vocal—members of the collectors and operators market Lionel was trying to reach. High prices, necessitated by the high costs of new tooling needed to produce these new products, were escalating at an alarming rate. These prices were driving Lionel's customer base to seek refuge in mail-order discounts and the swap meet free-lance dealers Lionel was trying to quash. No one can doubt Richard Kughn was a very moral man during his tenure, pursuing what he considered to be cheap undercutting of Lionel's hard work rather than lashing out for the sake of elbowing his way to the top. For almost 10 years he kept Lionel not only afloat, but constantly on the cutting edge of the hobby. But in the end, according to friends, he seemed almost relieved to be leaving the rough-and-tumble world of toy train commerce and returning to just being another collector.

Neil Young learned of Kughn's desire to sell and brought the idea to Martin Davis' investment firm of Wellspring Associates L.L.C. The firm's specialty was to invest in "turnaround" situations. Davis, the former CEO of Paramount, had operated as part of the Gulf & Western conglomerate, buying and selling dozens of companies. One stumbling block to the sale was the still-pending lawsuit filed by Mike Wolf. While the terms of the settlement were sealed, Mike Wolf was allowed to say he had been paid off by LTI.

Whatever can be said about the Kughn years at LTI, they were never dull and their legacy of innovation, marketing aggressiveness, and quality products were carried over into the next generation. Joshua would have liked Richard a lot.

In its "Collector Line" of 1992, Lionel Trains, Incorporated—under the hand of Richard Kughn—offered models of modern new trains. This Norfolk Southern Dash 8–40C with TOFC cars helped bring back semi-scale type models to the line and appealed to a younger audience by offering prototypes that could still be seen at trackside. *Lionel L.L.C.*

Lionel's *Commodore Vanderbilt* has been a mainstay in some form or another starting in O-27 gauge back in 1937, shortly after the prototype first was unveiled on the New York Central. This hefty brute of a scale model bears only a superficial resemblance to its tinny relative. Lionel took a fully detailed and configured Hudson chassis and shrouded it—which is how the prototype was created. Different versions of the $1,300, electronically equipped locomotive were offered in 1999. Aside from the standard silver, "weathered" silver, and black versions, a special run of 250 were offered in red and 250 in blue through selected Lionel dealers. A good lesson in how to manipulate a sure-thing sellout. *Fred M. Dole photo, courtesy The Choo-Choo Barn*

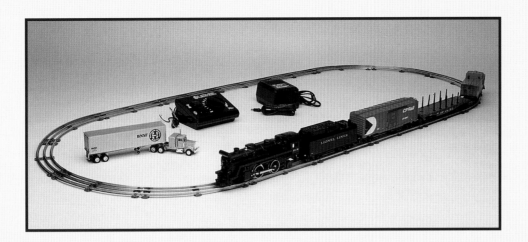

chapter 7
And Now, Lionel L.L.C.

On page two of the Lionel L.L.C. 1999 catalog, the copy reads, "It is flattering to be copied, but . . . copycats cut corners." Joshua Lionel Cowen would have loved that. Lionel's newest management picked up his torch with a flourish and followed the spirit of Joshua's 1905 marketing broadside against, "unscrupulous manufacturers [who] have endeavored to duplicate our outfits and sell our goods at lower prices." with a gentler, but no less pointed, "So, please, don't confuse us with those who would like to be like us."

Those who have carried the Lionel name forward after Joshua established its high-quality reputation have benefited from its recognition and virtually continuous presence in the toy train marketplace for 100 years. No other toy train manufacturer can make that statement. The name itself—though at times battered and bruised by bad decisions and market double crosses—has remained an armor-plated, Teflon™-coated, bomb-proof icon that has never been seriously challenged until the latter part of that hair-raising 100-year history. What a scary responsibility to carry into this new millennium. No one wants to be the last carriers of the flame, the last management that finally let Lionel join the bones of its beaten competition. Lionel

L.L.C. is making its run at keeping the flag flying in the most demanding marketplace in toy train history.

Oh, how that market has changed since the father-son bonding concept of the good old days and the feverish anticipation of each year's Lionel catalog. During the glory times of prewar years and the brief period of postwar success, the question wasn't, "Would you like a Lionel train, son?" but, "Which Lionel train do you want, son?" Owning and playing with a Lionel train was a rite of passage before discovering that girls were something more than snowball targets. Real trains were powerful juggernauts commanded by wise grandpas in blue-striped denim. Belching smokestacks meant progress and industrial might driven by captains of industry. Boys with "character" joined the Boy Scouts, listened to Jack Armstrong (the All American Boy on the radio), and operated Lionel trains.

Today, they laugh at the gross-out cartoon humor of *South Park* on television, battle a hundred different horrors on the video game screen, wander through the sometimes scary landscape of the Internet with their computers, and do their best to keep on the straight and narrow in a more challenging society. Being a kid isn't as easy as it once was. Options abound, but goal-seeking pressure has been accelerated. Operating a toy

With its oddball 2-4-2 Columbia-type steam locomotive, a Lionel starter set of the new millennium period looks surprisingly like starter sets a half century earlier—except for the Burlington Northern & Santa Fe 18-wheeler! *Lionel L.L.C.*

train no longer seems relevant in today's technology-driven, high-energy fast track. Most of today's railroads shun the public, half of whom hardly know that trains still exist. So, who's buying toy trains?

Today's toy train market is driven by an aging population of nostalgia-loving adults who collect and run joyful remembrances of their youth. These hobbyists are a blend of hearty individualists, quietly building large layouts and valuable collections, and more gregarious collectors and operators who thrive amidst the camaraderie of fellow hobbyists in clubs and organizations such as the Train Collectors Association and the Toy Train Operating Society. If they share a single trait that helps define the market, it's that toy train hobbyists view each manufacturer's product offering with a squinty-eyed speculation. They suffer no foolish decisions and are very vocal in both their praise and their damnation.

Between 1997 and 1999 Lionel L.L.C. used an interesting shotgun approach to create its latest market identity. That may sound strange for a manufacturer with Lionel's perceived horsepower, but there was stiff competition from builders who established their credentials before and during Lionel's Kughn years: the veteran Williams Electric Trains, turn-around champion K-Line (MDK), and the hard-charging Mike's Train House (MTH) with its huge investment in new tooling. In company with these fast track rivals, a misstep could be very costly.

Gary Moreau, 44, took over as both president and CEO of Lionel L.L.C. in January 1996 with a willingness to experiment and to understand an unfamiliar product. He came from Oneida flatware—knives, forks, and spoons—into an arms-folded, wait-and-see marketplace still smarting from the often perceived heavy-handed moves of LTI. Lionel's customer base expected sweeping changes from Moreau and his new management team. While the team was mastering its learning curve, baskets full of words came from the plant at Chesterfield, Michigan, but the changes were gradual—and many exacerbated already tense relationships between Lionel and its dealers—as if the Lionel people were trying to find a light switch in the dark.

In 1996, Lionel L.L.C. reverted to Lionel's roots and published the first fully illustrated catalog in over 30 years. Its 1997 catalogs featured "Classic" and "Heritage" lines which was a departure from the "Book 1" and "Book 2" division set up by the former LTI regime. This caused grumbling, but everyone eventually got on with their lives and those with a kind heart enjoyed the return to artwork reminiscent of the Fabulous Fifties over strictly straightforward photography.

Lionel catalogs usually led with one of their strongest cards, and the Classic catalog featured a Santa Fe Alco PA set on the cover, but inside it led with Thomas the Tank Engine™ in O-gauge for $130. The heaviest hitter was a brutish General Electric Dash 9 road diesel in Southern Pacific gray and red livery, or as a GE demonstrator in black with red striping. It was a stunning model as illustrated by the artist, featuring the prototype's unique trucks, correct panelwork, and dynamic brake housing. Inside, the Lionel model was equipped with dual motors and TrainMaster™ CAB-1™ remote control plus ElectroCouplers™ that permited uncoupling anywhere on the layout. These internal magnetic coil couplers brought back the self-contained concept of Lionel's first magnetic coupler of 1945. The TrainMaster™ TCC CAB-1™ control finally proved the concept of the "Electronic Set" of 1946. Its initial reception also met with a cool response.

By and large, Lionel customers are traditional model railroaders—especially those with a bank of postwar ZW transformer behemoths holding down the control end of their layout. Computer control of locomotives offers prototypical operation such as multiple locomotives independently running on the same track and use of Railsounds™, Crewtalk™, ElectroCouplers™, SignalSounds™ lighting and other desirable features. This unique control capability puts some operators off by adding a degree of untinkerable complexity to their railroading. In the same way that today's computer chip-controlled automobiles have challenged the home garage mechanic, some toy train operators have stripped out electronic reverse units and installed the old postwar E-type units in their place ". . . because they work better." Other hobbyists have layouts that are too small to take full advantage of TrainMaster™ controls and don't want to pay for what they can't—or don't want to use. To accommodate these operators, Lionel L.L.C. offered locomotives that can be "upgraded" to Cab-1™ control at a later date.

What if an operator wants to use the TrainMaster™ controls with a locomotive not made by Lionel? Some manufacturers have signed on to a program that Lionel offers allowing them to build motive power that is "TrainMaster™ Command Ready™" and use that compatibility as a marketing tool. While this charitable act of opening up Lionel's technology to its competition appears magnanimous, according to Mike Wolf the participating manufacturer must sign an agreement that forbids making any claims against Lionel's patents or concepts before they are told the costs of this retro-fitting or what is required of their hardware. There have been mixed reactions among toy train

President of Lionel L.L.C. from 1996 into 1999, Gary Moreau sits for a press interview shortly before he was replaced by Richard Maddox. Moreau did not have a toy train background but showed a desire to grasp the complex dictums of the marketplace as he piloted the company for Wellspring Associates, the holding company that purchased Lionel from Richard Kughn. Moreau was likeable and sincere, but his team could not overcome the over-promise and under-performance problems Lionel faced with its dealers.

builders, especially those developing their own walk-around command-control systems.

Other toy train offerings in the Classic line included a set of three goofy cars based on Warner Brothers cartoon characters, appealing to kids—or to collectors who would want to collect the whole set. Lionel had been down this road before with Walt Disney, creating cars with no basis in prototype railroading but providing the collector with a goal. Lionel L.L.C. policy, as stated by Gary Moreau, defined today's collectors as people who buy now for $200 and sell later for $300.

But, collecting cannot be confined to that narrow interpretation. The toy train collector's wife fills her étagère with Precious Moments™ figurines or antique Hummels™ while upstairs, Little Tommy's bedroom shelves are lined with Star Wars™ figures and his drawers are full of Pokemon™ cards. Collecting is an almost addictive hobby unto itself even without a strict investment motive. Lionel L.L.C. has fed this pleasant addiction with endless "sets" of commemorative rolling stock—sometimes falling short of promises, as when sporting logos were offered on a set of commemorative

boxcars. The offer fell through when the National Football League failed to sign on to the program. A current offering is the "Alien" series offering spooky cars such as the Area 51 9400-series boxcar with the head of an escaping alien bobbing in and out of a hole cut in the roof as the boxcar, stenciled "When empty, return to Roswell, New Mexico," rolls along.

A second Lionel Classic catalog was issued in 1997, and this one offered Walt Disney character cars and accessories as well as Warner Brothers funny nonsense to collect. You could also get another in the "I ♥..." series of boxcars exalting states in the U.S. This 1997 boxcar "loved" New York and was actually a model of a prototype that had been done up by the Delaware & Hudson several years ago. A set of short, or "baby" heavyweight plastic passenger cars rolled past beneath a billboard advertising Airex fishing gear (a fishing reel that is now a collectible in its own right, by the way). Alco PAs were the diesel passenger locomotive of choice hauling matching cars in New York Central colors instead of the Santa Fe "warbonnet" scheme. The other Alco PA in the catalog was the sole

What was once a simple 9400-series boxcar has been transformed into one of Lionel's "Alien" series. This one features an alien head that bobs up and down through the hole in the roof as the train rolls along. This series of cars is aimed at kids, but adults buy them for their eventual (and speculative) collectible value and to have something different running around the track. Coupled to it is a MADD 9700-series boxcar. This is from the "Donation Series" for Mothers Against Drunk Driving. They receive a few cents from each car sold. Buy a boxcar, do a good deed.
Mike Moore, Toys and Trains

A pair of scale Alco PA passenger diesels coupled back-to-back in A-A configuration wait on a siding. They are sold as a pair and are numbered 2000A and 2000B. These 1997 Lionel locomotives were issued in Santa Fe and New York Central (shown) liveries and are complete with command control and RailSounds™. *Mike Moore, Toys and Trains*

Lionel's No. 9823-2 flatcar is one of the "Peace" series—each with a different load—this one carries a model of Volkswagen phenomenally popular New Beetle against a "flower child" paint job. Flatcars are real revenue generators since they offer an infinite variety of loads for a low manufacturing cost. It is coupled to a "biohazard" tank car that is part of the "Radioactive Waste" series that has been going on for years. Put them all together for a very scary train. *Mike Moore, Toys and Trains*

motive power offered for the Gilbert American Flyer line in the back of the book. This was a big improvement over the few freight cars offered before. The S-gauge locomotive and a "Four-Pack" of passenger cars required a $700 commitment from the enthusiast while freight cars cost between $45 and $75 apiece.

Flatcar loads were out-sourced. Ertl™ and Corgi™ trucks and loaders are lashed to Lionel flatcars. The "Peace" series featured loads on a scale flatcar decorated with flowers at each end and, possibly, a new model Volkswagen or other vehicle on board.

Lonely Thomas was reunited with his friends, Annie™ and Clarabel™ the Passenger Coaches. Even the disgruntled railroad worker who fired packages out of the express car returned, this time emptying a FedEx boxcar with élan.

The Heritage catalog catered to the more serious operator who had little room for Thomas the Tank Engine™ whipping around his freight yards. A Hudson wearing Santa Fe lettering lead a consist of four "hand-weathered" boxcars and a caboose with Santa Fe logos made a splendid short freight for $1,300. The streamlined diesel *du jour* was the EMD F3 in an A-B configuration, and a Union Pacific GP9 diesel hauled an impressive load of six well-detailed and hefty ore cars plus a UP caboose around the layout for $1,250.

We only dwelled on prices with the previous catalogs to underline a simple truth about today's toy trains—trains they may be, but toys they ain't. While Lionel and the other manufacturers have continued to press home the marketing message that an electric train is a great child's toy, to achieve the absorbing play value of an average video game, much more of an investment than a $100 electric train starter set is required. Kids who have the most fun playing with toy trains are the ones who are allowed to play with Dad's toy train layout. These are the kids who are carrying on the next generation of the hobby.

Mike Moore, owner of Toys and Trains in Morton Grove, Illinois, is a long-time Lionel dealer. He offers an interesting bit of marketing insight . . .

"I have one set—the Norfolk & Western freight set—that sells for $99.95. It's an engine with no features: no headlight, no reverse, no smoke, and two cars. It has a loop of track and a little transformer. People come in, see the price, and are surprised they can get a Lionel set so cheap. In a week, they bring it back and ask for something with more features. I've sold this one set a half dozen times, but I've sold hundreds of the better sets each year. I tell parents, they aren't just buying the set, but should expect to come back and add accessories each year.

"We still do 70 per cent of our train business between November and January, but now we have 30 per cent year-round sales from adult hobbyists and birthday presents for kids. We used to do 100 per cent of train business in those three months and then put the trains away for the rest of the year."

Clubs that have Kids' Night or welcome teens into their meetings as new members are promoting the hobby to grow it beyond the happy collection of gray hair and pot bellies that surround many of today's club layouts. Parents who are considering buying a starter toy train set for their kids should consider this commentary in the final chapter of Gary Cross's book, *Kids' Stuff* (Harvard University Press):

". . . the alternatives of nostalgia for the toys of the past or passive acceptance of ever-changing fantasy toys solve nothing. We need to find playthings that give children a connection to the past and a constructive, but imaginative view of the future."

The nostalgia trap is a generally a yawning chasm of disappointment for parents who attempt to impose their well-remembered youthful pleasures on their kids. Trains hold little or no relevance for today's young people. Most kids have never seen an operating steam engine except in period movies. By the time a little O-gauge steamer, puffing smoke while towing three freight cars, makes its third trip around an oval of track, the interest is gone and so has a $100 investment. Now, take that same train and let Little Tommy —or Sally—run it on Dad's or Grandpa's layout, or the club layout, or even the club's traveling modular layout set up at the local mall, then the experience becomes an event. The kid and his or her train set has become part of the hobby—running rolling stock with the adults and starting their own layout. Even if the

train is made up of Thomas the Tank Engine™ and his two pals—Troublesome Truck 1™ and Troublesome Truck 2™—watch the kids' faces as their train rushes past the coal drags and passenger consists and big, snooty Hudsons.

With rolling stock featuring ostriches and aliens popping out of boxcars, fish swimming in a moving aquarium, glow-in-the-dark radioactive boxcars, stacks of bullion glistening in a boxcar window, or even Looney Tunes and Disney characters cavorting on cars and accessories, Lionel L.L.C. is trying to bridge that nostalgia/fantasy gap. But dropping at least $50 on one of these kid-oriented toy boxcars can require a bank loan to accumulate enough rolling stock to make up a train. One way of protecting that kind of toy investment is to introduce the young engineer to the fun of the hobby with membership in a club or access to the right-of-way on the big layout in the basement.

To keep this fantasy line going, Lionel L.L.C. introduced the ultra-streamlined gray *Phantom* futuristic locomotive in 1998. Supposedly designed by a group of rogue engineers in the 1920s, this imaginary streamlined locomotive represents their vision of the future.

This particular Lionel Norfolk & Western freight set, handsomely boxed with eye-catching graphics, has been sold at least six times at Mike Moore's Toys and Trains shop in suburban Chicago. Each purchaser of the set has been surprised that they could buy a Lionel set for as low as $99.95. However, on discovering that the little locomotive has no reverse, no headlight, and no smoke, every purchaser thus far has decided to return it and upgrade their purchase. If nothing else, the set has done its job as a door-buster. Most "starter sets" are hooks that lead to later purchases of rolling stock and accessories which pump up Lionel—and all the other manufacturers'—bottom lines. *Mike Moore, Toys and Trains*

Two collectible and homegrown Lionel cars are these two 6464-style cars decorated for Vapor Records and Hell Gate Bridge. The Vapor Records logo is rock singer Neil Young's recording label, and a number of the cars were knocked off for Neil's friends. The remaining cars were dumped into stores for purchase at about $100 at first and then the collectible price jumped to $300 in a short time. Now there is a series of Vapor Records cars in general distribution. The Hell Gate Bridge boxcar is a 1999 model that goes with the new Lionel Hell Gate Bridge model. Only enough cars were made to accompany the bridges. Buy the bridge—get the car. *Barry Stevenson Collection*

An entire background fiction has developed about this "Pratts Hollow Design Society (PHDS)" to explain the concept. The locomotives sold out. In 1999, they created a red version of the *Phantom* and promised a four-pack of passenger cars to be available in the summer of 2000—but in gray only. In this era of Japanese Bullet trains, German Mag-Lev, and the French high speed TGV, this set really targeted kids or the more adventuresome adult operator. In that same spirit, but more down-to-earth, Lionel L.L.C. also created a model of Amtrak's high-speed Talgo train for the 1999 Christmas season.

The author's HO modular railroad club often sets up in public places such as fairgrounds or shopping malls. When there are a lot of kids attending, we put a member's French TGV passenger set and send it off at a near prototypical 200 MPH. It fairly hisses down the long straights and hugs the wide-radius curves. The kids light up and follow it around the 20-module layout. The club member who operates the TGV throttle is 12 years old and an associate member in good standing.

In 1998, Lionel L.L.C. featured "Little Lionel'" nonmetal trains for pre-schoolers to run on "Lionel Softrack'" or wooden track systems like the popular Brio™ sets from Sweden. Competing with small die-cast automobiles, Lionel L.L.C. offered Big Rugged Trains™—non-motored replicas in 1:120 inch scale of Lionel locomotives including everything from the 4-4-0 diamond-stack steamer *General* from the 1860s to a bevy of F3s and GP9s in many railroad hues. Each is about five and a half inches long and came in a special stamped tin presentation box for about $30.

The Big Rugged Trains™ were originally licensed to Hallmark as ornaments, but their success caused Lionel to produce its own version. But, one dealer said about the product, ". . . I can't give 'em away. Maybe I'll do just that and give them to people for Christmas gifts." Not every marketing experiment is a roaring success.

Lionel L.L.C.'s approach, as its business plan matured through the late 1990s, was to experiment far afield from their primary customer base—the adult toy train market—and make its money from an eclectic shotgun blast of products working hard with marketing spin to convince this base that the kid-oriented and fantasy products were really desirable as collectibles. Today, their competitors are torn between letting Lionel's camel put its head into their tent or to go it alone with their own concept of better products, lower prices, and consistent rapport with toy train collectors and operators who are not stampeded by hype.

More and more "toy" trains are being manufactured off-shore with reduced labor and tooling costs. This next generation of three-rail trains are built to 1:48 scale (O-gauge scale is actually 1:43, but 1:48 has become the popular reference), just the same as their two-rail counterparts, or semi-scale adapted to tighter radius curves and employing deeper wheel flanges. They are exquisite models designed to run on either tinplate track with automatic couplers, or with scale couplers on "hi-rail"-style track with more realistic T-rail design and a black center rail that is less conspicuous than tinplate's shiny tubular rails. These prototypical beauties roll elegantly around 54- and 72-inch-radius

continued on page 150

A 1998-issued futuristic *Phantom* locomotive wheels silently past a stopped Santa Fe F3 A-B-A set. Lionel created a fictional secret society of railroad designers—the Pratt's Hollow Design Society—which came up with plans for this locomotive in the 1920s. This "train of the future" is a fiction with no known prototype, comes fully loaded with computer-controlled operation, full electronics and even "its own sound." A great idea for kids, it sells for over $400. In 1999, a "four-pack" of *Phantom* passenger cars were offered for another $400, but as of this writing had yet to put in an appearance. *Barry Stevenson collection*

At one time, Lionel licensed Hallmark to make die-cast trains to sell as ornaments. They were relatively successful so Lionel decided to market their own "Big Rugged Trains." These specially boxed locomotives—some 30 so far—are static decorations selling for $29.95. The quarter lying on the foam packing gives some idea of size. Mostly they are gathering spider nests on dealer shelves since their collectible value is virtually nil—for now. Many dealers are looking for creative ways to dispose of them. *Mike Moore, Toys and Trains*

Williams, MTH, K-Line, and Marx
—Among Today's Tough Competition

By the early 1960s, electric trains had lost their status as the Number One toy on nearly every American boy's Christmas wish list. Replaced by slot cars, model planes, rockets, and other high-tech symbols of the second half of the century, toy trains faded from the kid's toy market only to be resurrected by adults who were either seeking to hold onto memories of their youth or looking for an investment for the future. Adults who had grown up with electric trains knew the sentimental, collectible, and hobby value of these playthings from a simpler era, and there were several entrepreneurs ready and willing to keep toy trains alive and riding the high iron.

While Lionel struggled amidst bloodless coups within its organization, Jerry Williams and Fred Mill, members of the Train Collectors Association, were quietly making standard-gauge box-cab electrics and 2-4-0 steam locomotives for TCA members. Jerry went on to form Williams Reproductions in December 1971, preferring to reproduce old designs for new collectors or people who wanted to run classics without damaging valuable originals. Williams was taking a big chance with this venture. In the late 1960s and early 1970s there appeared to be almost no market for classic reproductions. Most manufacturers were offering only replacement parts for older trains, and many collectors themselves disdained to attach new parts to these vintage models, feeling that to do so affected the product's "purity," not to mention its value. So, Williams chose as his initial offering the highly desirable and rare Ives O-gauge No. 1694 model of an electric prototype locomotive. Sales far exceeded his expectations, and he soon followed with more models. Before long, Williams ran out of room in garage and moved his operations to an industrial park in Columbia, Maryland. He moved again in 1980 to even larger quarters and at the same time expanded to freight cars, purchasing dies from the Kusan Corporation. Two years later he developed a series of low-end O-gauge kits. By 1984, Williams had changed direction from reproductions and kits to products aimed at the middle- to high-range market. Like a cell dividing itself, Williams' organization helped spawn two other companies that catered to the emerging market of adult operators and collectors.

Mike Wolf, an employee of Williams since the age of 12, purchased the reproduction kits from his boss in 1984. Later, Jerry Williams would introduce Mike to See Yong Lee, president of Samhongsa, the Korean company building a reputation for fine brass locomotives and rolling stock. Wolf formed his own company called Mike's Train House (MTH), focusing on Lionel classics like the huge Standard Gauge 381E and its classical cousin, the 408E.

In 1987, Lionel, under the new ownership of Richard Kughn, decided to offer upscale brass productions rich in detail and asked Wolf to create steam locomotives and accessories. He responded with not only highly detailed steam locomotives but also Alco PA diesels and a lift bridge. Lionel eventually ended the agreement, leaving MTH with $750,000 of orders begging to be filled and Samhongsa waiting to continue production. Wolf filed a lawsuit against Lionel and won a settlement. MTH and its budget-priced Rail King line are more prolific than ever, with a line that includes 41 diesel and electric locomotives, 30 steam engines, and over 30 freight-car types. In 1999, MTH released its own hand-held Z-4000 Remote Commander™ that interfaces with its powerful Z-4000 transformer, putting MTH in head-to-head competition with Lionel's TrainMaster™ TCC Cab-1™ controller.

Another benefactor of Williams was MDK Incorporated, makers of K-Line Electric Trains, owned by Maury D. Klein. Maury grew up in Philadelphia and learned to love electric trains as he passed the display

Rounding the elevated turn with a squeal of steel wheels is a string of New York IRT (Interborough Rapid Transit) subway/elevated cars from Marx Trains. Although they look toylike (and such was and remains the charm of Marx), the three-car set offered a sound system that announced Manhattan line stations and made door-closing chimes. The current owners of the Marx name, Jim and Debbie Flynn, show the same flair for clever design as Louis, but are developing totally original products that are quickly snapped up. *Marx Trains*

windows of Wanamaker's department store in the 1950s where Lionel models ran every holiday season. He started his own business in 1978, offering O-27 track, competing heavily with Lionel in price without sacrificing quality. Between 1980 and 1985 his product line included 42-inch switches in O and O-27 as well as Marxville buildings and accessories (purchased from the Marx Company). By 1986 he was able to add O-27 freight cars to his catalog, having purchased Kusan car dies from Williams. The first train sets came out in 1987. His operation at Chapel Hill, North Carolina, now turns out O-gauge locomotives and cars that are excellent in their attention to detail and operational value, yet still priced at the low end of the market.

The Weaver Company of Northumberland, Pennsylvania, began operations in 1965 as Quality Craft Models, producers of wooden HO and O-gauge kits. Weaver now offers two types of rolling stock: the Ultra Line models produced by plastic injection molding, and the Gold Line with brass locomotives and aluminum passenger cars. One of its products is the Union Pacific 4-6-2 *Forty-Niner* steam locomotive, detailed right down to crewmembers in the cab.

Another name that survives from the 1920s is Marx. The company rose like a phoenix from the ashes in 1993 after its supposed demise in 1975. Jim and Debby Flynn asked Jay Horowitz, a fellow TCA member and president of American Plastics (owner of the Louis Marx & Co. name), to revive the train line. Horowitz wasn't convinced, so in 1993 the Flynns decided to license the name on their own. They began with maroon Canadian Pacific passenger cars with lithographed details. Unlike some of the other relatively new companies, the Flynns don't manufacture replicas of earlier models. Although they often use body styles and fabrication similar to original Marx items, all their designs are their own and they provide their own graphics. From time to time they do offer models of prototypes, such as the streamlined New York Central Hudson from the 1938 *20th Century Limited* and a set of 1950s-era

Chicago Transit Authority elevated cars, all running on O-27 track. Following the huge success of the Chicago set, their latest addition is a set modeled after New York elevated trains. Today's Marx products are aimed at the adult hobby market, and Marx prints a disclaimer on all its packaging stating that their products are not toys for young children.

Lionel's competition, apparently, is here to stay. These strong competitors have driven Lionel to reach down deep for new innovations, better manufacturing processes, and closer customer relations. As of this writing, Lionel is playing catch-up, but new management, new products, and promises are putting the company back on track. No matter what type of transportation technology invades our world, toy train collectors and operators will always be with us. According to a recent survey conducted by Kalmbach Publishing Company, model railroading is the fastest growing hobby in the country. Young people who are exposed to operating layouts at train shows, in the homes of collector-operators and in hobby stores are finding the hobby fascinating, challenging, and one that has been passed on into the twenty-first century.

A scale model MTH 0-8-0 Steamer chugs down a siding on the Choo-Choo Barn layout. Extremely accurate attention to detail is the hallmark of today's models created for the scale model hobbyist who is fast becoming the primary customer in three-rail railroading. *Fred M. Dole, courtesy The Choo-Choo Barn*

Continued from page 146

curves and still carry full electronics packages for sound effects and smoke.

Some say the hobby is maturing. Others see the new prototypical models, computer control, and operating realism as taking away the clatter-crash and swirling colors of toy fun that made the hobby so special. Fortunately, there is room for both right now.

All the manufacturers are fighting over an aging, but well-heeled market and trying to help grow its numbers by adding young people to the mix. Whoever figures out the magic combination wins. And, as seen before in the 1960s and 1970s, Lionel's iconic name is a huge marketing draw, but it is not bullet-proof. Lionel can lose.

A flurry of new products assaulted the 1999 market. Curiously, the locomotive builders grouped their shots at their customers' wallets. In the blink of an eye, MTH, K-Line, Lionel, and Williams all brought out their versions of the ubiquitous Hudson locomotive. This plethora of Hudsons was followed by a batch of *Crusader* steamers. This obscure stainless-steel shrouded prototype was introduced by the Reading Railroad in 1937 to power its new Philadelphia–Jersey City streamliner of the same name. Weaver outshopped a scale version of the 4-6-2 locomotive while MTH and K-Line created semi-scale models. Another popular prototype with the toy train designers was the GP38–2 produced by Lionel, MTH, Weaver, K-Line, and Williams.

Unique types were also offered, keeping everyone on their toes. While Lionel announced its first articulated locomotive, the massive Allegheny 2-6-6-6 created by the Lima Locomotive works in 1940 for the Chesapeake & Ohio Railroad, MTH offered a box-cab electric as part of its Premier Line, the 2,600-hp. P2 in New York Central livery. This was another relatively obscure prototype considering that only 22 were built. While Lionel moved toward more solid prototypes like the Electro-Motive SD60 and SD70 road diesels and the monstrous Union Pacific Big Boy 4-8-8-4 articulated steamer, MTH went fanciful with *The Wanderer*, a nineteenth century diamond-stack American type (4-4-0) built for the mixed genre science fiction/Western film, *The Wild, Wild West*.

Mike's Train House has invested a huge amount of cash in new products while many industry experts and pundits question whether the flood of new trains can be sustained without angering hobbyists with missed introductions or quality problems. Meanwhile, everything from trolley cars to small steamers, electrics, and a plethora of rolling

This "Gold Edition" Santa Fe *Valley Flyer* 4-6-2 Pacific-type steamer hauling a string of passenger cars can be had on either three-rail or—for the "adult" hobbyist—two-rail track. The Weaver model offers a can motor with a flywheel for low prototypical speeds and the exquisite detail only available on brass models. The fully appointed cab features both engineer and fireman figures. If you want the three-rail version with electronic sound and smoke, bring a check for $975. *Weaver Models*

stock are flying out the door at MTH's assembly plant in Columbia, Maryland.

Meanwhile, in Elmhurst, Illinois, Jim and Debbie Flynn's Marx Trains™ was keeping up with new freight rolling stock patterned after—but not duplicating—the realistic and fanciful models that once came from Louis Marx's Girard shops. While Marx Trains'™ output is relatively small, its models have a jewellike quality and strong motors for long-term operation. They reflect the best of the "toy" in toy trains.

Lionel L.L.C. has also called back some great locomotives of the past. The 4-8-2 Mohawk is on the high iron again, this time with prototypical "elephant ear" smoke deflectors and exquisite detail. The company has also brought back the 1/4-inch scale Hudson—a technologically updated revival of the original 1937 model—and a hefty scale version of that same Hudson, but with the *Commodore Vanderbilt* streamlined

shrouding. The Hudson, the *Vanderbilt,* and the new huge Allegheny use an infra-red link between the tender and the locomotive to provide computer chip-based instructions without a clutter of wires between the two units. The *Vanderbilt* engine is built just like the prototype by adding the shroud over a standard Hudson mechanism and is offered in shiny silver, "weathered" silver, or black. In 2000, there were plans to offer this $1,300 locomotive in both red and blue—with a run of only 250 of each. This guaranteed sellout has Lionel's approximately 2,000 dealers in a quandary over who will get one of the coveted 500 locomotives to peddle.

Lionel L.L.C. CEO Gary Moreau was content that his company was turning around. Though he came from selling Oneida flatware, as he learned about the hobby he was sure his plans were coming together. He was eager to keep what he judged to be winning momentum

This model of an Electro-Motive GP7—the first road-switcher produced by Electro-Motive—is a 1998 reissue of the popular Lionel GP7 of the 1950s. This version is loaded with features compared to its predecessor, which had a motor, a horn, and a light. This No. 2328 GP7, wearing a curiously fictitious Burlington scheme, is fully equipped with Command Control, Electro-couplers that can be operated anywhere on the layout, and the 2.5 edition of Lionel's digital sound system. *Mike Moore, Toys and Trains*

Representing the largest die-cast locomotive ever built by Lionel as of this writing (a 4-8-8-4 "Big Boy" was promised for December 1999), this Allegheny-type locomotive hunkers down on the tracks with 12 powered drive wheels of its 2-6-6-6 wheel configuration. The prototype weighed over one million pounds and was built by the Lima Locomotive Works as a mountain-hauler. Lionel's 17.5-pound, 32-inch brute is fully loaded with electronics, an infra-red tether between tender and engine systems, Railsounds™, and a price tag of $1,400. It is immaculate in execution and a real find for an operator with a layout big enough—minimum 54-inch-radius curves—to justify its size and drag capacity. *Mike Moore, Toys and Trains*

Dropped into a kid-style layout as a static display, this O-gauge Lionel 4-8-8-4 Big Boy steamer fills an entire siding with its 32-inch length. The semi-scale model is based on a UP prototype that, at 772,000 pounds and riding on 24 68-inch drivers, was billed as the "largest locomotive in the world." UP fielded 25 of these behemoths from 1942 to the end of the steam era in the 1950s. Lionel's version was promised for the spring of 2000 and carries a full electronic sound and function package for about $1,500.

moving into the year 2000. He saw a Lionel layout featuring not just trains running around tracks and accessories clattering, lifting, buzzing, and swinging, but also a cacophony of crew chatter coming from cabooses and locomotive cabs, clucking chickens and mooing cattle from stock cars, and instructions blaring from the switch towers and train stations. Sounds and animation were high on his priority list.

As he told an interviewer for the February 1999 issue of Kalmbach's *Classic Toy Trains* magazine, ". . . My objective is to have a vast majority of Americans think of Lionel, and think of Lionel as the ultimate gift, a great alternative to all of the other things I can give my child."

Unfortunately, it became not uncommon practice during Moreau's watch to advertise products and then not deliver them—or at least not deliver them on time. One example was the beautiful No. 770 Camelback steam engine—a relatively obscure prototype that had its crew cab straddling the boiler to allow for the huge firebox necessary for burning anthracite coal. This locomotive was offered as ". . . ready to meet the challenge

of your railroad layout today!" in the Vol. 1 1999 catalog, but was later promised for the spring of 2000.

Lionel should not be singled out for this failure—almost every manufacturer has made announcements, then fudged on actual release dates. However, discrepancies between promise versus performance at Lionel had become chronic since the Fundimension days, and dealers had become jaded whenever a new product was announced.

During the months of Moreau's reign, the bottom-line numbers were not there. Lionel was not meeting its sales goals as part of Wellspring Associates L.L.C. Rumors circulated that Lionel was about to be sold. A purge took place and several key executives were sent packing, but that was too little too late. Finally, on July 26, 1999, Lionel made the following announcement.

"Wellspring Associates L.L.C. announces the appointment of Mr. Richard N. Maddox as the President and Chief Operating Officer of Lionel L.L.C. effective immediately. Richard joins Lionel from Bachmann Industries where he was most recently, Senior Vice President Sales and Marketing."

So Gary Moreau ended his brief tenure with a buy-out of what remained of his five-year contract and Richard Maddox settled himself behind the CEO desk. Many Lionel dealers and hobbyists tossed their hats in the air with a whoop when they heard the Maddox name. Knowledgeable hobbyists proclaimed that Dick Maddox, a railroad guy with a background in retail, was largely responsible for Bachmann being judged "best of the best" in a recent readers' choice poll taken by Kalmbach's *Model Railroader* Magazine. Maddox started his career in model railroading at age 15 as a clerk in a hobby shop and advanced upward through wholesale and retail markets until he joined AHM— Associated Hobby Manufacturers—in Philadelphia as vice president of sales and marketing. From there, he moved to Bachmann Industries. HO scale modelers know Maddox from

the turnaround Bachmann made, winning *Model Railroader*'s Best Product of the Year Award for Bachmann's totally redesigned 2-8-0 Consolidation steamer. It won again with a beautifully detailed large-gauge Shay locomotive. To say the least, Dick Maddox has the confidence of his customer base.

He acknowledged the dynamics of the current marketplace, and company spokespersons promised more new locomotives would be produced in the ensuing 12 months than during Lionel's past ten years. While many traditional models will continue to be produced in the Michigan plant, Maddox and the production team predicted considerably more scale and semi-scale models will be produced in China and

A Pennsylvania GP9 road-switcher rolls past a freight depot on Bob Hanselman's garden railroad. This Lionel Large Scale diesel is powered by four motors, is lit inside and out, and takes up 22 inches of track space. It represents the latest offerings in Lionel Large Scale circa 1998— a major leap forward since the line was introduced in 1987 to very mixed reviews. *Mike Moore, Toys and Trains*

This Lionel Hudson was re-issued at Christmas in 1997 and represented a scale model featuring the same details as the famous 700E of 1937. It was designed to run on standard O-gauge track rather than special T-rail and has all the modern era accessories: smoke, computer sound, and a unique feature—an infra-red link between the self-contained electronics in the the big Vanderbilt-style tender and the locomotive. This model is fitted with "box-pok" drivers—an unusual touch. *Mike Moore, Toys and Trains*

Korea. Additional quality controls have been implemented at the plant to assure that what does go out the door meets Lionel's quality demands. The mass market, such as Toys-R-Us outlets, will continue to receive Lionel starter sets designed to move off busy shelves. Traditional Lionel dealers are looking forward to new products arriving and not just empty promises. The keen competition for this volatile and growing market niche has caused all the three-rail manufacturers headaches in this regard. As new products are announced each month, there's no way most dealers can keep everything in stock. To expand their pipeline, Lionel, K-Line, MTH, Williams, and the others have turned to the internet and direct sales through their web pages. This competes directly with over-the-counter sales as do the mail-order houses who advertise lower than over-the-counter prices in the hobby magazines.

As the new president of Lionel L.L.C. was settling into his job in October 1999, Martin Davis, the co-founder of Wellspring, passed away. Davis was a considered a pioneer in turnaround strategies for financially troubled companies. How his passing will affect Lionel's future remains to be seen.

Richard Maddox and Lionel need exciting products and increased sales to survive—and not just seasonal sales any more. The adult toy train hobby, with all its demands, its struggle to attract younger members, and its perceived brand loyalties, is the only game in town.

One hundred years have passed since Harry Grant and Joshua Lionel Cohen took a chance to liven up a toy shop window with a fan-motor-driven cheese box on rails. By 1902, the pair of window dressers were officially the Lionel Manufacturing Company and admitted that their "goods" also made good "gifts." From that point on, Joshua never looked back. As his name changed from Cohen to Cowen, so did Lionel's corporate designation change over the years, but to the buying public, the name "Lionel" meant "electric train." The name itself rose above its founder and all the hands at the helm who followed. The company's fortunes, as it continuously supplied electric trains to the public for 100 years, should be a case study in every business school in the country.

Lionel has survived competition, inflation, two world wars, the Great Depression, financial scandal, receivership, rampant nepotism, material shortages, off-shore production experiments, dubious corporate acquisitions, management blunders, marketing blunders, the decline of the railroads, Roy Cohn as CEO, loss of its distribution network, loss of its primary customer base, *Sputnik*, acquisition by a cereal company, spin-off to a toy company, purchase by a millionaire hobbyist, and the computer chip revolution. Today, the name Lionel still means "electric train."

Once Joshua Lionel Cowen got serious about growing his company, he was never seriously challenged by his competition. Ives, Dorfan, American Flyer—they